DATE DUE

Provincial Drama in America, 1870–1916 — A Casebook of Primary Materials

Edited by

Paul T. Nolan

Edith Garland Dupré Professor of Humanities
and Professor of English
University of Southwestern Louisiana

The Scarecrow Press, Inc.
Metuchen, N. J.   1967

Contents

Introduction

Most casebooks are intended to serve as substitutes for research. This one, <u>Provincial Drama in America, 1870-1916</u>, is not; rather, it is intended to direct the reader, largely by examples, into a number of controlled research projects that will call for him to make full use of all the various tools of research.

During the period from 1870 until the beginning of World War I, several thousand playwrights across the nation copyrighted over fifty thousand plays, most of which were never produced, and only a few of which--even many of the successfully produced ones--were ever published.

Although at this time it is not generally known, copies of many of these plays still exist; some in private collections, some in the Library of Congress. These plays are the primary documents now suggested for research projects.

One need not make any claims for these "forgotten" plays and their authors to recognize the worth of such research, both for its own value and because it offers interesting and challenging projects for the student being trained in research techniques. The information that such projects will make available will be, of course, of value to literary historians, critics, sociologists, regional historians, and the like as heretofore unexamined artifacts of an age. The advantage to the student working with such materials rather than with the conventional materials normally handled in research-writing courses is that with such work the beginning student is not competing with scholars with years of experience and special access to materials not available to the young student. The chance of publication, it seems to me, teaches the beginning student that the purpose of research is to make generally known that which was unknown before.

This casebook starts with a general argument for research in

provincial drama. Although all of the materials in this book are
centered around playwrights in the eleven-state area across the
South, the subject matter for like studies exists in every state, almost every town, in the United States. The argument is followed
by some excerpts from Dramatic Compositions Copyrighted in the
United States from 1870 to 1916, the basic bibliography of the primary source materials. The literary, historical, and popular articles that make up the text are examples of the kinds of writing that
may result from studying such materials. Some of these essays
are traditional research articles, with sources documented; some
are semi-scholarly articles; some are popular articles, even newspaper features. All, however, are written from research. It is
hoped that the variety of articles will not only suggest sources for
research, but the variety of written means open to the student to
report his findings. An attempt has been made, too, to suggest
some of the various kinds of markets to which the student may submit his finished paper.

Throughout this book, the page numbers for the original publication of the separate essays and checklists have been placed in
brackets for the convenience of those who would like to consult the
original work. Footnotes for "III, Sample Checklists," placed at
the end of the section, have been renumbered to run consecutively.
In the original publication of the Alabama and Arkansas lists, the
first note in each essay started with 1; in the Mississippi list (the
second of a two-part article), the numbering started with 15.

I am grateful to the various journals and publishers for their
permission to reprint works that originally appeared elsewhere. I
have indicated the original journal and publisher in the body of the
text.

I.   The Argument:
"Research Projects Waiting: The Forgotten
Dramas of Provincial America"
(Reprinted from <u>Western Speech</u>, [Summer, 1963], 142-50.)

Students of American culture can hardly be accused of neg-
lecting the study of the public verbal arts in the United States, neither their present practice nor their past history.   Editions of ora-
tions and plays, histories of big and little theaters, analyses of
speeches and dramas make their appearance at a rate that fully jus-
tifies the biblical warning that in the making of books there shall
be no end.

In spite of this tremendous activity, however, one large part
of the study of the verbal arts yet remains almost completely untouched.   Between 1870 and 1916 over 40,000 plays were registered
for copyright protection in the United States; and nine out of ten of
these have never been examined.   The neglect of these documents--
many of which were written by provincial playwrights and never
produced or published--has been so complete that one almost sus-
pects that our ignorance of them is intentional.

If one, for example, compares the attention given to the history of any public theater in America with that given to these plays,
written in the shadows of these theaters, one is forced to conclude
that cultural historians are far more concerned with the physical details of theater construction, the finances of theater management,
and the personal lives of touring actors and actresses than they are
with the nature of dramatic composition--the be-all and the end-all
for all theatrical activity.   No other body of American literature--
not the dime novels of Ned Buntline, not graveyard epitaphs, not
even the doleful verses of the languishing Southern belle--has been
so neglected.

In fact, this neglect is sometimes praised as an evidence of
critical taste.   American drama between the Civil War and World

War I, it is assumed, is better forgotten. How, the critic asks, could a pioneer society without formal theaters, without a leisure class, and with a Puritan bias against the theater have produced any drama that is worth anything? It is assumed, moreover, that the best of what drama was written was pro- [142] duced on the professional stage. And finally, it is argued that the stage in A- merica during these years was so bad that anything it produced had to be worthless.

It is not aside from the point, however, to remember that during this same period, the drama of western civilization was go- ing through a most spectacular revolution. What evolved from this revolution, "modern drama," is now ranked as being at least the third most important period in history, rivaled only by the glory that was Greece and the grandeur that was Elizabethan England. These are the years of Ibsen, Strindberg, Shaw, Becque, Haupt- mann, Wedekind, Tolstoy, Chekhov, Gorki, Rostand, Molnar.

America, it is frequently lamented, has not a single play- wright in this period who belongs with such worthies. Who, for ex- ample, would compare Americans like James A. Herne, Howard Bronson, Steele MacKaye, Edward Sheldon, or Augustus Thomas with an Ibsen, a Strindberg, a Shaw, or a Chekhov?

Those American scholars who defend the Hernes and the Bron- sons have pointed out, of course, that the American theater during these years, with its star system, its indifference to art, its gross commercialism, had a corrupting influence on the American play- wright. The comparison might not be so odious, they suggest, if instead of Belasco's theater and Frohman's theater, and the Klaw and Erlanger Syndicate, the American playwright had had Antoine's Theatre Libré, or die Freie Bühne, or the Moscow Art Theater to encourage better work.

It should be noted, however, that in their own time, American playwrights did not have to face such comparisons. The popular Europeans of that age, at that time, were not men like Chekhov and Shaw; rather they were W. G. Wills, Arthur Wing Pinero, Emile Augier, Victorien Sardou, Alexander Dumas, Mrs. Hodgson Burnett. If the creators of "modern drama" had not, by their plays, made

the art theaters necessary and through productions in such theaters
won their battle with the commercial stage, the plays of such men
as Chekhov and Shaw would now be buried under dust and indifference. George Buchner's Death of Danton, for example, although
written in the first third of the nineteenth century, was given little
critical attention until about twenty years ago.

If the theater itself is bad, it follows that it can produce only
bad drama; but it does not logically follow that all drama written in
that age--especially that unsuited for the bad theater--is bad. Such
an assumption has been made, however, by the drama historians of
America for the period from 1870 to 1916. Thus some 40,000 dramatic compositions written in that period and enough valued, at
least by their authors, to be copyrighted, have, in the main, been
lying untouched in the Library of [143] Congress, waiting patiently
for a critic or a research scholar in need of a project. It should
be said, rather, that these manuscripts were, until recently, "untouched." In the past few years, as the copyrights have expired,
these manuscripts have been examined by librarians to determine
whether they are worth the space. Since there has been little interest in them and since space is valuable, it has become the practice to destroy them.[1] Soon it will be impossible for scholars to
have any second guesses about the reasonableness of this neglect.

It is not being argued that all or even one of these plays is
the American equivalent of The Cherry Orchard or A Doll's House.
In my own examination of several hundred of these plays, I have
found only a few worthy of comparison with the best of the American
commercial drama of the age, none to compare with the best of Ibsen and Chekhov. It is argued (or perhaps merely suggested), however, that a possibility--however slim, the only possibility--for finding a superior American drama from this period lies in an examination of these manuscripts.

Ignorance of any such body of material, moreover--regardless
of its merits as artistic creation--seems inexcusable in an age when
the size of our research-training programs is such that research
problems are frequently created for the sole purpose of training the
student. Certainly all of the aims of research are better served

with projects in which the judgment is still waiting than with those in which the verdict has already been rendered. Even if a search and study of all of this material should result in the conclusion that the current prejudice against all of the American drama of this period is justified, it would be of value to know because of a reasoned judgment rather than to assume from a bias based on ignorance. Einstein, for example, did not begin his study of the assumption that the angles of a triangle always equal one hundred and eighty degrees because he expected to find one that contained more or less; and even the most violent anti-intellectual today will now admit the value of his search.

One might conclude, quite safely I think, that playwrights are a little more observant than most men, a little better trained to look at the scene and to hear the accent, a little more aware of the public issues and the general response to them. An analysis of the successful commercial plays of this age has been of value in understanding what might be called the [144] popular "national issues" and the general "national response" to them. Without arguing for the artistic merits of Uncle Tom's Cabin or Birth of a Nation, for example, scholars yet agree that to know the American temper of their time, one needs to know the assumptions--stated and implicit --in such works; and the works themselves are the best source.

The national temper, however, is not the sum total of all of the regional tempers; rather it is a compromise, something like each but never totally like any. If the plays of those writers who aimed for the "national audience" are valuable in understanding the "national temper," the plays of the provincial writers should serve a like purpose in understanding regional tempers. It is true that the provincial playwright, writing in New Orleans, or Little Rock, or Albuquerque, or Butte, might have imitated those plays that were then successful; he might have set his stage in any area of time and the world; he might have peopled it with ancient Greeks or too-modern Londoners; but in spite of himself, he would, also, have reflected his immediate environment. Sometimes, of course, in such now "forgotten" plays as Frederick Stanford's Stinger; or, The Arizona Carnival (the first play copyrighted from Arizona, 1882)

or Mary Isabelle Hassim's The Boomers (copyrighted from Blackburn, Oklahoma, in 1896), there is an obvious attempt made to in-
terpret the immediate environment; but even in plays such as Espy
Williams's Ollamus (set in Utopia) it is the problems of the immediate environment that are reflected in the theme and attitude of
the play. Ollamus, for example, clearly reflects the New Orleans
attitude toward such general problems as race and labor.

II

Even a hasty survey of the two-volume catalogue, Dramatic
Compositions Copyrighted in the United States from 1870 to 1916,
gives ample evidence of the interest in playwriting by citizens in
all parts of the United States during these years. Regional historians in every state can begin their search with the assurance that
their particular provinces will be represented.

Some states, it is true, are but slightly represented. Alaska,
for example, had only three residents who copyrighted plays from
that area during the years between the Civil War and World War I.
New Mexico had only five. Arizona had twenty. Oklahoma had
thirty-nine. Mississippi had thirty. Arkansas had thirty-nine.
Montana had thirty-six. Some states had hundreds--Louisiana,
Texas, Illinois, Missouri, California, Utah, for examples. [2] [145]

Some of these playwrights were, quite obviously, local citizens
who made one or two attempts to write for the theater, copyrighted
their efforts, and then, seemingly, never thought about their manuscripts or their literary ambitions again. Miss Hassim, for example, wrote only her single Oklahoma play, The Boomers. A
Southern actress touring Louisiana, Jennie Holman Krause, stopped
in a south Louisiana town, New Iberia, met and married a local
merchant, wrote one play, Another Woman's Husband, divorced Mr.
Krause, and then remained a resident of the area for the next fifty
years until her death in the 1940's. But after her one copyrighted
play, she limited her interest in theater to some activity with the
New Iberia little theater and to giving speech lessons.

A surprisingly large number of these playwrights had some
professional success. Arizona's first playwright, Stanford, for example, after Stinger, later moved to California and continued his

playwriting. At least one of his plays, Cupid Outwits Adam, had
an opening on Broadway and ran for eight performances at the Bi-
jou Theatre in New York in 1900. [3] Another playwright who started
his career in the provinces, Arthur Lee Kahn of Shreveport, Louisiana, was a popular Broadway playwright for two decades when he
wrote for David Belasco. [4] All of his plays, however, except those
in the copyright files, have disappeared. Titles of some of them
dot the standard histories of American theater. The Auctioneer,
for example--based on his experiences in Shreveport--is the play
credited with bringing David Warfield to popular attention; and, perhaps for this reason alone, the title is familiar to every American
theater historian, although it is to be doubted that anyone under the
age of sixty has ever had the opportunity to see it or read it.

Some of these playwrights, although achieving little or no success in the theater, were yet successful in other forms of literature, but their playwriting activity has largely been ignored even by
their critics and biographers. The stage interests of such men as
Henry James and Mark Twain have been duly noted, of course; but
they were only two of many. One minor local colorist, Tom P.
Morgan, for example, had hundreds of short stories and sketches of
the Ozarks folk published; but he also wrote about three dozen one-
act plays from his home in Rogers, Arkansas; and except for the
evidence of these plays in the copyright files, there is no other
mention of them. Stark Young, who has carved out for himself an
important position in dramatic theory and folk drama, started his
dra[146]matic work with a romantic tragedy, Guenevere in 1906,
when he was a young instructor at the University of Mississippi. Although the play was published, less than a half dozen known copies
of it now exist; and this past summer when I surveyed all of the
public libraries of his native state, I was unable to find a single
copy. Kate Chopin, George Washington Cable, Minnie Maddern
Fiske, Theodore Dreiser, for examples, wrote plays which are now
unavailable.

Some of the playwrights, although virtually unknown in literature, had reputations in other fields. The first New Mexican to
copyright a play, Capt. Jack Crawford, "the Poet Scout," is listed

in the Dictionary of American Biography for his exploits as a scout
in the Indian Wars and for his lecture tours for the various temperance societies.   Judge W. W. Howe, listed in the DAB for his
learned studies on the law, once lapsed into playwriting.

III

Although my examination of these "lost" plays has thus far
failed to justify itself by the discovery of any "lost masterpieces, "
I should add that this examination--the only one in progress to my
knowledge--has included less than one per cent of the available manuscripts.   Even with so limited a sampling, however, and with the
admission that not one of these plays in any way rivals a Cherry
Orchard, or Lower Depths, or Hedda Gabler, the search has not
been without some aesthetic pleasure.   None of the plays I have
read belongs in the same anthology with the great European plays
of the same period; but a few can at least justify their inclusion in
collections of such American plays as Paulding's The Lion of the
West, Sheldon's Salvation Nell, Thomas's Arizona, and Murdock's
Davy Crockett.

Young's Guenevere, for example, while inferior to Rostand's
Cyrano de Bergerac, is yet superior to most of America's romantic drama from Thomas Godfrey's Prince of Parthia to World War
I.   This play, however, was largely ignored when it was published
in 1906; and even though Mr. Young's later accomplishments should
have made a study of this play of some importance, Guenevere has
not been republished or produced in the last half century.

Capt. Jack Crawford, during the 1870's with the help of Sam
Smith, wrote a play, Fonda; or The Trapper's Daughter.   Crawford,
at the time, had achieved some attention when he appeared as an
"added attraction" with Buffalo Bill.   Alfred Dampier was interested in taking Fonda to his theater, the Royal Melbourne, in Australia and "declared [the play was] the best frontier picture play he
had ever seen, not excepting Davey [sic] Crockett. "   For financial
reasons and because of jealousy between the scout-actors, Fonda
never reached Australia.   So little concern has been [147] given to
the play, moreover, that the Library of Congress now has it listed
as The Trapper's Daughter by J. W. Fonda.[5]

Although it is unlikely that an examination of all 40,000 of
these forgotten manuscripts would result in an anthology of American drama that would reverse critical opinion about the worth of
the drama of this period, what would probably result would be some
revisions, some qualifications, about the nature of American taste
during these years.

In dealing with two productions of Greek tragedy in New York
during the nineteenth century (Antigone, 1845, and Oedipus, 1882),
Doris M. Alexander reviews the criticism dealt to both, largely objections to the form, materials, and nature of classical tragedy,
and concludes, "The tragic vision of Sophocles was far too distant
from the viewpoint of New York in 1882 . . . to be received with
enthusiasm by a wide public."[6] She suggests, too, that except for
a few college boys and Harvard professors, no audience existed in
America for such tragedy. While New Yorkers were rejecting Sophocles, however, a play written in imitation of classical tragedy,
Parrhasius by the New Orleanian, Espy Williams, was proving successful with audiences and critics in Memphis, San Francisco, Salt
Lake City, Denver; and its success was clearly the result of its
classical subject and form.[7]

In all the plays that I have examined--even those without literary or dramatic merit of the meanest kind--there is evidence of
a knowledge, a taste, a condition that has been ignored in those
cultural histories of America that assume that the only drama capa-
ble of indicating such taste is that which had some sort of national
success.

As early as 1914, for example, Sheldon Cheney in his The
New Movement in Theatre established the "debased American taste"
as one of the reasons that the United States had not taken its place
in drama with Europe. With the success of Eugene O'Neill and the
introduction of European "modern" drama into American theaters
came the now-established assumption that only the work of a few
brave innovators in the drama was responsible for the acceptance
of "new ideas" in drama by a hostile and indifferent American public. These manuscripts, however, show that before any public
movement toward the popularization of many of these "new ideas, "

somewhere, some place, a now unsung American provincial playwright was putting them into practice. [148]

Stark Young, for example, was writing one-act folk plays a-
bout Mississippi about the same time that the Irish theater was de-
ciding that Lady Gregory's plays were good theater fare. And
Young's plays--Addio, Madrette, and The Twilight Saint, for ex-
amples--are not only earlier examples of the folk play in America
than the better known North Carolina experiments of the 1920's and
the 1930's, but they also compare well with them as works of art.

Before the turn of the century, before the public movements
to establish a religious drama, almost a half century before Murder
in the Cathedral, Espy Williams was urging New Orleans church
groups to be concerned with the drama, both for the sake of religion and for the sake of the drama. In 1890 he wrote The Atheist,
a one-act play that utilizes the poetics of the medieval morality
play.[8] It is, however, traditional to credit the 1895 New York production of Everyman with being the pioneer in establishing the medieval morality play form as an acceptable one for the American
stage and with making it possible for later playwrights, like Eliot
and Irwin Shaw, to use the form in their plays at later dates.

In nondramatic matters, too, these plays offer evidence that
American taste was something other than the professional estimate
of it, frequently something better, something more catholic. In
1874, for example, Judge Howe wrote his one three-act comedy,
The Late Lamented. This play was produced in New Orleans and
later published. Although the play makes sport of the growth of
the ante-bellum Eden myth, there is no evidence of any objection
to it.[9] It is, of course, true that the myth itself as it appeared
in such works as Birth of a Nation has been examined; but what is
seldom noted is that Southerners were, also, aware of the growth
of this myth, and some of them did not approve of it. On the same
note, it should be pointed out that although many in the South ob-
jected to Robert Ingersoll's tirades against God and the South, Williams's The Atheist, written by a Southern, church-going Democrat,
makes Ingersoll the hero and defends his objections to religion. It
must be admitted, however, that Williams's dedication of the play

to Ingersoll in the first edition was dropped in subsequent editions.

It is not, of course, being argued that these "lost" plays contain the evidence to alter completely the history of cultural America during these years. Many of these plays simply add further documentation to those theses already held, and those plays that do offer some new light essen[149]tially do their shining on the footnotes rather than the text. It is argued, however, that a part of the cultural history of America--a part that has never been examined with any thoroughness--rests in these documents; and if historians, both dramatic and cultural, do not soon avail themselves of them, the loss, whatever it means, will be permanent. [150]

Notes

1. Recently, for example, I requested seven of these "lost" plays from the Library of Congress Photoduplication Service. All were by the same author, John W. Crawford; and all were listed in Dramatic Compositions Copyrighted in the United States from 1870 to 1916. As of this writing, I have received two of them, Dregs and Colonel Bob; I have been informed that two others are available, The Mighty Truth and The Trapper's Daughter, but they have not yet been sent; and the Library has no record of the other three. (Ed.'s Note: Since writing this, I have succeeded in finding all of Crawford's plays; and an edition of his full-length works has now been published: The Full-Length Dramas of John Wallace (Capt. Jack) Crawford: An Experiment in Myth-Making. The Hague: Mouton Publishing Company, 1966, 291 pp. [144]

2. The plays in Dramatic Compositions are indexed by title and author, but the address of the author at the time he applied for copyright is given with each entry. The totals given here are based on my count of these addresses. [145]

3. Burns Mantle and Garrison P. Sherwood, The Best Plays of 1899-1909 (New York, 1940), p. 370.

4. See my The One Act Plays of Lee Arthur (Cody, Wyoming: Pioneer Drama Service, 1962) and "A Southern Playwright: Arthur Lee Kahn," SSJ, XXVIII (March, 1962), 76-77, for accounts of the playwright's career. [146]

5. See Henry Blackman Sell and Victor Weybright, Buffalo Bill and the Wild West (New York, Oxford University Press, 1955), pp. 127-8, and "Forgotten Playwrights," New Mexico Magazine, XL (September, 1962), 37 and 39-40, for short accounts of Crawford as a playwright.

6. "Oedipus in Victorian New York," American Quarterly, XII (Fall,

1960), 417-21.

7. For a fuller explanation, see my notes on "Classical Tragedy in the Province Theater," American Quarterly, XIII (Fall, 1961), 410-3. [148]

8. See Paul T. Nolan, "A Southerner's Tribute to Illinois' 'Pagan Prophet'," Journal of the Illinois Historical Society, LI (Autumn, 1958), 268-273, for an edition of The Atheist and a discussion of its form.

9. Paul T. Nolan, "Playwright Judge Howe Pokes Fun at Antebellum Eden," Advocate (Baton Rouge, La.) Sunday Magazine, March 13, 1961, 3E. [149]

Suggested Readings

Dickinson, Thomas H., Playwrights of the New American Theatre. New York: Macmillan Co., 1924.

Gagey, Edmond, Revolution in American Drama. New York: Columbia University Press, 1947.

Hartman, John Geoffrey, The Development of American Social Comedy, 1787-1936. Philadelphia: University of Pennsylvania Press, 1939.

Hewitt, Barnard, Theatre U.S.A., 1668-1957. New York: McGraw-Hill Book Company, Inc., 1959.

Hughes, Glenn, A History of the American Theatre, 1700-1950. New York: Samuel French, Inc., 1951.

Quinn, Arthur Hobson, A History of American Drama from the Civil War to the Present Day. New York: Appleton-Century-Crofts, Inc., 1937.

Sayler, Oliver M., Our American Theatre, 1908-1923. New York: Brentano's, Inc., 1923.

II. The Basic Source:
The Bibliography of Primary Materials

(As the previous article indicates, the principal source for the unpublished dramatic manuscripts written in the United States from 1870 to 1916 is Dramatic Compositions Copyrighted in the United States from 1870 to 1916, published by the U.S. Printing Office in 1918. The following excerpts are from two pages of this two-volume work. The first shows the entries made for each play submitted for copyright; the second is an index of all the playwright's works recorded.)

1. The Index of the Plays

Dramatic Compositions lists all of the plays submitted for copyright alphabetically by title. This sample page (295) shows the information available: (a) title, A Carnival of Sports (sometimes followed by a descriptive subtitle: An Entertainment Representing Such Popular Sports as Tennis, Archery, Base-Ball, Boxing, Foot-Ball, Etc.); (b) playwright, "by Verend Minster," and the publisher -- "The Penn Publishing Company" -- if there is one and the date, 1891; (c) the owner of the copyright, Penn. Pub. Co., (d) the address of the copyright owner, Philadelphia; (e) the date of copyright, March 28, 1892; (f) the copyright number, 13520; and (g) the Dramatic Composition list number, 6267.

Each entry thus gives considerable information about the manuscript, its author, and the details of publication or nonpublication. The student selecting materials in terms of a particular location, Des Moines, Iowa, for example, should read each entry in terms of the copyright holder's address.

18

Carnival (A) of sports; an entertainment representing such popular sports as tennis, archery, base-ball, boxing, foot-ball, etc., by Verend Minster. Philadelphia, The Penn publishing company, 1891.

© Penn pub. co., Philadelphia; 1892: 13520, Mar. 28; 2c. Mar. 28.   6267

Carnival (The) of the elements; a play in which the names of the elements in chemistry are the characters, with music and songs, by E. H. Hazen.

© Edward H. Hazen, Des Moines; 1897: 60283, Oct. 25.   6268

Carnival of Venice; spectacular extravaganza in 2 acts, by S. T. Jack.

© Sam T. Jack, Chicago; 1895: 27663, May 21.   6269

Carnival promoter's troubles in Turkish bath.

© Benjamin Devault, Baltimore; D: 7942, Feb. 3, 1906.   6270

Carnival time. See Town (The) clown.

Cárnö (A); szinmü három felvonásban, irták Biró Lajos és Lengyel Menyhért. Budapest, Singer és Wolfner kiadása, 1913. 140 p. 12°.

© Nov. 22, 1912; 2c. Nov. 26, 1912; D: 31823; Hans Bartsch, New York.   6271

Carola; et drama i 3 akter og andre digte, af H. Jacobsen. 13 p. 12°. Printed.

© Henriette Jacobsen, Harlan, Ia.; D: 8459, Apr. 5, 1906; 2c. Mar. 7, 1906.   6272

Carolina; an American drama in 4 acts, by H. G. Donnelly. 4°. Typewritten.

© H. G. Donnelly, Plymouth, Mass.; D: 8148, Mar. 12, 1906; 2c. Apr. 9, 1906.   6273

Caroline, the caddie; a lyric comedy in 2 acts, by J. W. Harrington. Typewritten.

© John Walker Harrington, New York; D: 581, June 17, 1901; 2c. June 17, 1901.   6274

Carolyn of Metz.

© Francis Von Buhl, Lansing, Mich.; D: 6631, May 4, 1905.   6275

Caroms; farce-comedy drama. Typewritten.

© Wm. B. Dyer, Chicago; 1895: 13893, Mar. 9; 2c. Mar. 11.   6276

Carpathian (The) princess.

© Vivian Mitten, Lewiston, Id.; D: 4216, Nov. 9, 1903.   6277

Carpenter's (The) son. See Jarius Jordan.

Carpet-bagger (A); a play, by F. Standish.

© Frederick Standish, Lynn, Mass.; 1894: 44062, Sept. 20.   6278

—— a romantic political comedy in 4 acts, by Opie Read and F. S. Pixley. Typewritten.

© F. S. Pixley, Chicago; 1898: 57289, Sept. 29; 2c. Sept. 29.   6279

Carpet-baggers (The); a play in 5 acts, by F. S. Ganter.

© Franz S. Ganter, New Orleans; 1878: 680; Jan. 14.   6280

Carpet bags; a play in 4 acts.

© R. M. Taylor, New York; 1872: 9899, Sept. 13.   6281

Carranque; pasatiempo lírico, letra de V. de la Vega, música de los maestros Cereceda y Martf. Madrid [Sociedad de autores españoles] 1907. 27 p. 12°. [Libretto only]

© Ventura de la Vega, Madrid; D: 11483, Oct. 7, 1907; 2c. Oct. 7, 1907.   6282

Carrette, the waif; by Mrs. S. Johnston.

© Mrs. Sterrette Johnston, Salem, Or.; 1896: 47519, Aug. 21.   6283

Carriage (The) is waiting. 7 p. 4°. Typewritten.

© Grace Belle Delaney, Cincinnati; D: 6680, May 17, 1905; 2c. May 17, 1905.   6284

Carrick a Rede; a romantic Irish drama in 5 acts and 8 tableaux, by F. Percy.

© Frederick Percy, New York; 1880: 9530, June 22.   6285

Carrickmore; or, The blood test, a romantic original Irish comedy drama in 4 acts, with original songs and music, by J. F. Moran.

© J. F. Moran, Detroit; 1890: 15350, May 9.   6286

Carrie Arms; libretto for a musical farce in 2 acts, book and lyrics by A. N. C. Fowler. 63 p. 4°.

© A. N. C. Fowler, Glens Falls, N. Y.; D: 14164, Oct. 28, 1908; 2c. Oct. 28, 1908.   6287

—— music by Manuel Klein, book by A. N. C. Fowler, lyrics by Klein and Fowler. 58 p. 4°. Typewritten. [Libretto only]

© A. N. C. Fowler, Glens Falls, N. Y.; D: 10263, Apr. 3, 1907; 2c. Apr. 3, 1907.   6288

Carrie Nation; a farce in 1 act, by T. P. Bayer. 14 p. f°. Typewritten.

© Theobald Percy Bayer, New York; D: 5429, Aug. 12, 1904; 2c. Aug. 18, 1904.   6289

Carried away; farce in 3 acts, by L. Mackall. [72] p. 4°. Typewritten.

© 1c. June 1, 1911; D: 24381; Lawton Mackall, New Haven.   6290

Carried by storm; a proposed dramatic composition in 3 acts, by C. A. Loder.

© Chas. A. Loder, Philadelphia; 1893: 2872, Jan. 12.   6291

Carrienation; a travesty on the coronation.

© Felix Fair, Tarrytown, N. Y.; D: 1717, Apr. 9, 1902.   6292

After a student has found those playwrights with addresses in his area of study, he should then turn to the author's index at the end of the second volume (p. 2835), and he will here discover all the plays copyrighted by this same author. It is from this single source that the student of "lost" drama compiles his basic checklist.

2. Index of Authors

A. (M.) See Aldrich (Mildred)
A. (S. M.) See Mary Ambrosine (Sister)
A. B. C. See C. (A. B.)
Aaron (S. F.) Moonshiners. 30974.
Aarons (A. A.) Man from below. 27760.
Aarons (A. E.):
  Dancing dolls. 9723.
  Hotel clerk. 20352.
  Pink hussars. 36335.
Aarons (B. M.):
  Chinese romance. 7093.
  Home, sweet home. 20058.
Aarons (P. P.) Ethel Bowker. 12997.
Aaronson (D. D.):
  Aspiring detective. 2090a.
  At the christening. 52748.
  At the opera. 52754.
  Boys of the Golden brotherhood. 4869a.
  Jail up to date. 22429a.
  Levine & the law. 25180a.
  Moe Bloch's divorce. 30680a.
  Mutterzolb & son. 31477a.
  Shmoosers. 42138a.
Aaronson (S. F.) My old cotton plantation. 31670.
Abad (C.) Ahora si que va de veras. 628.
Abarbanell (J. R.):
  Creatures of the hour. 9051.
  Hardee, countess of Monte-Cristo. 18211.
  Ma. 26989.
  Model pair. 30573.
  My father's will. 31542.
  Rhody. 39323
  Rogues of New York. 39738.

Abati (J.):
  Alegres colegialas. 52611.
  Alegría de vivir. 734.
  Bendición de Dios. 52862.
  Cabeza de familia. 5766a.
  Café sólo. 53040.
  Cien doncellas. 7320.
  Corte de Risalia. 8584a.
  Debut de la chica. 10311a.
  Dichoso verano. 10801a.
  España nueva. 12933b.
  Hostería del laurel. 20314.
  Infierno. 54057.
  Mayo florido. 28920.
  Mea culpa. 28974.
  Mi querido Pepe. 29358a.
  Miser & the matchmaker. 29857.
  Orgullo de Albacete. 34341a.
  Pata de gallo. 35516a.
  Perros de presa. 35949.
  Piqueta. 36394a.
  Potro salvaje. 36908a.
  Sierra Morena. 55337.
  Tren rápido. 46913b.
  Vecinos. 48745a.
  Velón de Lucena. 55763.
  Viajes de Gulliver. 48925.
Abbamonte (S.) Patria e donna. 35547.
Abbé (C. S.) Berry Knap, antique. 3544.
Abbén (B.) Barnyard Macfidden instytoot. 3007.
Abbey (E. A.):
  Comedies of Shakespeare. 41781-41784.
  She stoops to conquer. 42015a.
Abbey (H. E.):
  Champagne & oysters. 6646.

III. Sample Checklists:

The four checklists given here as examples illustrate a few of
the ways in which the student may record his research from Dramatic Compositions. Each of these is for a particular state--Ala-
bama, Arkansas, Mississippi, and Oklahoma; but such lists may be
made--and are probably needed--for many separate cities: Rochester, New York; New Orleans, Louisiana; Little Rock, Arkansas;
and the like. For some editors, the editor of the Alabama Review,
for example, the bibliographical details are all that is important.
Others, the editor of the Arkansas Historical Quarterly, for example, like a combination of argumentative essay and bibliography.
Some, like the editor of the Chronicles of Oklahoma, do not particularly separate footnotes, preferring that the documentation be done
internally. Some value the footnotes above the text.

1. "Alabama Drama, 1870-1916: A Checklist"
(Reprinted from Alabama Review, XXIV [January, 1965], 65-72.)

Between 1870 and 1916 fifty-five residents of Alabama copyrighted seventy-one dramatic compositions. Perhaps because some
of these works are no longer extant and others exist only in manuscript form in the Library of Congress and only a few were published, they have been all but overlooked by both literary and social historians. Thomas M. Owen, for instance, listed four pages
of "Alabama authors" in his History of Alabama and Dictionary of
Alabama Biography (Chicago, 1921), including "every department of
literature--poetry, fiction, history, law, and science"--but made no
mention of drama.[1] His neglect was not due to ignorance. He was
aware that T. C. DeLeon was a native playwright and that other
writers, whom he mentioned for their other literary accomplishments, had written drama--poets like William R. Smith, Louis
DeV. Chaudron, and Margaret Henry-Ruffin. And, certainly, he

knew that his wife, Marie B. Owen, had herself written at least
two plays.

Nor has the neglect of Alabama playwrights been a conspiracy
on the part of other scholars. The consensus that American drama
before World War I was generally of low quality has simply led to
the supposition that drama written in the "provinces" (that is, in
the South), if there was any, should better be left lying, like the pro-
verbial sleeping dog. [65] Whether this aesthetic judgment is correct
will never be known, of course, until the plays are carefully studied, and the first step in that direction is to list them and make
known their bibliographical information and whereabouts. That is
the sole purpose of the following checklist. It is not intended to
be definitive, but it is hoped that it will stimulate research in an
area of Alabama literature which has up to now virtually escaped
the attention of scholars.[2]

Adams, Anna Byrne. Fathma, Daughter of the Beys. LC: D:134-
    88,[3] 49 typed pp. Copyrighted from Birmingham, Aug. 3,
    1908, by the author.[4]
Bell, Alonza Theodore. Home Sweet Home. No known copy.[5]
    Copyrighted from Birmingham, Sept. 7, 1891, by the author.
Beltzhoover, D. The Czar's Revenge: Opera in 3 Acts. No known
    copy. Copyrighted from Mobile, Aug. 1, 1870, by the author.
Boudousquie, Gabriel. The Poet: Tragedy in 3 Acts. No known
    copy. Copyrighted from Tuscaloosa, Dec. 31, 1868.[6]
Brenon, Frances St. John. The Intruders: A Farcical Playlet in
    1 Act. LC: D:15575, 14 typed pp. Copyrighted from Fair-
    hope, Apr. 9, 1909, by Herbert Brenon.
Brooks, Alice. Le Vipere: Drama in 5 Acts. No known copy.
    Copyrighted from Gadsden, Mar. 24, 1900, by the author.[7]
Calcina, H. F., and J. R. Calhoun. The Doctor and the Devil: A
    High Drama in 5 Acts Taken from the French During the
    Time of [66] Napoleon. LC: D:62507, 46 typed pp. Copyrighted
    from Mobile, Nov. 16, 1896, by the authors.
Carlysle, Frederick J. Bacio II: Overmastering Pride, Ruler of
    the Soul: An Original Play in 4 Acts. No known copy.

Copyrighted from Selma, Nov. 19, 1880, by the author.[8]

Chaudron, Louis DeV. The Duke and the Actors: Comedy in 5
Acts. No known copy. Copyrighted from Mobile, June 5,
1880, by the author.[9]

_____. A Game of Checkers: Drama in 5 Acts. No known
copy. Copyrighted from Mobile, June 5, 1880, by the author.

Claxton, Beaumont [T. C. Taylor]. In the Depths: Drama in 4
Acts. Dramatized from Mrs E. D. E. N. Southworth's Novel.
LC: D:29973, 85 typed pp. Copyrighted from Montgomery,
June 14, 1912, by the author.[10]

Cole, George Harrison. The Gray vs. The Blue: A Tragedy. LC:
D:8844, 28 typed pp. Copyrighted from Eutaw, Sept. 22,
1871, by the author.

Daly, William Oliver. Fortune's Fool: Sir Walter Scott's Kenil-
worth: Dramatized in 5 Acts. LC: D:7070, 57 typed pp.
Copyrighted from Mobile, Aug. 7, 1905, by the author.

_____. Twenty Minutes a King: Musical Comedy in 2 Acts
[Libretto only]. LC: D:13646, 52 typed pp. Copyrighted from
Mobile, Aug. 25, 1908, by the author.

DeLeon, T. C. Edged Tools: Comedy of American Life. No known
copy. Copyrighted from Mobile, Apr. 1, 1873, by the author.[11] [67]

_____. Life Insurance: Comedy of American Life. No
known copy. Copyrighted from Mobile, Apr. 1, 1873, by the
author.

_____. Mrs. Cob's Salon: Or the Maid and the Minuet:
Comedietta in 1 Act. No known copy. Copyrighted from Mobile, Apr. 20, 1896, by the author.

_____. North and South: Dramatic Comedy of American
Life. No known copy. Copyrighted from Mobile, Apr. 1,
1873, by the author.

_____. Through Fire and Water: Sensational Character
Comedy of American Life. No known copy. Copyrighted from
Mobile, Apr. 1, 1873, by the author.

Fitzgerald, P. A. Effie Gower: or the Forsaken: An Emotional
Drama in 5 Acts. No known copy. Copyrighted from Hunts-

ville, Nov. 15, 1876, by Mrs. Andrew Flynn.

Fordyce, E. W. _America._ No known copy. Copyrighted from Anniston, Oct. 3, 1908, by the author.

_____. _The Axiom._ LC: D:8228, 8 typed pp. Copyrighted
from Birmingham, March 26, 1906, by the author.

_____. _Dixie-Doodle: Theatrical Composition._ LC: D:110-
79, 19 typed pp. Copyrighted from Anniston, July 23, 1907.

Frohlichstein, Emanuel N. _As It Will Be in 1950: 1-Act Playlet._
LC: D:294444, 14 typed pp. Copyrighted from Mobile, Apr.
22, 1912, by the author.

_____. _True Friendship: 1 Act Playlet in 2 Scenes._ LC:
D:17547, 6 typed pp. Copyrighted from Mobile, Nov. 29,
1909, by the author.

Graham, Hamilton C. _Gray and Blue: Drama in 5 Acts._ No
known copy. Copyrighted from Selma, Apr. 9, 1888, by the
author.[12]

Greene, Frances Nimmo. _Speaking of Adam: Comedy in 3 Acts._
LC: D:41784, 136 typed pp. Copyrighted from Montgomery,
Sept. 20, 1915, by the author.[13]

_____. _The Ultimate American: Comedy in 3 Acts._ LC:
D:41784, 136 typed pp. Copyrighted from Montgomery, Sept.
4, 1913, by the author.

Hardman, Kathryn Stone. _United; Or, As a Woman Saw It: Play
in 5 [68] Acts._ LC: D:36672, 63 typed pp. Copyrighted from
Birmingham, Mar. 31, 1914, by the author.

Henry-Ruffin, Margaret Ellen. _The Bride: Play in 3 Acts._ No
known copy. Copyrighted from Mobile, Jan. 6, 1909, by the
author.[14]

_____. _The Heart of a Harp._ LC: D:8286, 54 typed pp.
Copyrighted from Mobile, Apr. 6, 1906, by the author.

_____. _The Leprechaun: Play in 1 Act._ No known copy.
Copyrighted from Mobile, Feb. 23, 1907, by the author.

Jackson, Mrs. Phillip. _Bitter Fruits: or Matrimony in Prospect
and Realization: Farce in 1 Act._ No known copy. Copyrighted from Alexander City, Dec. 9, 1893, by the author.

Jacobson, Isidor G. _He Stoops to Conquer: Comedy in Four Acts._

No known copy. Copyrighted from Mobile, May 24, 1894, by
the author.

Johnson, Lute Henry. Mary Carey of Old New York: Romantic
   Drama of Revolutionary Times. LC: D:34952, 76 typed pp.
   Copyrighted from Birmingham, Nov. 6, 1913, by the author.[15]

Lagman, Jonathan H. Way Down South: Character Comedy Drama
   in 4 Acts. LC: D:21607, 144 pp. Copyrighted from Mobile,
   July 26, 1910, by the author.

Lamar, Theodore J. The Agitator: Play in 5 Acts. No known
   copy. Copyrighted from Anniston, Aug. 1, 1904, by the author.[16]

Laughlin, Angus Prater. Fritz in America: Drama in Three Acts
   and Three Scenes. Decatur, Ala.: Valley Press, 1887, 80
   pp. Available in LC. Copyrighted from Courtland, May 13,
   1887, by the author.

Levy, Sidney P. The Love of Clifford: Romantic Drama in 4 Acts.
   LC: D:19359, typed ms. Copyrighted from Mobile, Mar. 24,
   1898, by the author.[17]

Lovell, Caroline Cowper. The Swayam--Vara: 1 Act Comedy.
   LC: D:43844, 17 typed pp. Copyrighted from Birmingham,
   May 8, 1916, by the author.

_____. Wuthering Heights: Drama in 5 Acts. LC: D:372-
   31, 126 typed [69] pp. Copyrighted from Birmingham, June 5,
   1914, by the author.[18]

MacKnight, James Arthur and J. Walton. Jamestown: Historic,
   Patriotic, Spectacular Drama in 4 Acts. No known copy.
   Copyrighted from Calera, Sept. 21, 1906, by James A. Mac-
   Knight and from New York, same date, by J. Walton Mac-
   Knight.[19]

McNutt, Hugh McGavock. The Dream: Play in 5 Acts. No known
   copy. Copyrighted from Bessemer, July 13, 1896, by the
   author.[20]

_____. Lucindy's Weddin': Comedy in 1 Act. No known
   copy. Copyrighted from Birmingham, Sept. 4, 1897, by the
   author.

_____. The Old Treasurer: Three-Act Drama. Bessemer,

Ala.: Bessemer Printing & Publishing Co., 1893, 70 pp.
Available in LC.   Copyrighted from Bessemer, Sept. 1, 1893,
by the author.

Martin, Mrs. Wade A.   Coward: Play in 4 Acts.   LC: D:36851,
21 typed pp.   Copyrighted from Birmingham, Apr. 27, 1914,
by the author.

Mullen, Len D.   Daisy; or The Doctor's Wife: Comedy-Drama in
4 Acts.   No known copy.   Copyrighted from Selma, Jan. 8,
1883, by the author.[21]

Nomaun, I. M.   Colonel Conyers; or A Tale of the South: Tragedy
in 9 Acts.   No known copy.   Copyrighted from Morrisville,
Feb. 7, 1896, by R. C. Morris.[22]

Owen, Marie Bankhead.   The Acting Governor: Drama in 5 Acts.
LC: D:33704, 125 typed pp.   Copyrighted from Montgomery,
July 3, 1913, by the author.

_____. The Deltan: Romance Play in 3 Acts.   LC: D:126-
44, 151 typed pp.   Copyrighted from Montgomery, Mar. 30,
1908, by the author.[23] [70]

Ritter, John P.   St. Elmo: Play in Prologue and 4 Acts, Founded
on the Novel, St. Elmo.   LC: D:10887, 84 typed pp.   Copyrighted from Mobile, July, 1, 1907, by Augusta Jane Evans
Wilson.[24]

Rivers, Lidie Auirett.   Just Life Itself: Drama in 3 Acts.   LC:
D:25804, 85 typed pp.   Copyrighted from Birmingham, Nov.
17, 1911, by the author.[25]

_____. Sour Grapes: Modern Drama in 4 Acts.   LC: D:
32153, 40 typed pp.   Copyrighted from Birmingham, Jan. 31,
1913, by the author.

Rubin, Daniel Nathan.   The Boomerang: Social Drama in 4 Acts.
LC: D:36948, 144 typed pp.   Copyrighted from Birmingham,
May 6, 1914, by the author.

_____. The Dedication: Drama in 3 Acts.   LC: D:45751,
91 typed pp.   Copyrighted from Birmingham, Dec. 28, 1916,
by the author.

_____. The Weakest Link: Drama in 4 Acts.   LC: D:423-
96, 99 typed pp.   Copyrighted from Birmingham, Dec. 2,

1915, by the author.

Rubin, Daniel N. and Benjamin Gross. Behind the Door: 1-Act
   Play. No known copy. Copyrighted from Birmingham, Oct.
   21, 1914, by the authors.

Ruff, Edgar and Dorothy Raynol. Cousins: 1 Act Comedy Dramatic Sketch. LC: D:15624, 16 typed pp. Copyrighted from Mobile, Apr. 15, 1909, by Ruff and from New York, same date,
   by Raynol.[26]

_____. Taming a Husband: 3 Act Musical Comedy. LC:
   D:7728, 37 typed pp. Copyrighted from Mobile, Dec. 16,
   1905, by Raynol.

Schinks, Robert Marcus. An Affair of the Family. LC: D:13319,
   30 typed pp. Copyrighted from Birmingham, July 10, 1908,
   by the author.

Sibley, Guy C. Columbus: Tragedy in 5 Acts. No known copy.
   Copyrighted from Mobile, Sept. 27, 1892, by the author.[27]

Smith, William R. Polyxena: A Tragedy. No known copy. Copyrighted from Tuscaloosa, Feb. 24, 1879, by the author.[28] [71]

Strauss, Rose. Bluffing It: Comedy in 3 Acts. LC: D:31155, 42
   typed pp. Copyrighted from Montgomery, Oct. 17, 1912, by
   the author.[29]

Taylor, Albert. Siege of the Alamo: Historical Drama in 4 Acts.
   No known copy. Copyrighted from Montgomery, Mar. 4, 1895,
   by the author.[30]

Turnworm [pseudo. for Mary A. Wolff]. Affinity and Duty; or
   Evangeline and Gretchen: Play in 1 Act. LC: D:34180, 34
   typed pp. Copyrighted from Montgomery, Aug. 16, 1913, by
   the author.

Vallee, William Albert. All Is Fair in Love and War: Military
   Specialty in 1 Act. LC: D:33985, 1 typed p. Copyrighted
   from Birmingham, Aug. 2, 1914, by the author.

Von Meybohn, H. A. A Good Touch: 1 Act Playlet. LC: D:24843,
   4 typed pp. Copyrighted from Birmingham, Aug. 2, 1911, by
   the author.

Wallick, James H. The Cattle Kings; or The Rival Ranchmen: A
   Melodramatic, Sensational and Equestrian Drama in 6 Acts.

No known copy. Copyrighted from Birmingham, Sept. 16,
1885, by the author. [31]

Weathers, E. W. The Intercepted Message; or, What Might Happen
If We Had War with Japan. LC: D:25105, 11 typed pp. Copyrighted from Woodlawn, Aug. 25, 1911, by the author.

Young, Martha. Old Turk: An Easter Drama. No known copy.
Copyrighted from Greensboro, Sept. 11, 1905, by the author. [32]

Zinn, William Henry. The Fair: Play in 5 Acts. LC: D:33047,
20 typed pp. Copyrighted from Anniston, Apr. 24, 1913. [72]

2. "Arkansas Drama Before World War I: An
Unexplored Country"
(With Amos E. Simpson, Arkansas Historical Quarterly,
XXII [Spring, 1963], 61-75.)

Literary historians and critics in dealing with the art of A-
merican drama commonly divide its history at World War I. Before the war lie the beginnings; only after the war comes the art.
Jordon Y. Miller in his American Dramatic Literature, [33] for example, gives seventy-three pages to the first two centuries of A-
merican drama and over five hundred pages to the drama of the
past forty years. Miller's chapter headings for American drama
from 1714 to 1918 constitute a brief history of America's dramatic
literature: "Early Theatres and Performers Before the Revolution, "
"A Permanent Theatre and the First American Plays, " "American
Writers and American Themes: 1800 to the Civil War, " "The Century of the Great Actor, " "The Birth Pangs of Realism: 1865 to
1900, " "The Period of Transition: The American Stage [61] From
1900 to 1914, " and "The Turning Point: 1914 to 1918. "

The reading of the dramatic history of America suggested by
these chapter headings--and it is the traditional one--views all of
American drama before World War I as a promise of the better
things to come, the plays of Lillian Hellman, Tennessee Williams,
Haines, the Heywards, Behrman, Thurber and Nugent, Carson Mc-
Cullers, Mary Chase, Eugene O'Neill, Arthur Miller. This account of the drama before World War I emphasizes, on the one
hand, the value of the plays as voices crying in the wilderness and,
on the other hand, their value as interesting historical artifacts

that reveal the playwright's reaction to his times, interesting documents for the cultural historian, if not of much value to the dramatic critic.

Professor Miller is patient and sympathetic with the playwrights of America in the years between the Civil War and World War I. He points out that the dramatists in these years had the almost impossible task of establishing themselves as artists: "Playwriting . . . was a long way from being a self-sustaining art."[34] The villain of the piece in these years--the antagonist of the playwright--was the professional theatre with its commercialism, its star system, its pandering to the worst tastes of the times. The "arrival" of American drama is described by Miller as a victory over the theater. "Not many years after 1914," he writes, ". . . the American drama was able to throw off the shackles of Daly and Belasco commercialism."[35] This victory, he points out, came following the European successes, starting with André Antoine's theater in France in 1887, with the Freie Buhne in Germany in 1899, with the Moscow Art Theater in 1898, with Strindberg's theater in Sweden in 1907, and with the Abbey Theatre in Dublin in 1904.

No serious student of American drama, to our knowledge, quarrels with this account of the development of [62] American drama. Certainly such a playwright as Eugene O'Neill came into prominence because of the Washington Square Players, and the Washington Square Players--which drew heavily on the plays of Shaw, Andreyev, Ibsen, Maeterlinck--drew its inspiration from the European theatrical revolution of the 1880's and 1890's.

There is, however, one point that needs re-examination. The revolt of the theater in Europe came because Chekhov, Strindberg, Shaw, Andreyev, Ibsen, and the others whose plays now make up "modern" drama needed a different kind of theater. In America the theaters imposed a change upon the playwrights.

If the "new" theaters of Europe had not popularized such plays as those of Chekhov and Strindberg, the history of European drama would consist of those plays successful in the European commercial theaters. Rather than Ibsen, Shaw, Chekhov, and Strindberg, the "major" dramatists for the period would now be listed as W.G.

Wills, Octave Feuillet, Arthur Wing Pinero, Emile Augier, Victorien Sardou, Alexander Dumas, Mrs. Hodgson Burnett. These
are the playwrights to whom the astute critic Henry James gave
his attention, if not his approval. [36] A comparison between the
Wills, the Sardous, the Augiers, and the Americans of the same
era, James A. Herne, Howard Bronson, Steele MacKaye, Edward
Sheldon, Augustus Thomas, is not an altogether unfavorable one
for the Americans; but to weigh the Bronsons and the Hernes in
the scale of an Ibsen or a Chekhov is almost to invite ignominy.
There is, of course, no reason why American commercial playwrights should be compared with European rebels against the commercial theater.

Shaw, Ibsen, Chekhov, and Strindberg existed as playwrights,
before the "new" theaters of Europe ever came into existence; and
while the works of their mature years may never have been born
without the help of the "new" theaters, their early works were created outside the theater. Without [63] the attention given them by later
theater success, however, we would probably be unaware of them
today; but they would still have been written and might exist yet.
If one were looking for Chekhov without the Moscow Art Theatre, he
would not seek among the commercial playwrights, quite obviously.
Rather, he would need to delve into the unpublished (and frequently
unproduced) manuscripts of plays written by the lonely playwright,
exiled from the theaters of his times.

American drama historians, however, have seen only the theatrical playwrights and have lamented that here only others like
Sardou are to be found, none like Chekhov. They have looked a-
mong those who made their compromises with the theaters for those
in rebellion against that theater. If American drama from 1865 to
1916 was in any way going through the same kind of rebellion that
Ibsen, Chekhov, and Shaw were waging, this drama was being created off-Broadway, far off-Broadway, as far as Little Rock, and
Fort Smith, and Newport, and Pine Bluff, Arkansas.

II

Strangely enough, however, even regional historians who are
willing to examine every scrap of newspaper doggerel seeking an-

other lost Emily Dickinson, have given but scant attention to their
playwrights, unless they also achieved national attention through
New York successes.   There has been a considerable interest in
the theater, but even among the theater historians, the local dramatists are given short shrift.   Walter Moffatt in an account of "First
Theatrical Activities in Arkansas,"[37] for example, makes only one
mention of an Arkansas playwright, John Field of Hempstead County.   Field in 1839 wrote what was probably the first play by an
Arkansan, **Bill Screamer; or, the Man of the West**.   "Unfortunately," writes Professor Moffatt, ". . . it did not give the native
drama a very auspicious beginning."   He cites a review from the
Arkansas Gazette (May 1, 1839) in defense: "It was wretchedly
butchered, and if it had any merit, we were unable to discover it." [64]

The American Guide Series' **Arkansas: A Guide to the State**[38]
gives four pages to the history of Arkansas theater, tracing it from
its beginnings in Little Rock in 1839 to the end of the 1930's, but
no mention is made of a single Arkansas playwright.   Jim P. Mat-
thews and V. L. Jones in **Arkansas Books**,[39] intended to "contain
all books, written by native Arkansans, books written by residents
of the state during a period of residence, books written about Arkansas . . . and those written for some local or commercial purpose," mention only two playwrights, Mrs. Bernie Babcock and Mrs.
Ellen Harrell Cantrell.   Fred W. Alsopp in **The Poets and Poetry
of Arkansas**[40] mentions two playwrights, Mrs. Babcock and Tom P.
Morgan; but it is not noted that either actually ever wrote a play.
Denham Wooten, in a series of articles titled "The History of the
Theater in Arkansas,"[41] probably the most complete account ever
compiled, gives no attention to the native playwrights and, in fact,
even seems to have some distaste for using Arkansas materials.   In
giving an account of a melodrama, **Kit, The Arkansas Traveler**,
which was produced in Little Rock on Feb. 3 and 4, 1859, Wooten
notes that the play had been a success in New York, but Arkansas
did not like it.   "The critics all agreed it was too full of pistol
shots, too bloody and too full of the gleam of the Bowie knife to be
realistic."[42]

The neglect of Arkansas playwrights is not, of course, a con-

spiracy of the historians and bibliographers. In the main the judgment has been that few American playwrights before World War I
are worth much mention. Those who achieved neither theatrical
success nor literary fame in another genre are worth nothing. Few
plays, until fairly recent times, were published; and few American
communities, even today, do much to encourage their local play- [65]
wrights by producing their works. Tom P. Morgan, for example,
wrote over two dozen plays. The Rogers Daily News: 1900-1950
Mid-Century Edition[43] reported, "Tom P. Morgan Well Known for
Short Stories," but made no mention of his plays, seemingly because his playwriting activity had received little attention from Rogers even during Morgan's lifetime.

III

Arkansas, however, had a considerable number of playwrights
before World War I. From 1870 to 1916, at least thirty-six residents of the state copyrighted dramatic compositions from Arkansas
addresses. Many of these plays apparently are no longer extant.
For a number of years it was possible to copyright a dramatic composition by submission of the title page alone. Many of these plays
exist only in the manuscript copy submitted to the Library of Congress for this protection. A few were published. Some of the
plays were written in the worst tradition of nineteenth-century commercial melodrama and farce. Some are little more than vaudeville skits. A few, like Sol Braunig's Nick Carter, The New York
Detective, are mere dramatizations of the popular potboilers of the
age; and others, like Tom P. Morgan's vaudeville skits, are attempts at local literature in drama.

The checklist of Arkansas playwrights was not prepared as a
summation of the history of Arkansas drama. At best it suggests
an awareness of a body of literature which may contain literary value and should be of importance to the cultural historian. In these
works, there is evidence of the aspirations, the frustrations, the
cultural interests, the humor, and the human concerns of a group
of Arkansans who set their hopes to paper in one of the oldest of
all civilized rituals, the drama. Henry F. Salerno in the introduction to First Stage: A Quarterly of New Drama explains that his

publication came into being to give unknown playwrights an opportunity to make their works public. [66] "The drama," he argues,"can
thrive only on a continuing tradition . . . Every practicing craftsman needs to know what is being done by his contemporaries--that
is, the experimental as well as the conventional, the . . . failures
as well as the marketable successes, the serious as well as the
slick. "[44] The historian would add to this argument that the "continuing tradition" needed by the craftsman extends back into time as
well as about him in space.

Checklist of Arkansas Playwrights[45]

Babcock,[46] Bernie. **Mammy: Drama in 4 Acts.** (New York:
  Neale Publishing Company, 1915), 102 pp., copyrighted by
  company from New York, Oct. 22, 1915, LC, D:42256. See
  below for Arkansas association.

_____. **Mary,** in **Arkansas Progress.** I, 20 (Oct. 24, 1914),
  LC: D:39041, copyrighted by author from Little Rock, Oct.
  24, 1914.

Blair,[47] Ernest F. **A Timely Confession: Military Dramatic**
  Sketch. 14 pp., typed, LC, D:21910, Aug. 29, 1910, copyrighted by author from Little Rock.

Bratton, Ocier S. **The Creation: A Play in 3 Acts.** 93 pp.,
  typed, LC, D:34411, Sept. 12, 1913, copyrighted by author
  from Little Rock.

Braunig, Sol. **Fate of the Dalton Gang.** No known copy, LC, D:
  1808, copyrighted by author from Little Rock, April 2, 1902.

_____. **Nick Carter, The New York Detective.** No known
  copy, LC, D:1764, copyrighted by author from [67] Little
  Rock, April 21, 1902.

Cantrell,[48] Ellen Harrell. **Freaks of St. Valentine; A Social Drama**
  in 4 Acts. 39 pp., Little Rock: Arkansas Democrat Co.,
  1893. Not copyrighted.

Cohn,[49] William Isaac. **The Blessed Runaway: Play in 1 Act.**
  19 pp., typed, LC, D:8554, May 18, 1906, copyrighted by
  author from Fort Smith.

_____. **The End of the Story: Play in 1 Act.** 31 pp.,

typed, LC, D:8555, May 18, 1906, copyrighted by author
from Fort Smith.

_____. The Little Boy with a Past: Playlet in 1 Act. 6
pp., typed, LC, D:8553, May 18, 1906, copyrighted by author
from Fort Smith.

_____. The Old Shoe: Play in 1 Act. 18 pp., typed, LC,
D:8552, May 18, 1906, copyrighted by author from Fort Smith.

_____. Patrick's Ward: Play in 4 Acts. 42 pp., typed,
LC, D:25304, Sept. 25, 1911, copyrighted by author from
Fort Smith.

_____. The Voice of the People: Play in 1 Act. 17 pp.,
typed, LC, D:8556, May, 1906, copyrighted by author from
Fort Smith.

Collins, [50] Whitney. The Last Round Up: A Story of the Plains.
87 pp., typed, LC, D:14757, Jan. 6, 1909, copyrighted by
author from Jonesboro. [68]

_____. Little Sister of the Streets: Play in 3 Acts. 78
pp., typed, LC, D:45263, Oct. 24, 1916, copyrighted by
author from Jonesboro.

Constant, Paul B. and E. James Kervin. Cross-Rays. No known
copy, LC, D:30084, copyrighted by authors from Pine Bluff,
May 18, 1896.

Corrington, S. B., Edgar A. Poe: A Tragedy in 3 Acts. No
known copy, LC, D:5233, copyrighted by author from Fort
Smith, May 1, 1876.

Crocker, [51] Philip Henry. Transformation: A Comedy Drama in 5
Acts. No known copy, LC, D:63773, copyrighted by author
from Newport, Nov. 15, 1897.

Crockett, Robert. One Girl Worth a Dozen Boys: A Drama in 2
Acts. No known copy, LC, D:15743, copyrighted by author
from Stuttgart, Mar. 19, 1895.

Everett, [52] Ruth. Cohen's Toy Shop: A 1 Act Comedy, Introducing
the Original Mechanical Doll. No known copy, LC, D:7932,
copyrighted by author from Elkins, Feb. 1, 1906.

Fisher, Isaac. Mile-Stones of Progress: From the Principal's
Lecture, Mile-Stones of Progress, Have You Counted Them?

No known copy, LC, D:4720, copyrighted by author from Pine
Bluff, Mar. 14, 1904.

Hammett, [53] R. W. In the Wilderness; or, A Romance of Christianity, In Forty Scenes. (Fort Smith: Thrash-Lick, 1896), 315
pp., LC, D:40781, copyrighted by author from Fort Smith,
July 13, 1896.

Harris, Irving. His Sister:[54] 1 Act Play. 13 pp., typed, LC, D:
30143, July 1, 1912, copyrighted by author from [69] Little Rock.

_____. The New Artist Model: 1 Act Playlet. 5 pp.,
typed, LC, D:30213, July 9, 1912, copyrighted by author from
Little Rock.

Hill, Jehu. Maid and a Drunkard on the Street: Drama in 5 Acts.
12 pp., typed, LC, D:23204, Jan. 27, 1911, copyrighted by
author from Fort Smith.

Hunt, [55] Samuel C. Three Wise Men: An Original Comedy in 3
Acts. No known copy, LC, D:16794, copyrighted by author
from Fort Smith, Mar. 25, 1895.

McCrary, [56] Ben. Intrigue: A Drama in Prologue and 4 Acts. 15
pp., LC, D:1911, Jan. 29, 1883, copyrighted by author from
Jennings Bros., Marshall, Tex., in 1883; and extension applied for from Hot Springs in 1910.

McKay, S. A. Molly Million: American Operetta. (Little Rock:
Democrat Printing and Lithographing Co., 1910), 31 pp. (libretto only), LC, D:21560, June 28, 1910, copyrighted by
author from Little Rock.

Morgan, Tom P. Actor and the Law. 7 pp., typed, LC, D:7973,
Feb. 10, 1906, copyrighted by author from Rogers.

_____. Alkali Ike[57] Drops In. 7 pp., typed, LC, D:7049, [70]
July 31, 1905, copyrighted by author from Rogers.

_____. All in the Family; An Original Monologue. 6 pp.,
typed, LC, D:14346, Nov. 21, 1908, copyrighted by author
from Rogers.

_____. The Bigness of Bill. 15 pp., typed, LC, D:10888,
July 1, 1907, copyrighted by author from Rogers.

_____. Cupid and a Wager; Vaudeville Sketch in 1 Act. 7
pp., typed, LC, D:7936, Feb. 2, 1906, copyrighted by author

from Rogers.

_____. Down at Uncle Polk's: Original Vaudeville Sketch
in 1 Act. 14 pp., typed, LC, D:6197, Feb. 9, 1905, copyrighted by author from Rogers.

_____. Everything Goes in Vod'ville: Comedy in 1 Act.
11 pp., typed, LC, D:11111, Aug. 5, 1907, copyrighted by
author from Rogers.

_____. Everybody Kisses Hattie: Comedy in 1 Act. 14 pp.,
LC, D:10617, May 22, 1907, copyrighted by author from
Rogers.

_____. Gentleman from Cheyenne: A 1 Act Comedy. 6
pp., LC, D:5103, May 31, 1908, copyrighted by author from
Rogers.

_____. He Was With Booth: Comedy in 1 Act. 9 pp.,
typed, LC, D:12648, Mar. 31, 1908, copyrighted by author
from Rogers.

_____. Her Father's Sword: Drama in 1 Act. 14 pp.,
typed, LC, D:10366, Apr. 17, 1907, copyrighted by author
from Rogers.

_____. The Joy of a Monologist: A Monologue. 7 pp.,
typed, LC, D:11998, Dec. 28, 1907, copyrighted by author
from Rogers.

_____. The Lady and the Sleuth: An Acrobatic Comedy in
1 Act. 5 pp., typed, LC, D:13074, May 28, 1908, copyrighted by author from Rogers.

_____. The Mollycoddle and the Lady Minstrel: A Vaude-
ville Sketch. 8 pp., typed, LC, D:13224, June 22, 1908,
copyrighted by author from Rogers. [71]

_____. Old Counselor Peavy: An Original Character Com-
edy. 11 pp., typed, LC, D:16631, Aug. 25, 1909, copyrighted by author from Rogers.

_____. Old Counselor Peavy: Original Comedy in 1 Act.
13 pp., typed, LC, D:24567, June 24, 1911, copyrighted by
author from Rogers.

_____. Old Sergeant Bundy: An Original Character Come-
dy. No known copy, LC, D:15824, copyrighted by author

from Rogers, May 11, 1909.

_____. The Reverend Snappy Halliday: A Vaudeville Sketch.
9 pp., typed, LC, D:11719, Nov. 12, 1907, copyrighted by
author from Rogers.

_____. The Sailor and the Rube: A Comedy in 1 Act.   7
pp., typed, LC, D:14229, Nov. 7, 1908, copyrighted by author from Rogers.

_____. Up Connecticut Way: A New England Character
Comedy in 4 Acts.   60 pp., typed, LC, D:5102, May 31,
1904, copyrighted by author from Rogers.

_____. Uncle Timrod's Little Game: Vaudeville Sketch in
1 Act.   7 pp., typed, LC, D:6897, July 3, 1905, copyrighted
by author from Rogers.

_____. Uncle's Littlest Girl: Vaudeville Sketch in 1 Act.
5 pp., LC, D:5650, Oct. 17, 1904, copyrighted by author
from Rogers.

_____. Undertaker and the Red Soubrettes: Sketch in 1 Act.
8 pp., typed, LC, D:8098, Mar. 5, 1906, copyrighted by author from Rogers.

_____. Verbosifantasticality: Monologue.   10 pp., typed,
LC, D:10637, May 25, 1907, copyrighted by author from
Rogers.

_____. Words and Women: An Original Monologue.   6 pp.,
typed, LC, D:13246, June 25, 1908, copyrighted by author
from Rogers.

Parish, Samuel C.   The Seven Blasts: Temperance Drama in 4
Acts.   (Mt. Ida: Seven Blasts Publishing Co., 1915), 32 pp.,
LC, D:40684, copyrighted by author from Mt. Ida, May 14,
1915.   [72]

Pierce-Lyman, Elizabeth.   Tesca: Libretto of a Grand Opera in 3
Acts.   30 pp., typed, LC, D:42000, Oct. 15, 1915, copyrighted by author from Little Rock.

Pritchard, Vergil Felton.   Fool for Luck; Or, The Mole, A Play
in 3 Acts.   37 pp., typed, LC, D:35344, Dec. 15, 1913,
copyrighted by author from Fayetteville.

_____. Zoka: A Farce Comedy in 3 Acts.   41 pp., typed,

LC, D:21862, Aug. 15, 1910, copyrighted by author from
Fayetteville.

_____. A Stolen Birthright: Play in 3 Acts. 35 pp.,
typed, LC, D:29356, April 12, 1912, copyrighted by author
from Fayetteville.

_____. A Struggle on Wall Street: Play in 3 Acts. 34
pp., typed, LC, D:29353, Apr. 8, 1912, copyrighted by author from Fayetteville.

Robbins, [58] Hiram. The Destruction of Hell: Operetta-Extrava-
ganza in 3 Acts. No known copy, LC, D:42603, copyrighted
by author from Little Rock, Aug. 21, 1895.

_____. Ingersoll's Destruction of Hell: Adapted to Opera,
Dramatic, Tent, or Out-Door Exhibition. No known copy,
LC, D:57445, copyrighted by author from Little Rock, Nov.
13, 1895.

Rogers, [59] Charles Smith. American Lords. No known copy, LC,
D:193, copyrighted by author from Hot Springs, Mar. 11,
1901.

_____. Knights of the Royal Arch. No known copy, [73] LC, A:
4079, [60] copyrighted by author from Hot Springs, Aug. 13,
1900.

Rose, G. B. Sebastian: A Dramatic Poem. (Buffalo, N.Y.:
Charles Wells Moulton, 1894), 93 pp., LC, D:19602, copyrighted by author from Little Rock, Apr. 16, 1894.

Ruble, Freda Slemons. El Paso, Down by the Rio Grande: A
Melodrama in 4 Acts. 52 pp., typed, LC, D:13523, Aug. 10,
1908, copyrighted by author from Monticello. (See also
Slemons, Freda, below).

Seibert, S.S. The Boodlers: A 4 Act Drama. No known copy,
LC, D:12453, copyrighted by author from Fort Smith, Feb.
14, 1908.

_____. The Brand: A 4 Act Drama. No known copy, LC,
D:12454, copyrighted by author from Fort Smith, Feb. 14,
1908.

_____. The Ways of Martins: 4 Act Comedy. No known
copy, LC, D:12586, copyrighted by author from Fort Smith,

Mar. 20, 1908.

Slemons, Freda. Joshua Copeland's Daughter: A Domestic Comedy in 4 Acts. 40 pp., typed, LC, D:3468, May 21, 1903, copyrighted by author from Monticello.

_____. Saint or Sinner: An Emotional Drama. 35 pp., typed, LC, D:3616, June 18, 1903, copyrighted by author from Monticello.

_____. The Sweetest Girl in Dixie: A Comedy Drama in 4 Acts. 40 pp., typed, LC, D:11163, copyrighted by author from Monticello, Aug. 12, 1907.

_____. Same as above, 32 pp., typed, LC, D:7797, Jan. 2, 1906. Copyrighted by author from Monticello.

Smyth, Louis N. Where Strife Held Sway: A Comedy Drama in 3 Acts. 37 pp., typed, LC, D:1908, May 20, 1902, copyrighted by author from Little Bay.

Thatcher, Eva. Twenty Minutes Till Train Time. No known copy, LC, D:33785, copyrighted by author and "Chenny," May 19, 1899, from Hot Springs. [74]

Varner, [61] William Iverson. Aurora Angelica: A Comedy in 2 Acts. No known copy, LC, D:36038, copyrighted by author from Varner, Aug. 1, 1894.

_____. Blossoming Youth: A Comedy in 4 Acts From College Life. No known copy, LC, D:36039, copyrighted by author from Varner, Aug. 1, 1894.

_____. Bottom's Dream: A Comedy Spectacular in 3 Acts. No known copy, LC, D:36040, copyrighted by author from Varner, Aug. 1, 1894.

Vredenburgh, Anna Van. The Grandest Pagan of Them All. No known copy, LC, D:6785, copyrighted by author from Hot Springs, July 7, 1905.

Williams, [62] Scott. The Phantom Beast; or, Seven Whiskies and a Bald Pate: Original Fantasty in 1 Act and 4 Scenes. 44 pp., typed, LC, D:43255, Mar. 6, 1916, copyrighted by author from Little Rock.

Withrow, N.H. A Night at Home: 1 Act Vaudeville Singing Sketch. 2 pp., typed, LC, D:28927, Feb. 13, 1912, copyrighted by author from Little Rock.

Witt, Louis. The Scab: Drama in 4 Acts. 51 pp., typed, LC,
D:33933, July 29, 1913, copyrighted by author from Little
Rock.

_____. The Servant: A Play in 4 Acts. 51 pp., typed,
LC, D:23855, April 5, 1911, copyrighted by author from
Little Rock.

Wood, [63] John P. The Drummer; or, Fun in a Railroad Station:
A Musical Comedy in 2 Acts. No known copy, LC, D:9842,
copyrighted by author from Fayetteville, May 29, 1883. [75]

3. "Mississippi Drama Between Wars, 1870-1916:
A Checklist and an Argument, Part II"
(With Katherine P. Finley, The Journal of Mississippi
History, XXVI [November, 1964], 299-306. Part I, a
restatement of the values of such a list, much like the
essay for the Arkansas drama article, was published
in the Summer, 1964, issue, 219-228.)

This checklist of Mississippi playwrights and plays was not
prepared as a summation of the history of Mississippi drama. At
best it suggests an awareness of a body of literature which may
contain material of possible literary and historical value. In these
works, there is evidence of the aspirations, the frustrations, the
cultural interests, and the human concerns of a group of Mississip-
pians who set their hopes to paper in one of the oldest of all civilized rituals, the drama. Henry F. Salerno in the introduction to
First Stage: A Quarterly of New Drama explains that his magazine
came into being to give unknown playwrights an opportunity to make
their works public. "The drama," he argues, "can thrive only on
a continuing tradition . . . . Every practicing craftsman needs to
know what is being done by his contemporaries---that is, the experimental as well as the conventional, the . . . failures as well
as the . . . successes, the serious as well as the slick."[64] The
historian should add to this argument that the "continuing tradition"
needed by the craftsman extends back into time as well as about
him in space and that every civilized person, not merely the "practicing craftsman," has the same need. [299]

A Checklist of Mississippi Playwrights[65]

Austin, Martha W.[66] Tristram and Isolt. Boston: The Poet Lore
Company, 1905, 64 pp. Copyrighted from Ocean Springs,
Miss., Oct. 2, 1905, by the author.

Battaile, Sallie C. Questions and Answers and Compositions and
Speeches for the Deestrick Skule. Unpublished. Copy in LC,
D:2433b, 13 pp. Copyrighted from Meridian, Miss., May 25,
1911, by author.

Bien, H. M.[67] The Feast of Lights; or Chanukoh: Three Character Poems and Grand Tableau Finale. Vicksburg, [300] Miss.:
Vicksburg Printing and Publishing Co., 1885, 27 pp. Copyrighted from Vicksburg, Miss., June 27, 1885, by author.

Boggs, Robert. Beneberak: The Spanish Jew: A Drama in Five
Acts, Dramatized from the Novel, A Step-Daughter. Unpub-
lished. No known copy. Copyrighted from Long Beach, Miss.,
June 13, 1903, by author.

_____. Luck Agin' It: Comedy in 1 Act with Song, He Has
Come to Get Married. Unpublished. No known copy. Copyrighted from Long Beach, Miss., Sept. 29, 1904, by author.

_____. Pet and Pert: A Comedy in 1 Act. Unpublished.
No known copy. Copyrighted from Long Beach, Miss., June
13, 1903, by author.

_____. Poor Lucinda Pearl: Drama in 5 Acts. Unpublish-
ed. No known copy. Copyrighted from Long Beach, Miss.,
April 6, 1903, by author.

Coflin, Frank S. The Wedding Bell: Comedy Drama in 5 Acts.
Unpublished. No known copy. Copyrighted from Quitman,
Miss., April 27, 1905, by author.

Cooley, Alice Kingsbury.[68] Did She Sin? An Original and Exciting Drama in 5 Acts. Unpublished. No known copy. Copyrighted from Natchez, Miss., Oct. 27, 1873, by author.

Cowan, Louise H.[69] Rajah Sindl. Unpublished. Copy in LC, D:
20073, 30 pp. Copyrighted from Greenville, Miss., Jan. 31,
1910, by author.

_____. The Reckoning. Unpublished. Copy in LC, D:
33516, [301] 31 pp. Copyrighted from Greenville, Miss., June 17,

1913, by author.

Dial, E. H.   The Queen of the East; or, The March of Progress:
A Play by One of the Oldest Inhabitants.   Printed: Meridian,
Miss., 1889, 12 pp.   Copyrighted from Meridian, Miss., May
29, 1889, by author.

Downing, A. Merle.   The Cain Man: Drama in 4 Acts.   Unpublished.   Copy in LC, D:28880, 61 pp.   Copyrighted from
Jackson, Miss., February 29, 1912, by author.

Falkner, W. C.   The Lost Diamond: A Thrilling Drama.   Unpublished.   No known copy.   Copyrighted from Ripley, Miss.,
March 29, 1883, by author.

Ferrell, Chiles Clifford.[70]   Sappho: Traverspiel in 5 Aufzugen,
von Franz Grillparzer.   Boston: Ginn & Company, 1899,
xxxxii, 143 pp.   Copyrighted from Oxford, Miss., Feb. 28,
1899, by translator.

Gaither, Francis O. Jones.   The Pageant of Columbus Within a
Masque of I. I. & C.:   Book of Words . . . Interpretive
Dances Written by Emma Ody Pohl.   Printed: Columbus,
Miss., 61 pp.   Copyrighted from Columbus, Miss., May 26,
1915, by author.

Gill, William.[71]   Full of Fun; or The Widow of Whymple: A New
and Original Farcical and Musical Comedy in 3 Acts [302] and 2
Scenes.   Unpublished.   No known copy.   Copyrighted from
Greenfield, Miss., Jan. 3, 1882, by author.

Hallback, William.[72]   A Hot Coon from Mississippi: A Comedy
Drama in 3 Acts.   Printed: Jackson, Miss., 17 pp.   Copyrighted from Jackson, Miss., July 23, 1902, by author.

Harris, Garrard.[73]   A Dream of Empire.   Unpublished.   No known
copy.   Copyrighted from Jackson, Miss., Feb. 13, 1900, by
author.

Henry, Louis.[74]   The Rajah of India; or, Marcelle: A Libretto.
Unpublished.   No known copy.   Copyrighted from Greenville,
Miss., Aug. 7, 1896, by author.

Hess, Fredrick.[75]   Mary of Magdala: A Drama in 5 Acts by Paul
Heyse, tr. from the German by F. Hess.   Printed: Pascagoula, Miss., 58 pp.   Copyrighted from Pascagoula, April 22,

1903 (printed Sept. 30, 1903) by translator.

Holt, Sara Barton.[76] The Radish King: A Drama in 5 Acts. [303] Unpublished. No known copy. Copyrighted from Woodville, Miss., May 28, 1887, by author.

Laird, Amy. The Little Puritan: A Comedy-Drama Playlet. Unpublished. Copy in LC, D:21795, 15 pp. Copyrighted from Water Valley, Miss., Aug. 15, 1910, by author.

Marks, L. Newman. Night of the Garter: A 1 Act Scintillant Satire. Unpublished. Copy in LC, D:16509. Copyrighted from Christian, Miss., Aug. 6, 1909, by author.

Minnis, Paul. Letka: A Drama in Four Acts and Fourteen Scenes. Unpublished. No known copy. Copyrighted from Aberdeen, Miss., Oct. 5, 1885, by author.

Mosgrove, Herbert Logan.[77] The Mississippian: A Drama in 5 Acts. Unpublished. No known copy. Copyrighted from Gulfport, Miss., March 29, 1909, by the author.

Richards, Matsy Wynn. One Wonderful Dream: Mother Goose Phantasy. Unpublished. No known copy. Copyrighted from Greenville, Miss., Aug. 9, 1915, by author.

Richardson, Norval,[78] and Johnson, W. A. Panama: A Musical Comedy in 3 Acts. (Libretto only.) Unpublished. Copy in LC, D:8075. Copyrighted from Vicksburg, Miss., Feb. 28, 1906, by Richardson. [304]

Samek, Dan. Tommie, The Orphan Boy. Unpublished. Copy in LC, D:17944. Copyrighted from Holly Springs, Miss., Jan. 15, 1910, by author.

Smith, Lelia May. Out at Old Aunt Mary's; or, A Visit from the Riley Children: Arrangement of the Riley Poem. Unpublished. Copy in LC, D:45335. Copyrighted from Hattiesburg, Miss., Nov. 3, 1916, by author.

Stern, Caroline. "The Queen Decides," in At the Edge of the World. Copyrighted from Greenville, Miss., April 14, 1916, by author.

Tindall, John Benton.[79] The Fountain: Play in 3 Acts. Unpublished. Copy in LC, D:37129, 151 pp. Copyrighted from Webb, Miss., May 26, 1914, by author.

White, John McElroy.   Craps; or Ten Lights: A Negro Dialect
Dramatic Composition.   Unpublished.   Copy in LC, D:14944,
9 pp.   Copyrighted from Meridian, Miss., Jan. 29, 1909, by
author.

_____. Napoleon Bonaparte: Historical Play in 3 Acts.
Unpublished.   Copy in LC, D:33838, 39 pp.   Copyrighted
from Meridian, Miss., July 18, 1913, by author.

_____. Napoleon Bonaparte: Drama in 5 Acts.   Unpublish-
ed.   Copy in LC, D:30378, 44 pp.   Copyrighted from Meridian, Miss., July 27, 1916, by author.

_____. Pineywoods: A Dramatic Composition Representing
the Dialect of the Pineywoods District.   Unpublished.   Copy
in LC, D:15885.   Copyrighted from Meridian, Miss., May 14,
1909, by author. [305]

Williams, Joseph John. [80] Curzon Sisters, Flying Butterflies.   Unpublished.   Copy in LC, D:9676, 5 pp.   Copyrighted from
Jackson, Miss., Dec. 17, 1906, by author.

Wright, Charles E.   Contrasts: Society Drama in 3 Acts.   Unpublished.   Copy in LC, D:25574, 27 pp.   Copyrighted from
Vicksburg, Miss., Oct. 23, 1911, by author.

_____. Gwynplaine: A Romantic Play of the Seventeenth
Century.   (Dramatized from Victor Hugo's novel, By Order of
the King.)   Vicksburg, Miss.: W.A. Jewell, 1910, 37 pp.
Copyrighted from Vicksburg, Miss., June 3, 1910, by author.

_____. Talked About: A Comedy Drama in 4 Acts.   Vicks-
burg, Miss.: Vicksburg Printing and Publishing Company,
1895, 54 pp.   Copyrighted from Vicksburg, Miss., Dec. 6,
1895, by author.

Young, Stark. [81] Guenevere: A Play in 5 Acts.   New York: Graf-
ton Press, 1906, 82 pp.   Copyrighted from University, Miss.,
Dec. 15, 1906, by author. [306]

4.   "The Boomers: Oklahoma Playwrights Opened the Territory"
     (Reprinted from The Chronicles of Oklahoma,
          XLI [Autumn, 1963], 248-252.)

Oklahoma has always been proud of its pioneers, especially

of its pioneer women. Bryant Baker's memorial statue, The Pioneer Woman, in Ponca City is probably the best known tribute to
the pioneer in the United States. And the contributions of the pioneers have long been the subject of story and song. The politi-
cians have been honored in C. W. Allen's The Sequoyah Convention;
the oil men, in such works as W. L. Connelly's The Oil Business As
I Saw It; the cattlemen, in E. E. Dale's Cow Country and the Range
Cattle Industry; the Indians, in Angie Debo's And Still the Waters
Run; the city-builders, in Debo's Tulsa: From Creek Town to Oil
Capitol; the frontier newspaperwomen, in Mrs. Tom Ferguson's
They Carried the Torch; and the list could be continued to include
almost all of those who made the Oklahoma "Run" one of the
world's great adventures in pioneering.

But among the pioneers, there was one hardy band, led by a
woman; and Oklahoma has not even left a shovel to show where they
were buried--the playwrights.

Kenneth C. Kaufman and Spencer Norton, writing of the dramatists of Oklahoma for the two editions (1941 and 1956) of Oklahoma: A Guide to the Sooner State, both comment on the accomplishments of such post World War I Oklahoma playwrights as Lynn
Riggs, author of Green Grow the Lilacs, Cherokee Nights, and Rus-
set Mantle; and Mary McDougal Axelson, the author of Life Begins.
They mention that Fleta Campbell Springer, in addition to her novels,
also wrote "a play." But neither mentions a single play or playwright before World War I, and both Kaufman and Norton are a-
mong the most devoted chroniclers of the state's literary history.
[248]

This neglect of this one aspect of Oklahoma's cultural history
is not difficult to understand, and it is a neglect which most of the
states in the Union share. Before World War I, it is generally
agreed, American drama was in a "low state," a state caused in
large part by the bad practices of the stage. Anyone who wrote
for that stage, it is argued, had to commit offenses against dramatic art that made their plays, at best, second-rate. And the "best"
of the nineteenth-century American plays--dramas like Herne's
Margaret Fleming--are judged to be inferior to their European con-

temporaries like Ibsen's <u>Hedda Gabler</u> and Chekhov's <u>Cherry Or-</u>
<u>chard.</u>

Before World War I, moreover, Oklahoma produced only a
few playwrights who had any success on this "bad" stage. And, the
argument runs, although the stage was "bad," only those plays that
were successful on it were any good at all. Oddly enough, with the
"conditions on the American stage," Europeans like Ibsen and Chekhov could not have produced what they were writing, but if any of
the stay-away-from-the-stage American playwrights were writing
like them, their work was then ignored, and it is now forgotten.

Whether the playwrights of Oklahoma were too bad for the stage
or too good, they were busy. From the opening of the Cherokee
Strip in 1893 until the outbreak of the First World War, Oklahoma
had at least thirty-nine playwrights who wrote at least forty-one of
their dramas while residents. And they, at least, thought their works
had enough merit to justify copyrighting them. These plays now
constitute what is probably the largest body of "neglected" literature
in Oklahoma's history.

Pioneer Woman, Playwright Style

The author of the first play copyrighted from Oklahoma was a
woman who might well have served as a model for Baker's statue,
Mary Isabella Hassim. She came to "Old Oklahoma" in 1889. Sev-
en years later she celebrated this event in her play, <u>The Boomers;</u>
<u>The Opening and the Settling of the Cherokee Strip.</u>

The play was copyrighted from Blackburn, and no known copy
of it still exists. It was, apparently, her only dramatic composition. At least, it was the only play she ever had copyrighted.

Six more plays were written and copyrighted from Oklahoma
before the turn of the century. Five of them, all written by two
brothers, George and Warren Noble, were copyrighted in 1897 from
Guthrie. Like <u>The Boomers,</u> all five are now among the "lost"
drama of Oklahoma. Their titles are known, however, and suggest
that the Nobles were interested in the drama for the sake of entertainment. Four of the plays are comedies: [249] <u>Dad's Angel,</u>
<u>Baby Mine, Gay Mr. Tompkins,</u> and the <u>Yankee Genius.</u> Their

fifth play was a melodrama, The Train Wreckers. All were three or four-act plays, suggesting that some of them, at least, must have been written before 1897.

Only one other play was copyrighted from Oklahoma in the nineteenth century. J. Frank Gudarian copyrighted Paradise Regained from Hennessey in 1898. It, too, is a "lost" play; and like Miss Hassim and the Noble brothers, Gudarian apparently wrote no other works for the theater beyond his Oklahoma composition.

Into The Twentieth Century

During the first fifteen years of the twentieth century, Oklahoma playwrights must have been as common as corner drugstores. Every town seems to have had at least one.

Oklahoma City had five. Two were women: Lena Blackburn, author of The Sheath Gown Girls, "a musical comedy in one act," 1908; and Edna Sutton Stark, the author of two plays: Via the Heart, "a play in 1 act," 1912, and Diamonds Seven, Hearts Eight, "a play in 1 act," 1915. The other three playwrights were men: Felix Hunter, author of By Chance, a one-act play, 1911; Courtenay Morgan, the author of One Christmas Eve, a "dramatic sketch," copyrighted January 3, 1910, and Innocent Widow, a "play in 4 acts, dramatized from Delpit's novel, Coralie's Son," copyrighted January 27, 1910; and William L. Tucker, the author of The Struggle, "a Heart-Interest Drama in 4 Acts," 1912.

Norman had three playwrights: Arthur O. May and Lew Sully, authors of Limb of the Law, 1914; and Mary E. Waddington, who copyrighted two plays from Norman in 1908--Al Douglass, King and The Return--and one play from Purcell in 1911, When Daughters Will.

Five Oklahoma towns had two playwrights each. Stillwater had Marion Hughes, author of Three Years in Arkansas, 1906, and L. J. Jardot, author of Oklahoma, 1903. Shawnee had Charles Patterson, author of The Lost Heiress, 1900, and We Wo Yonk, author of Chief Black Hawk's Revenge, 1911. Ardmore had Herbert Butzow and Jack Burnett, authors of The Gallery God, 1911. Hobart had William and Henry Ellis, the authors of Who Is He?, 1907.

Anadarko had two playwrights who listed their names simply as "Spahn & Corson," when they copyrighted their only play, The Tale of the Comet, 1909.

Over twenty other Oklahoma towns had at least one playwright each during these years. For four towns, the only playwright was a woman. Sulphur had Anna Burgess, author of [250] Money Against Money, 1909. A year earlier, in 1908, Miss Burgess had copyrighted her only other play, War of Money, from Chicago. Perry had Norma A. Lucy, author of The Crook, 1911. Muskogee had Isabel S. McLaughlin, author of The Question, 1911. The same year, Mrs. McLaughlin also copyrighted another play, My Wife's Daughter, from Washington, D.C., apparently her only other dramatic work. Ada had Mrs. Cannie West, author of A Man's Love; or Driven from Eden, 1913.

All of the other "town's only" playwrights were, apparently, men. (Occasionally women used men's names in the hopes of getting a more favorable hearing for their plays.) Tulsa had Don Louis Anchors, author of The Coachman, 1909. Dewey had James Baughman, author of The Little Mountaineer, 1908. Tyrone had Stephen Champlin, author of Adam Killjoy, 1904. Pryor Creek had John J. Dege, author of The Moor of Venice, "a revised edition" of Shakespeare's Othello, 1915. Pawnee had Gordon Lillie, author of Statehood at Pawnee Bill's Ranch, 1908. Mangum had W.C. Marble, author of The Heartsearching, 1913. Bomar had George Rhodes, author of Cupid's Arrow, 1910. North McAlester had Simeon Sites, author of The Turkey Maiden, 1914.

Durant's only playwright, W.A. Sterrett, should be of special interest to collectors of pioneer accounts. He wrote and copyrighted two plays in 1912, both about Oklahoma: Opening of Oklahoma and Opening of the Cherokee Strip.

Capitol Hill's only playwright, Ira N. Terrill, also turned to Oklahoma history for his only play, A Purgatory Made of a Paradise, 1907, "a tragedy in 3 acts, depicting early day scenes in Oklahoma."

Enterprise and Quinton had to share their "only playwright," Charles T. Wilkerson. In 1910 he wrote Beautiful Friend in Enterprise. In 1911 he moved to Quinton for his second and last play, The Clutch of the Vampire.

Geary, for a time in 1909, had for its "only playwright" one of the most prolific stage writers in the country, Junie McCree. McCree wrote and copyrighted one play there, Hebrewing and She-wooing. For the ten years before and after his Geary residence, however, he copyrighted at least eighty-eight other plays, running from After the Barber's Ball to Yit, Yat, and Yay. All of the plays, other than Hebrewing and Shewooing, were copyrighted from New York. Presumably McCree was a writer-actor traveling with one of the many road shows criss-crossing the state when he did his one Oklahoma dramatic composition.

Others of these playwrights did some writing for the stage, in addition to the plays copyrighted from Oklahoma. Champlin, [251] for example, after his play written in Tyrone in 1904, went to New York where he wrote and probably sold ten other plays, most of them one-act compositions intended for the vaudeville circuits. Only one of his plays, a three-act farce, Who Did It?, according to the Best Plays records, ever had a Broadway opening. It ran for eight performances at the Harris Theatre in New York, opening there June 9, 1919.

It is, however, in the forty-one plays written in Oklahoma that the best chance for recovering some "lost" Green Grow the Lilacs lies. Whether it was Terrill blaming "purgatory" on the opening of the Indian lands to white settlers or Mrs. West blaming it on "a man's love," it is in these plays, written on the scene at a time when the pioneer experience was still as fresh as bread from the oven, that the local playwrights were putting the Oklahoma adventure on record.

Some of these plays still exist in the writer's manuscript copies in the Library of Congress. Copies of most of them, however, if they now exist at all, are probably at the bottom of the trunk in the attic or in the vault with the family papers. Whereever they are, however, they are real materials for a monument in the making for Oklahoma's forgotten pioneer, the playwright. [252]

Notes

1. II, 888-891. [65]

2. The list has been checked against Dramatic Compositions Copy-
    righted in the United States from 1870 to 1916 (Washington,
    1918).   See also this writer's "Research Projects Waiting: The
    Forgotten Drama of Provincial America," Western Speech,
    XXIV, 142-150 (Summer, 1963).

3. This number indicates that a copy was deposited with the Li-
    brary of Congress (LC) and given a dramatic (D) number.   As
    the copyright expired on some of the plays (twenty-eight years),
    the manuscripts were destroyed.   Therefore, not all plays for
    which numbers are available are still on deposit.

4. Adams, the daughter of the Rev. Dr. William H. and Anna
    (Byrne) Mitchell and the wife of Sam Adams, a planter and
    merchant of Florence, was a student at the University of Ala-
    bama from 1893 to 1895 (Owen, III, 12).

5. Some plays were copyrighted on the basis of the title page only,
    as was this one.

6. Boudousquie wrote at least one other drama, Saturnalia: A
    Tragedy, copyrighted from New Orleans on June 22, 1906 and
    Jan. 14, 1907.

7. Brooks was possibly a member of the James T. Brooks family.
    He was mayor of Gadsden, 1882-1885 (ibid., II, 222). [66]

8. Carlysle applied for a copyright on this work a second time,
    Nov. 18, 1882, again from Selma.

9. Owen (II, 889) mentions Chaudron's collection of poetry, Madam
    la Marquis (1892).

10. Taylor wrote and copyrighted ten other plays (not from Ala-
    bama), using the pseudonym of Beaumont Claxton for all of
    them.   One, In Old No'th Ca'lina . . . , was published in
    Carthage, Mo. in 1904.   He was possibly the son of William
    Henry Taylor, an Alabama planter (ibid., IV, 1653).

11. DeLeon, who was born in South Carolina on May 21, 1839 and
    died in Mobile, March 19, 1914, is one of the best known of
    Alabama's writers (Benjamin B. Williams, "Thomas Cooper De-
    Leon: Alabama's First Professional Man-of-Letters," Alabama
    Historical Quarterly, XXIV, 40-51 [Spring, 1962]).   During
    1870-1871 he copyrighted nine other plays from Baltimore and
    New York City.   Brander Matthews collaborated with him on
    one play, Hand to Hand, which they copyrighted from Saratoga,
    N.Y., on Aug. 14, 1871, but George C.D. Odell, Annals of the
    New York Stage (New York, 1937), IX, 162, records that it was
    "a complete failure." [67]

12. Graham was an editor, a member of the Alabama legislature,
    and a circuit clerk. Born in North Carolina, July 20, 1840,
    he moved to Dallas County, Ala. after the Confederate War and
    was on the staff of the Selma Times (Owen, III, 688).

13. Greene, a teacher and novelist, was born in Tuscaloosa. In
    1911 she became editor of the woman's page of the Birmingham
    News. Two years later she was named head of the Birmingham
    Public Library, but resigned to "devote her entire time to writ-
    ing." Her novels include Arthur and His Court, Into the Night,
    One Clear Call, The Right of the Strongest, and The Devil to
    Pay (ibid., III, 700-701). [68]

14. Henry-Ruffin, born Aug. 26, 1857, was the daughter of Thomas
    and Mary Henry of Mobile. She wrote John Gildart, a story in
    verse; North Star, a novel of early Norway; Eden on the James,
    a story of the Jamestown settlement; and The Shield of Silence,
    among other non-dramatic works (ibid., IV, 1472).

15. Johnson copyrighted seven other plays, all from Colorado ad-
    dresses, between 1898 and 1913.

16. Lamar, the son of Theodore Jemison Lamar, was "a labor
    leader, founder and editor of The Labor Review" (ibid., IV,
    1003-1004).

17. This is a dramatization of Bulwer Lytton's novel, Paul Clifford.
    Between 1908 and 1913 Levy copyrighted seven other plays from
    Pensacola, Fla. [69]

18. This play is a dramatization of Emily Brontë's novel by the
    same name.

19. MacKnight copyrighted three other plays, all from New York
    City: Stanley (1890), Cuba Free (1896), and On the Klondike
    (1897).

20. McNutt was a Birmingham businessman and accountant (ibid.,
    IV, 1139).

21. Len D. Mullen has not been identified. H. F. Mullen, born in
    Tuscaloosa in 1838, was the first physician in Selma, opening
    practice there in 1862. He saw service with the Confederate
    States Army, and in 1865 was elected city physician, but re-
    tired in 1866 (ibid., IV, 1256-1257). The title of the play,
    The Doctor's Wife; the similar family name, Mullen; and the
    address, Selma, suggest a probable association with the com-
    position of this play by either Dr. Mullen or a member of his
    family.

22. I. M. Nomaun ("I'm no man") is obviously a pseudonym, and
    there is no record of a Morrisville in Alabama in 1896.

23. Owen, born Sept. 1, 1869, near Macon, Mississippi, also wrote novels, including Yvonne of Braithwaite (1929) and Children of the Night (1937). The Acting Governor was first filed for copyright on Feb. 28, 1908, but a copy of the play was not submitted until July 3, 1913. Owen and M. Mayo copyrighted another play, The Transgressors, from a general "United States" address on Sept. 21, 1909. [70]

24. Ritter's play is a dramatization of Augusta J. Evans Wilson's novel, St. Elmo (1888). Another of her novels, Beulah, was dramatized and copyrighted by Alice E. Ives and filed from New York City on Aug. 8, 1910.

25. Rivers copyrighted one other play, Naomi, from Cleveland, Ohio, Aug. 12, 1911.

26. Ruff copyrighted eight other plays from New York City between 1909 and 1913.

27. Sibley was either Guy Sibley, Sr., a saw mill operator in Mobile, or his son, Guy Sibley, Jr., who was a student at the time (ibid., IV, 1557).

28. Smith (1815-1879) was a distinguished lawyer, statesman, poet, soldier, and president of the University of Alabama. Another of his plays, Aaron Burr: A Tragedy, although never copyrighted, was produced, with Smith playing one of the roles (ibid., IV., 1597-1598). [71]

29. Strauss was probably a member of the prominent Leopold Strauss family of Montgomery (ibid., IV, 1632).

30. Taylor, a former soldier in the Confederate States Army, settled in Montgomery. His father, William Henry Taylor, was an early Alabama planter (ibid., IV, 1653-1654).

31. Wallick copyrighted a number of other plays from other states after 1889, several about Sam Houston.

32. Young was among the state's most successful prose writers. In addition to her own fiction, essays, and poetry, she also collaborated with Joel Chandler Harris on Songs and Ballads of the Old-Time Plantation.

33. (New York, 1961). [61]

34. Ibid., p. 36.

35. Ibid., p. 53. [62]

36. See Henry James, The Scenic Art: Notes on Acting & the Drama, 1872-1901, ed. by Allan Wade (New York, 1957). [63]

37. Arkansas Historical Quarterly, XII (Winter, 1953), 327-32. [64]

38. (New York, 1941), 115-118.

39. University of Arkansas Bulletin, XXV (July 15, 1931), No. 8.

40. (Little Rock, 1933), pp. 109-110 and 134.

41. Arkansas Gazette Sunday Magazine, issues Nov. 17 through Dec. 22, 1935.

42. Ibid., Dec. 15, 1935. [65]

43. July 1, 1950, 4D. [66]

44. I (Winter, 1961-62), 3.

45. All the items in this checklist have been checked against copyright files listed in Dramatic Compositions Copyrighted in the United States from 1870 to 1917 (Washington, 1918).

46. Mrs. Babcock, one of the best known of Arkansas writers, was born in Ohio, but came to Arkansas as a young woman and remained there until her death in 1962. Most of her success in writing came after World War I. As late as 1948, one of her plays, The Soul of Ann Rutledge, was produced in Conway by Miss Leona Scott at Arkansas State Teachers College. Mrs. Babcock attended the opening night performance.

47. Blair wrote at least one other play before World War I, A Sensational Mistake: Dramatic Composition, Vaudeville Sketch, 6 pp., typed, LC, D:5964, Dec. 24, 1904, which he copyrighted from Springfield, Mass. [67]

48. Cited in Arkansas Books, p. 7.

49. In addition to the six plays copyrighted in Arkansas, Cohn wrote at least three other plays before World War I: Becky: A Play in 4 Acts, 68 pp., typed, LC, D:14425, Dec. 1, 1908, copyrighted by the author from New York; The Citizen of the World: A Play in 4 Acts, no known copy, LC, D:10560, copyrighted by the author from New York, May 14, 1907; and The Little Working Girl: Play in 4 Acts, 45 pp., typed, LC, D:25384, Oct. 3, 1911, copyrighted by the author from Fort Smith, Kansas. The authors have checked this carefully and believe "Kansas" should read "Arkansas."

50. Collins also wrote at least one play while residing out of state: The Girl Without a Chance: Story of the White Slave Traffic, 40 pp., typed, LC, D:35621, Jan. 12, 1914, copyrighted by the author from Chicago. [68]

51. Crocker wrote two other plays out of state: The Plungers: A

Play in 4 Acts, 68 pp., typed, LC, D:14337, Nov. 21, 1908;
The Professor: Comedy Drama in 5 Acts, 83 pp., typed, LC,
D:6249, Feb. 8, 1905, both copyrighted by the author from
Chicago.

52. Miss Everett wrote at least two other plays out of state: A-
gainst This Nation, no known copy, LC, D:4660, copyrighted by
the author from New York, Feb. 27, 1904; and Good Hawk's
White Daughter: A Melodrama in 4 Acts, 121 pp., typed, LC,
D:8440, Apr. 28, 1906, copyrighted by author from New York.

53. Arkansas Books, p. 14, records of this play, "Not in dramatic
form; mostly sermonizing." It was, however, copyrighted as
a "dramatic composition."

54. Arkansas: A Guide to the State, p. 34, records that a Mamie
Harris, born in Belleville, Ark., and reared in Dardanelle and
Ola, "gained fame as a singer." We have found no evidence of
a family relationship. [69]

55. Hunt copyrighted at least two other plays out of state: Casey's
Four Hundred: Comedy in 3 Acts, no known copy, LC, D:
53803, copyrighted from Indianola, Ia., by Wm. Tripplett, J.F.
Cassel, and the author, Aug. 23, 1899; and Friends of Free-
dom; or, Cuba's Struggle for Liberty, no known copy, LC, D:
25615, copyrighted by author from Omaha, Neb., Apr. 23,
1898.

56. McCrary copyrighted three other plays out of state: Aaron and
Theodosia; The Fate of the Burrs, A Drama in 5 Acts, 69 pp.,
LC, D:1664, copyrighted by author from Salt Lake City, Mar.
29, 1902; Osceola; or, The Sorrows of the Seminoles: A Drama
in 4 Acts, LC, D:23312, copyrighted by author from Snohomish,
Wash., July 30, 1889; and Twin Dairy; or, Uncle Kit's Decora-
tion Day: A Drama in 5 Acts, LC, D:55722, copyrighted by
author from San Francisco, Nov. 30, 1894. According to a
letter from Donald C. Holmes, Chief of Photoduplication service, June 6, 1961, Intrigue is McCrary's only play "now located
in the Library of Congress."

57. Tom P. Morgan was said to be Rogers' "Best known citizen for
many years." He wrote a series of Alkali Ike stories for a
newspaper syndicate, and his stories were also published in
Life, Judge, Puck, Golden Days, Leslie's Weekly, Saturday
Night, and Youth Companion. Rogers Daily News: 1900-1950
Mid-Century Edition, July 1, 1950, 4-D. Alsopp, Poets and
Poetry of Arkansas, writes of him, "He was one of Arkansas's
most versatile and original journalists, the author of more than
350 worthwhile poems . . . ." [70]

58. Robbins copyrighted two plays out of state: Scouts of the Plains:
An Original Drama, no known copy, LC, D:12218, copyrighted
by author from Cincinnati, Oct. 24, 1873; and Wild Bill; or,

Life on the Border: A Sensational Drama in 5 Acts, no known copy, LC, D:4790, copyrighted by author from Cincinnati, May 3, 1873.

59. Rogers, on Oct. 23, 1882, copyrighted one play, Jack: A Comedy Drama in 3 Acts by Charles Gaylor, from "United States," LC, D:17627. Gaylor was the author of over two dozen plays, most of which were produced professionally. At least one of Gaylor's plays, Out in the Streets, had two separate New York runs, in 1895 and 1898. John Chapman and Garrison P. Sherwood, The Best Plays of 1894-1899 (New York, 1955), p. 127. On Apr. 30, 1885, Rogers and N.D. Roberts took out a copyright for The Alarm Clock: An Original Musical Comedy in 3 Acts, written by Rogers, no known copy, LC, D:9871. They listed their address as "United States." [73]

60. The "A" preceding the copyright number indicates that copyright was secured on the presentation of a published manuscript. [74]

61. Varner, with a 1940 population of 5, is a crossroads filling station and store. Arkansas: A Guide to the State, p. 227.

62. Williams copyrighted two plays out of state: The Deserter: Dramatization of Robert Buchanan's Novel, The Shadow of the Sword, by Scott and League Williams, 36 pp., typed, LC, D:38908, Nov. 24, 1914, from West Park, Ohio; and The Love Locket: Play in 4 Acts, Dramatization of the Novel Phyllis by the Duchess, with Liberties, 34 pp., typed, LC, D:43465, Mar. 29, 1916, from West Park, Ohio.

63. On Jan. 8, 1884, a play by Wood, A Wedding Party in a Railroad Station: A Musical Comedy in 2 Acts, no known copy, LC, D:193, was copyrighted by F.N. Wood, United States. [75]

64. Henry F. Salerno, First Stage: A Quarterly of New Drama, Introduction. I (Winter, 1961-62), 3. [299]

65. This checklist was compiled from the copyright information recorded in Dramatic Compositions Copyrighted in the United States, 1870-1916 (Washington: U.S. Printing Office, 1918). In the entries marked "copy in LC," the copyright number, "D . . .," indicates that at the time of application for copyright, a copy of the manuscript was submitted to the Library of Congress. Copyright protection, however, extends for a period of twenty-eight years, and it may be renewed for an additional twenty-eight years. To our knowledge all of the plays listed are now in the public domain, but persons seeking to use plays copyrighted after 1907 should, of course, write to the U.S. Copyright Office for official verification. Not every play listed "copy in LC" is still in the files there. The Library of Congress copyright officials explained to us that after the expiration of copyright protection, the original manuscripts are sent

to the Library of Congress general collection. Sometimes the
manuscripts are retained as part of the general collection, but
sometimes they are destroyed. Several efforts were made to
secure a copy of W. C. Falkner's The Lost Diamond (see entry
on list) without success. In 1883 it was permissible for an author merely to submit the title page for copyright list; thus it
is not unlikely that a manuscript of the play was never in the
Library of Congress.

66. Martha W. Austin seems to have been only a summer resident
    of Mississippi. She was born in New Orleans, La., a daughter
    of Major John E. and Shaulline Yerger Creath Austin, and was
    educated at Newcomb College, New Orleans, and subsequently
    took special lectures in psychology at Radcliffe College, Cam-
    bridge, Mass. She was for a time on the staff of the New
    Orleans Picayune. E. A. Anderson and Joel Chandler Harris,
    eds., Library of Southern Literature, XV (New Orleans: Mar-
    tin and Hoyt, 1910), pp. 13-14. A selection from Part III,
    Scene 1, is on pp. 6136-6139.

67. H. M. Bien (1831-1895) was also the author of Ben-Beor, an
    historical story divided into two parts, the first a counterpart
    of Ben-Hur and the second a companion romance to The Wan-
    dering Jew, which was published in Vicksburg, Miss., and
    Baltimore, Maryland, in 1892. He also wrote: Oriental Leg-
    ends (1883), Samson (1885), Purim (1884), What is Judaism
    (1888), and Solar Night (1887). Library of Southern Literature,
    XV, pp. 34-35. An edition of The Feast of Lights was made
    available this year in the University of Kentucky Press micro-
    card Series A. Rabbi Bien, before his work as a Jewish
    religious and educational leader, worked in Port Henry, New
    York. On Jan. 13, 1875, he copyrighted another play, George
    Washington: A Dramatic Tribute to the Great Centennial of
    American Independence in 4 Acts, A Prelude and Grand Finale
    (unpublished and no known copy) from Fort Henry. [300]

68. In addition to Did She Sin?, the only play which she copyrighted
    in Mississippi, Alice Kingsbury Cooley also had two other
    plays copyrighted: The California (no known copy), copyrighted
    from Alameda, California, Dec. 3, 1893; and Borrowed Till
    Midnight: Original Drama in 5 Acts (no known copy), copy-
    righted from Alameda, Sept. 19, 1898.

69. In addition to the two plays copyrighted from Mississippi,
    Louise Henry Cowan also wrote at least three other plays:
    Belhaven, The Future City (no known copy), copyrighted from
    Weatherford, Texas, Dec. 24, 1906; The Sword of Chivalry (no
    known copy), copyrighted from Chevy Chase, Md., April 23,
    1907; and Yolande (no known copy), copyrighted from Chevy
    Chase, Sept. 7, 1907. [301]

70. Chiles Clifford Ferrell (1865-1915) was a professor at the Uni-
    versity of Mississippi from 1893 to 1908. Born in Greenville,

South Carolina, Ferrell was educated at Vanderbilt University
and the University of Leipzig (Ph. D., 1892). In addition to
his translation of Grillparzer's Sappho, he was, also, the author of Teutonic Antiquities in the Anglo-Saxon Genesis, 1893.
Who Was Who in America, 1943, Special Library Edition, I,
p. 393.

71. William Gill (1844-1917) apparently wrote only this one play,
Full of Fun, from Mississippi; but he was most active in the
general American drama of the period. Alone and in collaboration with others, he had twenty-five other plays copyrighted during the period from 1879 to 1907. These plays, all of which
were copyrighted from New York and Boston, include such works
as Our Goblin (1879), Arcadia (1886), and M'zelle (1907). Gill
was born in Boston, Mass., and worked with various New York
newspapers. He is credited with rescuing the Poe cottage at
Fordham, New York, from "threatened destruction" in 1889 and
helped to establish Poe Park as a memorial to the Southern
poet. In 1903 he founded the Edgar Poe Society. In addition
to his plays (some of which are still retained by the Library of
Congress in typed copies), he was the author of The Life of
Edgar Allan Poe, The Evolution of the Peace Movement, and a
dramatization of Robert Louis Stevenson's Dr. Jekyll and Mr.
Hyde. Who Was Who in America, I, p. 456. [302]

72. In addition to his one Mississippi play, A Hot Coon from Mississippi, William Hallback was the author of at least two other
plays: Going to the Reception (no known copy), copyrighted
from Lancaster, Pa., Jan. 6, 1908, and Uncle Remus' Return:
Dramatic Musical Composition, 4 pp., copy in LC, D:22095,
copyrighted from New York, Sept. 10, 1910.

73. Garrard Harris (1874-   ) was born in Columbus, Georgia,
and educated at the University of Georgia and Millsaps College,
Jackson, Miss., from which he was graduated in 1902 with the
LL. B. In 1906 he married Mary Lou Sykes of Aberdeen,
Miss. He was a reporter, city editor, and editorial writer on
Southern newspapers; practiced law at Jackson, Miss., 1903-11;
asst. editor of the Mobile (Ala.) Register, 1911-13; a special
agent for the United States Department of Commerce from 1913
to 1917; and a member of the Mississippi National Guard for
thirteen years, retiring with the rank of major. In addition to
this one play, A Dream of Empire, he was, also, the author
of Joe the Book Farmer (1914); Central America as an Export
Field (1915); The Treasure of the Land (1917); and numerous
trade articles and popular fiction in American magazines.

74. Louis Henry is obviously Louise Henry Cowan (see above). It
is interesting to note that in this, her first play, The Rajah of
India, she seemed to feel the need of a masculine name; but in
the other two plays, written fourteen and seventeen years later,
she used her own name.

75. This translation seems to be the only dramatic work done by
    Frederick Hess. During this same period, one other Ameri-
    can, however, was also working with the plays of Paul von
    Heyse. An Emanuel Lederer, New York, during the years
    1901 to 1907, edited six of the plays in German, none of which
    was Mary of Magdala.

76. Sara Barton Holt, in addition to her one play copyrighted from
    Mississippi, also copyrighted two from New Orleans, La.:
    The Great Trust Company: A Drama in 4 Acts (no known
    copy), Sept. 15, 1890; and A Start to Calcutta: A Drama in 3
    Acts (no known copy), Dec. 1, 1892. [303]

77. Herbert Logan Mosgrove, in addition to this one play copyright-
    ed from Mississippi, also wrote at least one other: A Ken-
    tucky Heroine; or, Among the Moonshiners: A Drama in 5 Acts
    (no known copy), copyrighted from Sturgis, Kentucky, Dec. 1,
    1898, by author.

78. Norval Richardson (1877-1940) was born in Vicksburg, Miss.,
    and educated at the Southwestern Presbyterian University,
    Clarksville, Tenn. He was the second secretary of the Amer-
    ican Legation at Havana, Cuba, 1909-1911; the secretary and
    later charge d' affaires at Copenhagen, Denmark, from 1911 to
    1913; secretary at the American Embassy at Rome from 1913
    to 1920, at Santiago, Chile, in 1920, at Lisbon from 1920 to
    1922, and at Tokyo from 1922 to 1923. He resigned from
    government service in 1924. In addition to his one play written
    in Mississippi, he was the author of numerous magazine stories
    and "sketches" and of several professional and literary works:
    The Heart of Hope (1905); The World Shut Out (1919); Pagan
    Fire (1920); Cave Woman (1922); My Diplomatic Education
    (1923); That Late Unpleasantness (1924); Pirate's Face (1928);
    Mother of Kings (1928); Dream Boat (1929); Third and Last
    (1934); Forgotten Lady (1937); and Living Abroad (1938). Who
    Was Who in America, I, p. 1031, and Library of Southern Lit-
    erature, XV, p. 369. While with the American embassy in
    Rome, Richardson copyrighted The American Ambassador: Com-
    edy in 4 Acts (copy in LC, D:40885), 151 pp., copyrighted from
    Rome on May 5, 1915, by author. [304]

79. John Benton Tindall, in addition to the one play he copyrighted
    from Mississippi, also copyrighted one other: The Triple Part-
    nership: Play in 3 Acts (copy in LC, D:40929), 32 pp., June
    14, 1915, from Memphis, Tenn. [305]

80. Joseph John Williams, in addition to the one play copyrighted
    from Mississippi, was also the author of The Boy from Kerry:
    An Irish Comedy in 4 Acts (no known copy), which he copy-
    righted from Seattle, Wash., Dec. 17, 1891.

81. Stark Young (1881-1963) was for a half century one of Missis-
    sippi's most distinguished men of letters. His career in the

theater as critic, teacher, playwright, and translator has been
the subject of any number of essays and full-length critical
studies (see Edwin Duerr, The Length and Depth of Acting,
New York: Holt, Rinehart and Winston, 1962, pp. 451-467,
for example); but at the present time no full-scale study of his
total work in the theater, let alone his full career as a man of
letters, has been done. Of interest in association with his
career as a Mississippi playwright, however, two works in addition to his Guenevere should be consulted: Addio, Madretta
and Other Plays (Chicago: Charles H. Sergel and Company,
1912), and Viva Mexico: Comedy in 1 Act by Young and A. S.
Burleson (copy in LC, D:24160, 15 pp.), 1911. Although these
plays were copyrighted at the time that Young was serving on
the faculty of the University of Texas, they are ones in which
he is still working very closely with Mississippi materials.
Although Young continued his interest in Mississippi and general
Southern materials in his other works, like So Red the Rose,
his plays after 1920 reflect more his interest in European drama than in Southern life. [306]

IV. Editions

One of the advantages of working with hitherto unpublished primary materials is that the primary document, the play itself, has value. In fact, the first work necessary after the plays have been tabulated and the playwrights identified is an edition of the work. The three plays here included were published for various reasons. The first, The Last of the Hargroves by Lee Arthur, was published by the Pioneer Drama Service (Cody, Wyoming) in 1962 to be used by theatre groups interested in doing old-fashioned melodrama. The second, The Dregs by J. W. Crawford, was published in the New Mexico Quarterly as evidence of native interest in dramatic experimentation. The third, The Atheist by Espy Williams, was published because its subject matter, the life of Robert Ingersoll, is of historical interest.

1. An edition of The Last of the Hargroves (Reprinted from The One Act Plays of Lee Arthur: The Sardou of Shreveport. With an Introduction. Cody, Wyoming: Pioneer Drama Service, 1962.)

"An Introduction"--(Part III, which deals with the three one-act plays in the collection.)

Arthur's work in the one-act play, if the extant works that make up this collection are any evidence, differs from his full-length plays in the same way that a movie audience differs from a Broadway play audience. It has less glitter; the characters are from lower levels of society; and love and happiness come unaccompanied by wealth and social success. The first two--The Last of the Hargroves and Settled Out of Court--were written in 1906 at the beginning of Arthur's one-act-play writing career and thus are a little closer to the sympathies that one finds in his full-length plays. The last, Burglary a la Mode, was written in 1913, just before Arthur departed New York and the Broadway stage for Hollywood

60

and the nickel audiences of the new motion picture theaters, and it
shows a shift in class sympathies from the rich, powerful and successful to the poor outcasts of society.

The three plays seem to be a fair sampling of the kinds of
plots and settings with which Arthur dealt throughout his career.
The Last of the Hargroves not only uses some names from We-Uns
of Tennessee, but like the earlier play, it suggests that union of
North and South, the patching of old wounds, will come to the New
South through love and education.   Like We-Uns of Tennessee, too,
it is a melodrama that makes an attempt to use folk materials.
Settled Out of Court, like Putting It Over and Baby of the Family,
is a situation [10] comedy; but unlike the first two, which are set in
New York, in this play Arthur uses his early experiences when he
was a lawyer in the southwestern town of Shreveport, Louisiana, to
give the play some touches of local color.   Like The Fox, Burglary
a la Mode is superficially a protest against legalized injustice; but
here Arthur truly--not merely verbally--sides with the "little man"
against the organized forces of unjust legal and business interests.

No record exists as to how these three plays fared on the
stage, but the lack of such a record is not surprising.   During the
years before World War I, the professional theatre in the provinces
made tremendous use of such short plays, and little attention was
given to them or their authors.   George M. Cohan, for example,
sold skits of this nature to other performers as a means of picking
up a few extra dollars, and the skits that he and his family performed, The Professor's Wife and Money to Burn, both written by
Cohan, were largely considered "material"--like jokes and tricks--
rather than dramatic pieces.   It was only in the art theater that the
one-act play was treated with any seriousness.

The short play in the commercial theater, however, probably
had a considerable influence on the playwright for the amateur theater.   Such plays as Burglary a la Mode were a part of every traveling show, and if they seldom had New York productions, they
were yet popular in New Orleans, Shreveport, Dallas, Salt Lake
City, and Denver.   The short play, moreover, became the standard
fare of the first amateur theaters and of the high school and small

college theaters.

If these three plays by Arthur are indicative of the kind of
short plays that were then coming into popularity, they suggest that
the amateur and academic theaters were interested in drama that
had many of the ingredients of the standard full-length melodramas
and situation comedies and very little kinship with the kind of lyric
mood pieces of the art theater. All three of these plays, for example, have clearly defined "situation plots." In each there is a
sharp reversal of fortune which is always associated with some
skill or unforeseen good fortune of the hero. In The Last of the
Hargroves, for example, the tragic folk elements, alike in many
respects to those in Lady Gregory's Workhouse Ward, Synge's Riders to the Sea, and even Saroyan's Hello Out There, are not the
point of the drama, but [11] simply the background music. Arthur
is committed, primarily, to showing that his folk, in spite of their
folkways, may yet possess the "aristocratic" virtues, and the author is committed to rewarding these virtues, not with poetic respect for the tragic essence, but rather with material well-being.
Like Grandpa McCoy in the current television series, Arthur's
characters find that environment only affects the superficials--lan-
guage and costume. The internal effects of environment--the habits
of thought, the rhythm of life--are quickly ignored. "It's a hell of
a way of endin' a feud, but I recon it's fur the best," Lige Monroe
concludes when the two young lovers, the last members of the feud-
ing families, decide to bury their old hatreds and marry.

Unlike the one-act art drama of the same period, these commercial one-acters give their audiences a great deal of action: a
shooting, a hold-up, an escape. In fact, in both The Last of the
Hargroves and Burglary a la Mode, one is struck by the visual aspects of the drama. Burglary a la Mode, with its use of the motion picture cameraman, suggests that Arthur had in mind a use for
his one-act plays in the motion picture theater; but it is not only
this reference to the motion picture industry that indicates this conclusion. All of the plays have the same kind of action-filled drama
that was, and is, popular on the non-artistic stage, and all depend
heavily on what is seen, rather than on what is heard. All three,

in fact, would still be mildly successful with high school audiences.

The methods of characterization in these plays also differ vastly from those used in the art-theater one-act plays. In such plays as Maeterlinck's The Intruder and Lady Gregory's Workhouse Ward, for examples, one discovers the true nature of a character not by a new revelation through action but by a contemplation of the depth of the character's external habits. Our surprise in the artistic one-act drama comes with the realization that the external habits of the characters are rooted in their souls. We are surprised that they are what they appear to be. In this respect, the analysis of character in the artistic one-act play is like the analysis of a flower: as we peel back each petal, we find the wonderful variations within the whole. In Arthur's one-act plays, however, the surprise comes in that characters are not what they seem. In The Last of the Hargroves all the characters defy by their actions what they appear to be in the [12] opening of the drama. The rough mountaineer, violent and bigoted, is finally revealed to be kindly and logical. The thieves in Burglary a la Mode finally appear to be the only honest folk, and the police are the most dishonest. The whole sense of the inevitability of character that one finds, for example, in Riders to the Sea is intentionally violated in such plays as these.

Although one might argue that these plays are attempts at realism, since Arthur selected his episodes from the commonplace --a mountain feud, a cheap theft, a law case--any examination of them shows immediately that they are, in fact, attacks upon realism. They are not intended to show "life as it is," but rather to suggest that although life sometimes appears grim, beneath that grimness there is an easy way to avoid the fates and find happiness.

This intent largely controls the theme of the plays. All three of the plays are obviously intended for audiences who hope to leave behind them the environment that has shaped them. Neither what one is nor the times in which he lives controls one's destiny; rather a trick, practiced by a small-town lawyer or an ex-convict, is the final solution. There is no need, as in the plays of Lady Gregory,

O'Neill, or Maeterlinck, for one to come to terms with his environment. When the "break" comes, the lovers will be ready. They will seize the opportunity, find wealth and happiness, and live happily ever after. [13]

The Last of the Hargroves
By Lee Arthur

Characters: Lige Monroe

Ben Buckner (Young Ben)

Virginia Hargrove (Viny)

Time: Early Evening in September

Place: Cumberland Mountains in Tennessee

Scene: A Deserted Hut

The hut is built of rough logs. There is a large stone fireplace up-stage center; door, left of fireplace. Small window R. 2nd E. with shutter that opens off S. The sash has only a few panes of glass in it, broken. Door L. 2nd E. Rough table R. of C. There are the remains of a broken bench in front of table; the walls of the hut are eight feet high. There is a gable roof of rough hand-made shingles ten feet high. The chimney which is seen above roof has almost fallen to pieces, and the stones are lying on the roof. The side walls of the hut are five feet from the wings. The wings R. and L., borders above roof, show rough mountain scenery.

As curtain rises: Stage is empty. Lige Monroe, a rough mountaineer, fifty years old, enters L. of C. He is a fine specimen of manhood, tall and rugged. He carries a rifle and he has a stone jug strapped across one shoulder and a crude hunting bag across the other.

Lige: (He walks about cautiously looking to see if the hut is empty, gets on his knees and looks up the chimney, rises and

walks to door L. and 2nd E.   Opens it, looks off stage.
He closes it then he exits to door L. of C.   Opens it and
calls off S.)   Viny---Viny---Stop that star gazing and come
in hayr. [14]

Viny: (Off L. of C.)   I'm comin', Lige, just as fass as my legs
will fetch me.   (Enters L. of C.   She is a mountain girl,
18 years old.   She is almost exhausted and has a rifle in
her hand which she is dragging.)   Lige, I'm almos tucker-
ed out.   (Sits on table, lays rifle beside her)

Lige: Be you-uns hungry?

Viny: I don't spec a little vittles would hurt me.

Lige: (Takes hunting bag from his shoulder, hands it to Viny)
Hayr is some corn pone and fried spar ribs Widow Gopher
giv me.

Viny: (She takes bag and eats food during the following)   Don't you-
uns want a snack, Lige?

Lige: All I'm hankerin fur is a chaw of terbaccer.   (Takes plug
out of pocket, bites off piece and chews it)   Is you-uns cold,
Viny?

Viny: A little fire would feel moughty good.   (Lige takes jug from
his shoulder, breaks bench into pieces, builds fire and
lights it.   There is a soft red glow from fire which lights
stage.)   How long is us-uns going to stop hayr, Lige?

Lige: The moon will be out fore long, then we-uns will start on
the trail again.

Viny: I can't walk any further tonight.   Lige, please let's stay
hayr 'till morning.

Lige: If you-uns don't kill young Ben tonight, you-uns may have to
        wait a long time for you get another chance of ending the
        feud.

Viny: Are you sartin that young Ben is the only one of the Buck-
        ners that's livin?

Lige: Yes, an you-uns is the last of the Hargroves.

Viny: What kin is he to the Buckner that killed gran-dad an start-
        ed the feud? [15]

Lige: Young Ben is his gran-son.

Viny: I don't s'pose I ever seed Young Ben.

Lige: Well, if you-uns did, you-uns was too young to remember
        him.   He was just a lettle shaver when he was took away
        from hayr.

Viny: Who was it that took him away?

Lige: I don't know the man's name, but I been tole he was power-
        ful rich.   He was up in the mountains huntin deer and he
        seed Young Ben, and when he larned that Young Ben was an
        orphan he took him to the city to raise and edicate him.

Viny: And this is the fust time Young Ben has been hayr since
        then?

Lige: Yes, I bin watchin and waiting fur him, and when I larned
        that he was hayr, I come straight home and tole you-uns, an
        I'm not a goin to close my eyes as long as he's in these
        mountains.   When your mammy was dyin an giv you-uns to
        me to bring up, she made me swar that when you-uns was
        big enuff to toat a bear gun, and thur was a Buckner livin'

I'd help you-uns find him.   I'm goin to do my best to keep
that swar, an I want you-uns to keep yours.

Viny: (She gets from table, stands on stage)   Yes, I'll keep the
swar I made my mammy.   If I ever set my eyes on a Buckner I'll kill him.

Lige: (He goes to her, shakes her hand)   Now you-uns is talkin'
like a Hargrove, and I'm powerful proud of you-uns.

Viny: You-uns is sartin ef you-uns sees Young Ben you-uns will
know him?

Lige: Know him---Why I'd know a Buckner ef I seed him any whar
this side of Hell.

Viny: We-uns has been lookin' fur him fur three days.   Maybe we-
uns is on the wrong trail. [16]

Lige: He passed Widow Gopher's place jess a lettle while fur we
was there.

Viny: I didn't hayr her say nuthin 'bout Young Ben.

Lige: She didn't want to skeer you-uns---She took me aside an
tole me that Young Ben was looking fur you-uns.

Viny: Does you-uns think he's toatin a bear gun fur me?

Lige: Yes---the feud is begun agin, an it won't end 'till Young Ben
or you-uns is dead.

Viny: (Sinks her head on table in despair)   God help me-

Lige: Be you-uns afeerd of a Buckner?

Viny: No. (Grabs gun quickly, unlocks breech, examines it to see
if it is loaded) I'm not afeerd of nobody. (Sits in front of
fire and cleans gun with her apron)

Lige: (Takes seat beside her) Then tell me when I called you-uns
to come in hayr tonight, why you-uns was gazin at the stars,
with a sickly grin on you-uns face. When folks does that,
thars one of two things that ails them---they's moughty a-
feerd uv someone or they's head over heels in love.

Viny: You-uns can rest easy. I ain't afeerd.

Lige: Then what was you-uns a star gazin fur---ugh?

Viny: Tain't no harm doin that is they? Why I thought God Almighty he put the stars in Heaven for folks to talk to, when
everything was dark and they was in trouble.

Lige: Be you-uns in love, Viny?

Viny: Is we-uns going to start on the trail agin soon?

Lige: Now don't try to change the subject, Viny. I asked you-uns
if you-uns was sweet on some fellow. [17]

Viny: Now you-uns is starting agin. You-uns is always trying to
run me about bein in love with somebody. I jess can't look
on a man 'less you-uns thinks I's dead gone on him.

Lige: (Coaxingly) Now come and tell me. I ain't goin to run you-
uns anymore. Once I used to set nite after nite gazin at the
stars, 'till me jug of mountain dew was empty, and the sun
was shinin in my face.

Viny: Wus you-uns tellin them 'bout someone you-uns loved, Lige?

Lige: Ugh-ugh---Nobody else would listen to me. (Takes out plug of tobacco)

Viny: When wus that, Lige?

Lige: It was a long time ago---Long afore you-uns was born, Viny. It was just after I hayrd that you-uns daddy an mammy wus goin to be married.

Viny: You-uns loved my mammy, Lige?

Lige: Ugh-ugh---an maybe ef I hadn't been so no'count an triflin ---I mought have been you-uns---(Wipes tear away from his eye with back of his hand and bites tobacco fiercely) Sufferin wild cats but I'm powerful thirsty.

Viny: You-uns wouldn't have to coax me to take a drink of water.

Lige: Thar must be a spring 'round hayr some whar. I'll see if I can't skeer up some. (He gets jug, exits to door L. of C., turns to Viny) You-uns ain't afeerd to be left alone?

Viny: (Rises, holds out gun) As long as I got this fur company, I ain't afeerd of nobody livin---But, I hayrd folks say this hut was haunted. Lige, did you-uns ever hayr it was haunted?

Lige: Yes, but spirits don't pester folks that keeps their promises to the dead. Is you-uns gun loaded? [18]

Viny: Yes---I was just lookin at it a mite ago.

Lige: Well, keep you-uns eyes and ears open, and you-uns hand on the trigger. Remember Young Ben is lookin fur you-uns, and all the Buckners were powerful good shots. (Exits L. of C. carrying jug. He closes door.)

Viny: (Looks about stage cautiously with gun in both hands to win-
        dow R., places gun on window sill, leans on it, looks off
        right) Lige was show right, when you-uns in love, thar
        ain't nobody will listen to you-uns, without pokin fun at you-
        uns, ceptin the stars. (She holds out both hands, looks up)
        You-uns is shinin so bright tonight, you-uns must see him
        ---. Tell me ef he loves me, as much as I love him.
        (Ben Buckner enters L. 2nd E. He is 22, gentle appear-
        ance, wears riding suit. He closes door. It makes a
        noise. Viny grabs gun, turns quickly, aims it at him.)
        Who's thar?

Ben: (Throws up both hands) Don't shoot.

Viny: (Lowers gun, exclaims with a pleasant smile) Oh---It's you-
        uns---

Ben: Well, this is a fine reception to give a fellow after he's been
        searching these mountains three days for you. (Exits to her,
        shakes her hand heartily)

Viny: I's moughty glad to see you-uns agin, an I'm sorry I could-
        n't come to meet you-uns as I said I would.

Ben: You're not half as sorry as I am. (They sit on table facing
        audience, the moonlight from window shines upon them) I
        was awfully worried when you didn't meet me at Old Eagle
        Rock. I thought that you were ill or in trouble---But thank
        Heaven I've found you and you're all right.

Viny: It's a down right shame I caused you so much trouble. [19]

Ben: Why I was only too glad that I had an opportunity to show
        how much I really cared for you.

Viny: Honest injun---Do you-uns really care so much fur a nobody like me?

Ben: A nobody---If I heard anybody else say that, there would be trouble.

Viny: And there's no other gal back in the city, whar you-uns come from, that you-uns care fur?

Ben: No one, that I'm losing any sleep over.

Viny: Not anyone, you-uns cares a teeny, weeny, little bit fur.

Ben: No---but I'm afraid you're getting tired of me.

Viny: I ain't no sech thing.

Ben: Then why didn't you meet me at Old Eagle Rock, as you promised?

Viny: I jus couldn't come---I'd been looking fur somebody.

Ben: Who have you been looking for?

Viny: You-uns wouldn't know if I tole you.

Ben: A man?

Viny: Y-e-s

Ben: You love him?

Viny: No---I hates him, an when I finds him I'm goin to kill him.

Ben: (Horrified) You're going to commit a murder?

Viny: We-uns jess call it gettin' squar, up in the mountains.

Ben: Has he wronged you? [20]

Viny: No, but his folks wronged my folks, an now he's lookin' fur
       me an if I don't kill him he'll kill me.

Ben: But why are you engaged in this feud, you're really only a
       child?

Viny: (With indignation) I ain't no chile---I'm big enough to toat
       a bear gun.

Ben: But you're a woman.

Viny: There ain't no Hargrove living 'ceptin me to carry the feud.

Ben: How long has it been going on?

Viny: It started long 'for I was thought uv---. Thar was a fuss
       over a yaller dog an my gran-daddy was shot---. That was
       what begun the feud. All I remembers uv it was when my
       daddy was killed, and then brother Bill---. He was chasin
       a rabbit when they got him. I was playin eye-spy with my
       baby sister when she was struck in the head with a minnie
       ball.

Ben: (Horrified) Good God---what an outrage.

Viny: It sure was onry to kill a lettle bit uv a gal like her, with
       sech a moughty big bullet. They mought hav been decent
       'nough to use a smaller one---, then thar was only me and
       mammy left.

Ben: Was your mother killed by one of the same family?

Viny: Yes---they took her away frum me. When she was burry-
       ing lettle sister---I forgot to tell you-uns that while the feud

was going on we-uns didn't waste all our bullets--thar was some uv them folks burried on tother side of the fence that divided our two places.

Ben: And one of these men is looking for you now to kill you.

Viny: He sure is. [21]

Ben: Tell me the name of the brute and I will settle matters with him---(He grabs gun from her)

Viny: No-no---you-uns mustn't mix up in this fuss---. I's got to do it myself---I made a swar to my mammy when she was dyin' that if I ever seed him, I'd kill him.

Lige: (Off C.) Open the door.

Ben: (Starts, raised gun to shoulder) Who's that?

Viny: It's only Lige.   He took me when I was a lettle gal to raise. (Crosses to door L. of C., opens it) We-uns got company, Lige.

Lige: (He enters door L. of C., has rifle in one hand and jug in the other.   He also carries wood for fire under each arm. Viny closes door.   Lige stares at Ben.) Whar did you-uns meet him, and what's his name?

Viny: (Breaks into hearty laughter) Well, if that don't beat the devil.   We-uns met more'n a week ago at Old Eagle Rock and every time I's seed him since then, we-uns has been so busy talking, I forgot to ax his name---(Convulsed with laughter) Say stranger, what's yer name?

Lige: (He drops jug and wood, puts his gun to his shoulder, aims it at Ben) God Almighty, gal--I jes came in time to save you-uns, it's young Ben.

Viny: (Horrified) No-no---Lige, it can't be him.

Lige: It won't do you-uns any good to lie now.   I knows you-uns,
        Ben Buckner---.

Ben: Yes---I'm Ben Buckner.

Lige: Come, Viny, take this gun.   (He keeps gun leveled at Ben's
        head, his eyes fixed on him and his finger on the trigger.)
        If you-uns as mech as bat an eye, I'll blow you-uns brains
        out.   [22]

Viny: (Runs and grabs gun, puts it to shoulder, aims at him) You-
        uns lied to me---.   You-uns pretended that you-uns loved
        me and all the time you-uns was waitin for a chance to kill
        me, as the rest of you-uns folks killed mine.

Ben: I was a child when I was taken away from here---So help
        me God---I never heard anything about this feud until you
        told me tonight.   If you had only mentioned the name of my
        family I would have had a chance to explain.

Lige: Why did you-uns come back to the mountains?   Why was you-
        uns lookin fer her?

Ben: I came back to look after the property I inherited---I was
        looking for her because I love her and---

Lige: He's lyin, Viny, don't you-uns believe him.

Viny: No-no---, Lige, I believe he's tellin the truth.

Lige: That don't make no difference---I'm goin to make you-uns
        keep the swar you-uns made to yer mammy---thars no use

wastin time talkin--pull that trigger.

Viny: I can't do it, Lige---I love him---.

Ben: And I love her.   There's been enough blood shed already.
Let's forgive and forget.

Lige: (Crosses to Viny, fixes his eyes upon her, sticks his finger
in her face) Ken you-uns forget when you-uns daddy was
killed and you-uns baby sister---?

Viny: (Hysterically) Stop--Lige--stop---

Lige: I ken see the pough lettle critter lyin thar now, with a big
hole in her haid.

Viny: For God's sake, stop---I can't listen to any more. [23]

Lige: I ain't goin to let up 'till you-uns do your duty to the dead.
I ken hear them cryin for vengance now and you-uns must
help them. (Noise of the wind heard off S. , Viny shows
fright.) Did you-uns hear that?

Ben: It was only the wind.

Viny: No--no---It was my mammy's sperit. She's come back to
haunt me.

Lige: Yes---an she's goin to hant you-uns 'till you-uns keep the
swar you-uns made her. If you-uns don't, you-uns won't
have any rest as long as you-uns live. She'll hant you-uns
sleep, she'll hant you-uns when you-uns is awake. (Noise
of the wind is heard again. Shutter on window R. closes
with a terrific bang)

Viny: (Frantic with fear) Don't hant me, mammy----don't hant me

---I'll keep my swar---(Aims gun at Ben) Defend you-unself, young Ben--defend you-unself. (Fires gun. Ben staggers and falls on stage. She screams and drops gun, runs to Ben, kneels on the stage beside him)

Lige: You-uns has kept you-un's promise an killed him.

Viny: No-no--he mustn't die--I love him--I love him. (She puts her head to his heart.) He's alive, he's alive. (Puts her hands on each side of his face, raising his head) Speak to me, young Ben---speak to me---say that you-uns will for-give me.

Ben: (Opens his eyes, speaks faintly) You're a game little girl.

Viny: Say that you-uns will forgive me.

Ben: I'm the one who should ask forgiveness for the wrong my people have done you and your family.

Viny: Is you-uns badly hurt?

Ben: (Raises himself with his right hand. Viny [24] assists him. He feels his left shoulder.) It doesn't pain me. I think the bullet only grazed my shoulder.

Lige: Viny, come hayr.

Viny: Lige, I want to stay hayr and nurse him. (Lige crosses to Viny, takes her roughly by the hand and pulls her to her feet, drags her away from Ben) I can't leave him, Lige. I love him, Lige, I love him---I love him. (Ben rises, walks to table, leans against it.)

Lige: (He stands between Ben and Viny, holds rifle toward her) You-uns must end the feud hayr and now.

Viny: (Pleading) Lige, he loves me and I love him. You-uns loved my mammy, you-uns knows how much it hurt when you-uns lost her. (Holds out her hands) I asks you-uns, Lige, in the name uv that love, please have pity on us.

Lige: (He looks at her a moment, then at Ben, drops gun, crosses to Ben) Let me see the woon. (Takes out pocket knife, rips Ben's coat, examines his shoulder.)

Viny: (Crosses to Ben) Lige, please go fur a doctor.

Lige: (He ties his handkerchief around Ben's shoulder) It taint nuthing but a scratch---You-uns don't need a doctor, what you-uns need is a parson.

Viny: (Throws her arms around Ben's neck and kisses him.) You-uns is willin fur us to be married?

Lige: It's a hell of a way of endin a feud, but I recon it's fur the best. (Takes chaw of tobacco.)

(Curtain)

[25]

2.   An edition of The Dregs

(Reprinted from "J. W. Crawford's The Dregs, A
New Mexico Pioneer in the Short Drama," New
Mexico Quarterly XXXIII [Winter, 1963-64], 388-
403.)

One spring night in 1963, an audience at the University of
Southwestern Louisiana in Lafayette watched a performance of The
Dregs by John Wallace Crawford. It was the first performance of
the play in almost a half century, and for those in the audience interested only in the content of an art form, The Dregs was, at
best, an interesting museum piece, a bit of Americana, a prohibition drama in the style of Ten Nights in a Barroom and The Drunkard, a play that would be wonderful farce if "played straight." For
those in the audience interested in dramatic form itself, on the
other hand, the "weaknesses" of the play--its melodramatic diction,
its trick ending, its stereotyped characterization--were simply elements that obscured, but did not hide, the real theatrical merits of
the play.   Any thoughtful evaluation of the play suggests that the
form that Crawford created for The Dregs--like the forms that O-
dets used in Waiting for Lefty and Beckett used for Krapp's Last
Tape--is one full of artistic possibilities and should be studied as
a pioneer form in the short drama.

Crawford himself probably did not understand the possibilities
of the form he created. By 1907, when he copyrighted The Dregs,
he had built a reputation as a "Western poet," calling himself "Captain Jack, the Poet Scout"; and in both his poetry and in his other,
conventional, plays, he used his literary talents to create a picture
of himself as the "representative man of the West"--brave, adven-
turous, gentle with women and children, a friend of wild nature,
and intolerant of savages, Mormons, cigarettes, dime novels, and
draft-dodgers. He was distinguished from the other Western scouts
only by the fact that he was a working poet and a professed prohibitionist, two aspects of his career that he worked into almost
everything he wrote. [388]

I

Crawford was born in County Donegal, Ireland, on March 4,

1847, the son of John Austin and Susie Wallace Crawford. The father, a Glasgow tailor, had been something of a political revolutionist and had fled Scotland for Ireland to escape arrest "for some
seditious utterance. " He had met and married Miss Wallace, the
daughter of another Scotch exile, in Ireland. The 1840's and '50's
were distressing years for Ireland; and to add to the difficulties,
the father became a drunkard.[1] In 1854, "to escape from dissolute
associates, " he came to America, finding work as a coal miner in
Minersville, Pennsylvania. The family waited in Ireland for four
years; but when it became obvious that Crawford was not going to
return, Mrs. Crawford went to Pennsylvania, found her husband,
and brought the children to America in 1858. Captain Jack, then
eleven years old, found employment in the mines at one dollar and
seventy-five cents a week.[2]

With the outbreak of the Civil War, the elder Crawford enlisted in the Union Army. Captain Jack tried to enlist, but he was
twice rejected because of his youth. Finally, before his sixteenth
birthday, he was accepted for service in the 48th Pennsylvania Volunteers. At Spottsylvania, on May 12, 1864, he was badly wounded
and sent to Saterlee Hospital in West Philadelphia. At this time,
he was illiterate; but a Sister of Charity taught him to read and
write during his convalescence. Later when he was a public lecturer, he often told the story of writing his first letter to his mother.
After recovering from his wounds, he was sent back into action; and,
on April 2, 1865, he was again wounded, this time at Petersburg.
After his recovery, the war was over and he returned home. A
short time later his mother and father died, his mother exacting a
deathbed promise from him that he would never touch liquor, another episode that he used often in his public lectures.[3]

Crawford remained in Pennsylvania for the next five years.
In 1869 he was married to Anna Marie Stokes of Numidia, Pennsylvania; and a short time afterward, he went west to the Indian country of the Dakotas. He was variously employed and during the Indian uprisings was named chief of a citizens' group, the Black Hills
Rangers. It was with this position that he became known as Captain
Jack. Crawford is said to have been one of the first seven men to

enter the Black Hills region after the Custer expedition of 1874; and
by April 25, 1876, he was well enough established in the area to be
listed as a member of the [389] Board of Trustees of Custer City. During the Sioux War of 1876, he was employed as a scout for the
army, serving under Generals Merritt and Crook; and on August 24,
1876, he succeeded William F. Cody (Buffalo Bill) as Merritt's chief
of scouts. [4]

   In the fall of 1876 Buffalo Bill was touring the country with a
play, Life on the Border, which he alternated with his standard
show, Scouts of the Prairie. He starred Captain Jack in Life on
the Border. [5] Although this experience in show business suited
Crawford's ambitions, he was not, as he later wrote to Buffalo Bill,
pleased with his treatment as a member of the company. His salary was too low, he complained; and, moreover, he said that Buffalo Bill, while drunk, had seriously wounded him in a reenactment
of the Yellow Hand--Buffalo Bill fight and had, moreover, left him
stranded and "at death's door" in Virginia City, Nevada. [6]

   While recovering from this wound in Virginia City, Crawford
collaborated with a Sam Smith, who had written one successful play,
Struck Oil. The product of this collaboration--Fonda; Or, The
Trapper's Dream--was taken to San Francisco with Captain Jack in
the starring role. Alfred Dampier, a manager of the Theater Royal Melbourne, saw Fonda and suggested to Crawford that he bring
the play to Australia for a season. It was planned that the cast
would include five American Indians, the first to be seen in Australia. Crawford, however, needed five hundred dollars for ex-
penses; so he "thought of the offer of help from the man [Buffalo
Bill] who had left him stranded and at death's door...." He wrote
to Cody, received assurances that the money was available for him,
and made his plans. The money never arrived, however; and Crawford was forced to leave show business for other employment. [7]

   He accepted an offer to scout for General Hatch, then warring
with the Indians in New Mexico and Arizona. For the next ten
years Crawford spent most of his time scouting for the army; but
he seems, also, to have started his career as a public lecturer, to
have done some prospecting, and to have started some ranching ac-

tivity. In 1886, he was retired as an army scout and was appointed by Robert Lincoln, "then secretary of war, as a reward for his services to the government,"[8] custodian of Fort Craig, New Mexico.

From all accounts, it was Mrs. Crawford and their children who took care of the duties at the fort while Captain Jack roamed the country in search of fame and fortune. He maintained a ranch near San Marcial, did some mining in New Mexico and Colorado, and gained some [390] reputation as a popular lecturer, especially for prohibitionist causes.[9] In 1898 he went to Alaska for the Gold Rush, but after two unsuccessful years there, he returned to the United States to open a play in San Francisco.[10] Although for the next seventeen years of his life he maintained a legal residence in New Mexico and dressed the role of the "Western Scout," after his Alaskan adventure Crawford spent most of his time lecturing, writing, and acting in the Midwest, East, and South. On February 28, 1917, he died in New York, just a month after the death of Buffalo Bill. He is buried in the National Cemetery in Brooklyn.[11]

II

Although Crawford did not learn to write until he was sixteen years old, once he had learned he seems to have spent every free moment in his "literary development." As early as 1876, when a Captain James E. Smith[12] met him in the Dakotas, Captain Jack already had a regional reputation for his verses, and some of his prose accounts of the Indian wars had been published in the city newspapers of Chicago and New York. In 1879 he borrowed money to bring out a collection of his verses: The Poet Scout: A Book of Song and Story, which proved popular enough to be twice republished, in 1886 and 1891, in enlarged versions. In 1886, too, he had published a second volume of verse, From Darkness Into Light and Other Poems. In 1893 appeared yet another volume of verse, Camp Fire Sparks; in 1904, a fourth work, Lariattes; in 1905, a fifth, The Broncho Book; and in 1908, a sixth, Whar' the Hand o' God Is Seen.

During these years, too, he wrote more than a hundred short stories and articles for various small publications. In all of this work (and frequently he used the same poem in several different

volumes), Crawford argued for the simple rustic life, for the colo-
nization of the West by military rule, for a life of sobriety, free
from the taint of cigarettes, dime novels, and liquor. He championed various causes: aid for the veterans and orphans, prohibition,
the rights of the miners. His heroes were General Grant, McKinley, Harrison, Teddy Roosevelt, Taft, Wild Bill Hickok, Custer,
and Billy the Kid. His villains were Cleveland, Wilson, pacificists,
drunkards, formal religionists, Indians who would not be tamed,
writers of dime novels. Always, however, the personality of Captain Jack, the Poet Scout, was Crawford's main con[391]cern. He was
always the real hero--honest, sober, sane, second only to Wild Bill
with a gun, second to no one on a horse; and he was always modest.

Crawford thought of himself primarily as a poet, but poetry
was for him only a part of the characterization that he was creat-
ing--the dialogue of his hero, Captain Jack. The character that he
created--a man of giant ego, little tolerance, and great success in
all endeavors--is more the result of faulty poetics than of his private character. Crawford wanted fame and fortune; and, although
he complained bitterly about the untruthfulness of the dime novelists, his notions of fame and fortune were largely based on the
standards found in the dime novels. His plays had for him two re-
sponsibilities--to be successful as theater and to popularize the
character of Captain Jack; and although he seems to have had little
real success with any of them, from his first experience with the
theater, he was continually composing and revising his dramas.

After the failure to finance the Australian tour of Fonda, he
kept the manuscript and revised it with a new title, California
Through Death Valley, copyrighted in 1879. Under this title, the
play seems never to have been produced, but as The Trapper's
Daughter, it was a starring vehicle for Texas Jack (John B. Omohundro) at the Adelphia Theater in Denver on March 16, 1880. [13]
The character of the scout, the hero of the play, is an idealized
portrait of Crawford; and in the only extant copy of the play--the
author's copyright manuscript in the Library of Congress--he is
called "Jack Crawford, " and he is a poet and a scout. In 1888,

Crawford copyrighted this play again, this time under the title of
Fonda; or, The Trapper's Dream. [14]

The following year, 1889, he copyrighted another play, Tat;
or Edna, The Veteran's Daughter, a border drama in four acts. No
known copy of this play exists; but another play, The Mighty Truth;
or, In Clouds or Sunshine, a drama in three acts, copyrighted in
1896, is obviously the same play revised. For this play, Crawford
announced that he had the help of James Barton Adams, a Western
newspaperman and poet. Crawford said that Barton "did the real
literary work on Tat while . . . he did the gymnastics and hurdles
with an occasional song." Judging from the play and Crawford's
poetry, however, Barton's part in the writing of the play was probably more a question of cutting than of writing. As in Fonda,
Crawford, the Poet Scout, is again the hero; and it is the same
character, but a few years older. He tames the wild Indians,
saves the pure maiden, and reforms a fellow [392] scout, Bill
Wilde, all the while reciting his poetry and his pathetic tales and
teaching the other characters in the play to do the same.

In 1908 Crawford copyrighted his last full-length play, Colonel Bob: A Western Pastoral, which he wrote in collaboration with
a Marie Madison, who by then had written several mildly successful
melodramas. Colonel Bob is a characterization of the "mature"
Jack Crawford. Crawford was at the time over sixty, and evidently
the play was written for him; but the character of Colonel Bob appears to be in his late thirties or early forties. The New Mexico
scene--the wild woodland that taught Colonel Bob the lessons of nature and humanity--plays a large part in this drama, as does the
Alaskan scene; but in the play, in contrast to the hard facts of
Crawford's life, Alaska opens its treasures to the Poet Scout, Colonel Bob.

The year before he copyrighted Colonel Bob, in 1907, Crawford had copyrighted The Dregs--seemingly the only one-act play he
ever wrote. From all existing evidence, he used The Dregs, which
he subtitled "A Monologue," as a part of his performance on the
lecture platform. It is interesting to note, however, that in writing
his autobiography for the various volumes of Who's Who in Amer-

ica, he listed himself as the author of all his various volumes of poetry, of his short stories, but of only three of his plays: Fonda, Tat, and Colonel Bob. No mention is made of The Dregs.

III

The Dregs is the only one of Crawford's works that does not star the Poet Scout. Even when he wrote his poem about the death of General Custer, it was less about Custer than about Crawford. In The Dregs, however, he uses materials that had become closely associated with him throughout his career. The final speech of the play, for example, "The Toast to Women," had been included in two of his volumes of poetry and had been one of his favorite pieces for recitation on the platform. But the only character to appear in the play, Frank, is never the person that Crawford saw himself to be, although he may well have been the person that he sometimes unconsciously longed to be--educated, wealthy, a student; and the person he sometimes feared he would become--unsuccessful and a drunkard.

The main action of the drama--the fall of a young man from a fortunate position to disgrace through the evils of alcohol--is admit[393]tedly melodramatic. The relentlessness of the fall--in some respects like a Greek tragedy--is weakened by the quick and mountainous load of catastrophes--loss of job, loss of child, loss of wife, loss of self-respect, loss of mind, loss of life. The other characters of the play, although they appear only by inference, are stereotypes: Ted and Jim, the good friends; Bill, the bartender; Mary, the faithful wife; the little boy. The dialogue is that odd mixture of cliché, pretentious rhetoric, and folksiness that makes the most seriously expressed sentiments seem a burlesque of themselves. The ending seems to be a most amateurish attempt to save a "happy ending" from a bad mess at all cost.

In spite of these faults, however, The Dregs is a remarkable drama. Crawford, judging from his notes to the actor, had given considerable attention to the working out of the theatrics; and in the space of about fifteen minutes, he makes his characters--not merely Frank, but all the characters who people Frank's dream--come alive. By the intensity of the pacing, Bill, Mary, the members of the crowd, all take on flesh and blood.   Like Euripides' Medea, we may not believe that they are realistic, but we know they are there. And the dream device, which at first seems merely a convenient way of ending the drama, upon reflection becomes the heart of the play.   Unfortunately Frank's dream is not so profound an experience as Tom Wingfield's memory of The Glass Menagerie; but this fault is Frank's, not The Dregs.   The device, itself, is a good one.

Although even the most ardent admirer of Captain Jack Crawford would have to admit to a thousand faults in this play, yet The Dregs, for all its faults, is a most interesting theatrical experience, quite unlike anything else written by Crawford and quite unlike anything else in the American theater of its time. [394]

Notes

1. "Crawford, John Wallace (Captain Jack)," Dictionary of American Biography, IV (1930), pp. 522-23.

2. Leigh Irvine, "Biographical Sketch," in The Poet Scout: A Book of Song and Story.   St. Paul, Minn.:   Price-McGill.

3. Ibid., p. xi.

4. DAB, IV, pp. 522-23.

5. Henry Blackman Sell and Victor Weybright, Buffalo Bill and The Wild West.   New York: Oxford University Press, 1955, pp. 127-28.

6. Permission to use this letter and other unpublished materials in the Crawford family collection was given to me by Mrs. Buford Richardson, Crawford's great-granddaughter, Socorro, New Mexico.   I am grateful to her and to other members of Crawford's family and his friends for considerable aid.   I would especially like to acknowledge my debt to Miss Dorothy Virgin, Santa Fe, New Mexico, for countless aids.

7. An unpublished, untitled manuscript in the Crawford family collection.   It was written sometime around 1905 and seems to have been an introduction given of Crawford before one of his lectures.   The author is unknown.

8. Ibid.

9. DAB, IV, pp. 522-23.

10. "Captain Jack Is Going: His Play To Be Put On In Frisco," Dawson Daily News, June 15, 1900, 1.

11. "Capt. Jack Crawford Dead," New York Times, Feb. 28, 1917, 11.

12. A Famous Battery and Its Campaigns, 1861-'64: The Career of Corporal James Tanner in War and Peace, Early Days in the Black Hills with Some Account of Capt. Jack Crawford, The Poet Scout. Washington: W. H. Lowdermilk & Co., 1892, pp. 218-20.

13. Herschel C. Logan, Buckskin and Satin: The Life of Texas Jack. Harrisburg, Pennsylvania: Stackpole Press, 1950, p. 100.

14. The only extant copies of any of Crawford's plays are those that were submitted by the author for copyright protection. The typed manuscripts of four of these plays are still on file in the Library of Congress: "Fonda; or, The Trapper's Dream, by J. W. Crawford, New York, D:32709, Nov. 19, 1888"; "The Mighty Truth; or, In Clouds Or Sunshine: A drama in 3 Acts, by Capt. Jack Crawford, 90 pp., typewritten, San Marcial, N. M., D:2585, Jan. 6, 1896"; "The Dregs: A Monologue, by J. Crawford, 11 pp., typed, San Marcial, Mexico [sic], D:11354, Sept. 16, 1907," and "Colonel Bob: A Western Pastoral in 5 Acts, by M. Madison and J. Crawford, 91 pp., typed, Chicago, Ill., D:12696, Apr. 7, 1908." [395]

The Dregs
A Monologue by John W. Crawford

The scene is a student's room. There is a mantle L. with
an open fireplace in which a fire is smouldering. On the mantle is
a picture of a pretty young woman and a glass of water. A round
table stands L. C. on which is a half-empty bottle and three wine
glasses. Armchair near fireplace and other furniture to make the
room appear comfortable and well-to-do. A window upstage shows
a snow-covered landscape without. Door L. in F. If possible, a
calcium light should be used for effects; and otherwise the whole
monologue should be played in an otherwise dark house except where
stated that lights should be "turned on full." If calcium is not ob-
tainable, a strong lamp with reflector can be used.

As the scene is disclosed, Frank is discovered at door looking off L., the moonlight shining full on him. Lights of stage on
full. (Voices of young men heard singing gradually dying away.)

Frank: (Calling after supposed friends.) Goodnight, boys, see you
    tomorrow. Goodnight. (Voices reply and take up singing a-
    gain, die away in the distance.)

Frank: (Closes door and goes over to fireplace rubbing his hands
    over the coals and singing to himself.) "For we are jolly
    good fellows, Yes, we are jolly good fellows, As nobody can
    deny." (Puts hand to his head as if dizzy.) Whew, I'm
    dizzy. The cold air and the sudden heat--it isn't good to sit
    so near the fire. (Moves back to table.) But what's cosier
    than a bottle between friends and a blaze to cheer on a cold
    winter night like this. Jolly boys, Ted and Jim. Good whole-
    some fellows. They know how to drink and when to quit. So
    do I. No danger of becoming a drunkard when a fellow can
    quit at the right time. (Takes up his half-filled wine glass.)
    Why, they even stepped off with half a glass behind. That
    shows self control and the gentleman. Well, I'll have a night-
    cap and go to bed. Here's to your [396] future lives, Fellows.

May you never want for what you've left in the glass. (Then
turns to picture on the mantle.) And here's to you, sweet
Mary, and the day I'll call you mine. I'll drink to you, my
other heart, in sparkling ruddy. (Drinks all that is in the
glass.) How it warms a man. It creeps through the veins
like love and warms the heart, though it dulls the brain.
(Sings softly.) "For we are jolly, good fellows . . ." (Falls
asleep singing.)

(Very far away in the distance the voices of the others are
heard completely dying away. The scene becomes dark. Lights all
out, during which time Frank quickly puts on top coat and evening
hat. When calcium is turned on, he is standing in what is apparently a barroom. Scenery of same can be dispensed with, but can
be used if procurable.)

Frank: (Addressing supposed companions.) Hello, Boys, have a
    drink. Don't go. It's early yet. My wife don't complain.
    Why should yours? Give me the dice box, Bill. I'll show
    you how badly I can throw and pay the price of drinks for my
    folly. (Throws dice and laughs.) See? I told you so. A
    whiskey straight, please. Wine has lost its flavor, and, say,
    Boys, I was drunk last night. Think of it. I, who boasted I
    knew when to quit--I was under the table. But my lady never
    knew it. She thought I was sick, poor girl; and this morning
    she was worrying about my hollow eyes and pale face. I felt
    ashamed, and I ought to feel ashamed now, but I couldn't go
    by somehow. The odor of this place draw me in. I wonder
    if you fellows know how much the smell of liquor has to do
    with making a drunkard? I believe if liquor were odorless, it
    wouldn't be half so hard to pass a rum shop. (Turns suddenly
    in surprise.) Why, little one, what are you doing here? This
    is no place for a lady. Yes, you're right. It's no place for
    a gentleman either. Yes, I know. I didn't feel well, and I
    thought I'd take a little brandy before I came home. Run a-
    long. That's a dear girl, Mary. I'll come in a minute. Just

as soon as I settle this little bill. Run along, Dear, and
wait outside if you like. Run along now. I . . . .

(The light is turned off, and when again turned on, Frank is
seen very drunk, feeling in his pockets and speaking to a supposed
wife.)

Frank: I haven't any money. Don't be a fool, Mary. Don't sniv-
el. I hate tears. It's weak and foolish to cry when it can't
be helped. [397] Well, it can't, I tell you. I didn't get drunk pur-
poshly. It was an . . . acci . . . accident. I was cold,
and the plashe was warm, and the schtuff went to me head.
Hic. I'm sorry, but I'll go an' borrow it if the little fellow's
sick. You can't be without money, I know that; an' I love the
little one, even if I don't deserve him. Oh, I know I don't,
Mary. I don't deserve him or you. I'm a beasht, or I
wouldn't have come home like thish. I know it. Don't worry,
Kid. I'll do better. Before Heaven, I'll do better. Jusht
give me another chance. I'll borrow the money. Wait here.
(Staggers away.)

Light is turned full off. When again turned on, Frank is L.
C. in pleading attitude.

Frank: Say, Bill, lend me a dollar, will you? The little fellow is
sick, and I've spent all my money here. Yes, I lost my job
today. That's true, but I'll get it back tomorrow all right.
Where did you hear about it? Bad news travels fasht, don't
it? Well, never mind; I'll find another plashe if I don't go
back to the old one. Jusht lend me a dollar, will you? I
need it badly, Bill. Haven't got it? Why, Bill, you've got a
drawer full of money there. It's yours. Why I've spent a
barrel of money here, but I won't lower myself by begging you
for a single cent. Jim will let me have it; don't trouble yourself, Bill. (Staggers over to R.) Say, Jim, can't you lend
me a dollar? Yes, it has come to this, even though we used

to boast we'd never be drunkards. You're drunk now, and
we've both been drunk at this table many a time together. So
for the sake of old times, lend me a dollar, Jim. Haven't
got it? I believe you, Boy, for I know you'd let me have it
if you could. (Turning angrily to C.) Good heavens, Mary,
haven't I told you many a time never to come here after me?
I'm not drinking. God help me, I'm begging--begging for you
and the boy. Yes, even that. What do you want? What?
(Shrieks.) What? (Staggers upstage.) Bill, Bill, tell me
what she said. Did she say my boy was dead? That neither
she nor he needs me any longer? Is that what she said, Bill?
Can it be true? Mary, Mary, for the love of heaven, wait
for me. (Staggers across to R.C.) I'm sober as a judge.
You needn't turn from me. Tell me the truth, or are you
just trying me? The boy isn't dead, is he? He isn't cold
and silent. Don't tell me, Mary. Don't tell me those little
hands will never lead Papa home again . . . those little lips
will never welcome me with [398] their beautiful smile. Don't tell
me I've murdered . . . murdered him, Mary. Yet I have.
I've murdered my boy--my beautiful boy. There's nothing to
live for now. Yes, there is, Mary. I'll live for you. Listen, Mary, if you'll forgive me, I'll promise never to touch
another drop. Yes, I know, I've promised it a hundred times,
but I'll keep my word now. You believe me, don't you, Mary?
What? You won't give me another chance? You never want
to see my face again? Mary, Mary, you don't need me, but
I need you, Mary, more than ever. For the sake of the boy,
won't you give me another chance? Mary, don't go like that
. . . don't go like that. I'll try . . . Mary . . . Mary . .
. . God help me now. (He is overcome with emotion.)

Lights are turned off and in darkness Frank changes, by turning coat wrong side out. The actor wears a coat which is good on
one side and ragged on the other, thus enabling him to make a
quick change. In pocket, have a little powdered charcoal, which by
dexterous application to face and neck can give a grizzled appear-

ance to character, but this must be practiced so as to know just how to apply it in the dark. Then apply a little cornstarch to hair at the temples. Have a soft tattered hat in pocket also. This change must be made quickly and when the light is again turned on, Frank appears as a fallen sot and speaks in a husky voice. As light is turned on stage, Frank is at extreme R. in darkness and saunters into the full light, as though entering a barroom.

Frank: Hello, Bill, never expected to see me again, did you? Yes, I know this is a rather tony place for me now, but I found a quarter, and I thought I'd like to spend it here, to try to awaken old dreams with the sight of old faces once more. Give me a whiskey straight--one of the old timers. Say, Bill, what's become of Ted and Jim? Gone to the bad? Ted's reformed, has he? I'm glad of that. He has more sand than I. What, Jim's dead? Poor old Jim. He always went the pace whatever he set out to do. Say, Bill, do you remember the last time I was in here? It's been ten years, but it seems like a hundred. I lost them both that night, Bill, the boy and Mary, for she left me as I deserved, and heaven took the little one away--as I deserved. I haven't heard of her since. (Looks suddenly to R. in a startled manner.) Great heaven, Bill, there she is as sure as I'm [399] alive. That's Mary, and isn't she dressed? She looks like a swell, Bill. I wonder if she'd speak to me. (He approaches his supposed wife and speaks to her.)

Frank: Mary. Mary, I know you, so you needn't turn away. I may be a fallen drunkard, but I've still got a right to ask how you came by such finery, for you were my wife once. You remember that? (Staggers back.) Married? Married to another man. And you've forgotten that you ever cared for me. I suppose you've forgotten the boy, too, for maybe you have other children? You have--and you never think of us now? Ah, yes, you think of him, but not of me. I don't blame you. I'm not worth a thought. I never was a good husband, and I

hope you have one such as you deserve. God bless you,
Mary, I haven't a hard thought of you. Only I might have
been a better man if you'd given me another chance when I
needed you most. Yes, I know. You were tired of giving
me chances. You gave me many, but one more might have
won the day, when we lost our boy. But I suppose it wasn't
worthwhile. Goodbye. I won't keep you standing here. People will wonder at us; so go on your way and may all the happiness on earth be yours. You are drinking life's cup of happiness where it is sweetest, and I am draining its dregs. It's
not likely we'll ever meet again. Goodbye. Goodbye. (Stands
looking off R.)

Frank: There she goes, and I almost hated her once because she
would not let me wreck her life. Yet she leaves me now with
tears in her eyes. God bless her. But they were tears of
pity--not regret. Why should she regret? Why should she?

(Light goes out. In the darkness the actor darkens under the
eyes and quickly puts on unkempt grey wig. When light is again
turned on, he is seen old and broken.)

Frank: (Staggers to C., laughs croakingly.) Bill, it's me. Somehow, I'm like a bad penny. Give me a drink for old times,
Bill. Anything as long as it's strong--anything. Ah. (Drinks.)
That's like an oasis in the desert of my soul. It's many a
day since I tasted such stuff as that. Say, Bill, do you know
what brought me here today? I saw her again--Mary, my
wife. And I saw the man she's married. I'm glad she left
me, Bill, for he's the right kind of man to protect a [400] woman.
I never was. But, Bill, the old loneliness stole around my
heart like a hungry hand, clutching and tearing it out of me,
and I've come creeping back to the old scenes in hope of finding some crumbs of comfort in their memory. Bill, I don't
know what's been wrong with me, do you? I just think I
didn't care. No matter how much I protested I wanted to be

better, I think I loved myself more than all the world.   And
that's why I couldn't reform.   A drunkard is the meanest ego-
tist on God's green earth.   He starts with an over-weening
confidence in himself--thinking he has enough self-control to
stop when he will, though he drink as he will.   Why, he's
only dealing out the rope to hang himself.   That's why he gets
to be a drunkard.   And, by and by, he begins to pity himself.
And the more he pities himself, the more he loves himself;
and the more he loves himself, the more he indulges his ap-
petite.   His selfish egotism grows stronger as his manhood
wanes.   The drunkard is proud of his fall.   Don't believe the
man who tells you he is ashamed of it, as long as his inebri-
ated state makes him an object of pity or interest to others.
Say, Bill, give me another drink?   I've got a pain in my
heart I don't like.   Don't laugh.   I have a heart, and it's ach-
ing--aching just as hard as a heart can ache if it is aching
only for myself.   Somehow I can't get the sight of the little
one's face from before me today.   He seems to haunt me.   I
see his eyes everywhere.   And, Bill, I heard them whispering
at the station house when they pulled me in.   Someone said I
was getting daffy.   Do you believe it?   I'd rather die than go
to the madhouse, Bill, and that's what's in store for me, if I
go to the hospital with the horrors much more often.   I believe
I will die.   God help me, I believe I'm dying now.   Oh, you
can laugh, but if you knew how tight that hand is clutching at
my heart and how hard it is for the old thing to beat, you
wouldn't wonder.   Bill, have you a heart?   Dying?   What if I
am?   The world won't miss me.   I won't leave a bubble on
the surface of its life.   Not a soul will care--or see what I
might have been, what I might have done in the world with my
talents and my chances.   God gave me great talents, Bill, and
I wasted them as I wasted a sweet woman's love.   Now I'm
dying like a weak . . . dying . . . . (Laughs hollowly.)   That's
a strange thought--dying.   (Rubs his eyes.)   See how the light
fades and see how the mocking faces grin at me in the shadows.
(Begins to rave.)   See how the clouds lower over me.   They

are holding back the wild horses.   They mean to turn them
loose on me.   Hold them back, for God's sake, hold them
back.   Don't you know [401] they'll trample me to death, you fools.
They are coming--coming.   See them . . . hundreds . . .
aye, thousands.   Hear the thunder of their hoofs.   See their
flaming eyes and see . . . . Mary, Mary, where are you?
Give me your hand.   Save me, save me from all this awful
darkness and terror.   Save me.   Where is my boy?   All is
darkness.   Even my boy is not there, but I hear the horses
coming.   Hear them?   They are coming--coming--the horses
of the night . . . .

(He falls dead in C. of stage.   Light goes out full.   Actor
discards wig and with a cloth well greased with cold cream or vas-
eline wipes stains thoroughly from his face, turns coat and throws
hat from stage.   All lights turned on full show him asleep in his
chair before the fire as in the beginning on the monologue.)

Frank: (Springing to his feet in terror.)   The horses . . . the
         horses . . . . Stop them.   Oh God, Mary . . . Mary hold
         me . . . hold me . . . I . . . I . . . . (He looks around
         then wakens thoroughly, but appears dazed.)   Where am I?
         Merciful heaven be praised.   It was a dream.   (Laughs.)
         Thank God for that.   And Mary (kisses her photo), sweet girl,
         she wouldn't help me.   Oh, I know better than that.   She
         would never let go of me.   But after all, what does it mean?
         Isn't it the truth?   Isn't it possible it could be me?   Of
         course, the wine went to my head.   And I thought I knew
         when to stop.   There is only one time for me, and that is
         now and forever.

(Takes bottle by neck in one hand and Mary's photo in the
other.)

Frank: Mary, sweetheart, this pledge is to you.   I've drunk my
         last drop, forever more, amen.   (Breaks the bottle on the

hearth and rises addressing the picture.) Mary, darling
Mary, never again shall I drink to your health in that which
may send your husband reeling home to abuse whom he should
love and cherish. Never again in that which may send a
mother's boy to a drunkard's grave and maybe her girl to a
life of shame. No, not that, but rather (takes a glass of water from the table) in God's life-giving water, pure as her
chastity, clear as her intuitions, bright as her smile, sparkling as the laughter of her eyes, strong and sustaining as
her love. In the crystal water I will drink to her, that she
may remain queen, regent in the empire she has already won,
grounded deep as the universe in love, [402] built up and enthroned
in the hearts of the world. I will drink to her, the full-blown
flower of creation's morning, of which man is but the bud and
blossom--to her, who in childhood clasps our little hands and
teaches us the first prayer to the great All-father; who comes
to us in youth with good counsel and advice; and who, when
our feet go down into the dark shadows, smoothes the pillow
of death as no other can, to her who is the flower of flowers,
the pearl of pearls, God's last, but God's best gift to man--
woman--peerless, pure, sweet, royal woman. I drink to your
health in God's own beverage--cold, sparkling water.

(Drinks and holds up glass in a toast to the audience.)

Curtain

Note: This edition of The Dregs is based on the typed copyright
manuscript (1907) in the Library of Congress; and, except for minor corrections in punctuation and spelling, it follows that manuscript. [403]

3.   An edition of The Atheist

(Reprinted from "A Southerner's Tribute to Illi-

nois' 'Pagan Prophet'," Journal of the Illinois

Historical Society, LI [Autumn, 1958], 268-283.)

Robert Green Ingersoll, the Illinois "Pagan Prophet," holds a
paradoxical position in the history of nineteenth-century American
thought.   One of the country's most popular public speakers, he
championed the most unpopular subjects.   A political spokesman for
"McKinley Republicanism," American imperialism and laissez-faire
social and economic rule, still he was the darling of the liberals,
the socialist-minded, the internationalists. [1]   Now, with the discovery of the "lost manuscripts" of Espy Williams, [2] once [269] labeled
"The South's Leading Dramatist," [3] the paradox of Ingersoll's reputation
grows.   Although Ingersoll attacked the South with the full arsenal
of his verbal guns, he was the man selected by the South's "leading
dramatist" as the model for the hero in a play called The Atheist.
The play itself was dedicated to Ingersoll, but this fact, if ever
widely known, has long been forgotten, since the only readily available copies of the work do not carry the author's dedication.   The
rediscovery of the original manuscript and the light which it throws
on Ingersoll's reputation are the justification for its republication,
almost seventy years after it was written and, until now, forgotten.

Much of Ingersoll's general popularity in America in the last
quarter of the nineteenth century was, of course, due to his ardent
defense of Republicanism.   As Harry T. Peck pointed out at the
time of Ingersoll's death, "Colonel Ingersoll delivered his attacks
on Christianity before audiences made up in part, at least, of in-
telligent, serious-minded, influential men and women," men and
women who approved of his statements on politics.   "The political
partisan had won a hearing for the professional agnostic." [4]   C. H.
Cramer sums up the problem faced by these partisan Republicans:

> Would his Christian Republican friends, who admired
> Ingersoll the Stalwart in campaign years, resort to bil-
> lingsgate again when Ingersoll the Agnostic took the plat-
> form after the political canvass was over?   Most of
> them found it impolitic to do so . . . after 1876.   Solid
> Republicans . . . found it expedient to put in a token

appear[270]ance when he appeared during off-election
years to discuss science and religion on his regular
cross-country tours. [5]

Some of Ingersoll's popularity, especially with writers and
artists, was the result of his defense of free thought. Walt Whitman, for example, disagreed with most of his pronouncements on
domestic politics and foreign affairs. [6] Yet he attended when Ingersoll spoke, and described Ingersoll as a "master pilgrim" who, with
Huxley, "could unhorse the whole Christian giant."[7] Ingersoll was
often praised by men who disagreed with his politics, such men as
Vice-President Adlai Stevenson, Hamlin Garland, Edgar Lee Mas-
ters, and Mark Twain. [8] The latter, for example, felt so kindly
toward the Illinois pagan that when he received word of Ingersoll's
death, he wrote to Miss Eva Farrell, Ingersoll's niece, "Except my
daughter's, I have not grieved for any death as I have grieved for
his. His was a great and beautiful spirit, he was a man--all man
from his crown to his foot soles. My reverence for him was deep
and genuine; I prized his affection for me and returned it with
usury."[9] As this letter indicates, Ingersoll's reputation with such
men as Twain and Whitman rested, in part, at least on his affection for them; but unless the man also meant something, his approval would not have.

Ingersoll's appeal to Republicans and liberals cannot, [271]however,
have been the basis of his appeal to Espy Williams. Williams was
neither a Republican nor, in matters of religion or letters, basical-
ly a liberal. Born in New Orleans in 1852 of parents of north-
eastern origin, Williams was a Southerner both by birth and sympathy. Even later in life, when his success as a playwright made
friends suggest to him that he follow the steps of his friend, George
Washington Cable, and move north, Williams preferred to remain at
home. Moreover, although Williams was only a boy at the time of
the Civil War and not in sympathy with slavery, the war cost him
the two things he prized most, education and a full dedication to
letters. The financial difficulties which his family faced because of
the war forced Williams to withdraw from school at the age of sixteen, when he was within one term of graduation from the New Or-

leans high school, to enter business life.   Even though he was successful as a New Orleans financier, [10] he remained committed to
literature, and even on his deathbed busied himself with trying to
complete a drama, obviously intended to be his magnum opus. [11]

   Williams, of course, shared some tastes with Ingersoll.   A
part of the Illinoisan's charm was that he was so catholic in his
tastes that it was almost impossible for a civilized man not to
share some of them.   Like Ingersoll, Williams was strongly influenced by Shakespeare.   Like Ingersoll, who was [272] enough attracted
by the stage to be flattered by proposals that he become an actor,
Williams, too, loved the theater.   Moreover, Williams, like Ingersoll, was the product of a stern religious background; and although
he reacted to the extent that he never held regular church member-
ship, he was not anti-religious and encouraged his children to take
active roles in church work.   Williams, in fact, looked upon the
church as a worthy place for the support of values, and in one of
his unpublished addresses, "A Union of the Church and Stage," he
suggested that if the theater would take a more active interest in
religion and if the church would take a more active interest in theater, both would profit.   Like Ingersoll, too, Williams was sympathetic to the Jews.   In adapting F. Marion Crawford's novel The
Witch of Prague for the stage, Williams, for example, not only
rooted out Crawford's anti-Semitism, but transformed it into a pro-
Jewish idea.   In the novel, Kafka, a Jew, with the help of the Jewish community--pictured as violent and selfish people--poses a
threat to the leading character.   But in Williams' adaptation, Unorna,
Kafka is a Christian, and the Jewish community is pictured as gentle and generous.   Its support, in fact, is what saves the leading
character from the Christians led by Kafka.

   As a Southerner, of course, Williams could not have helped
being offended by Ingersoll's attacks on all things Southern.   Although he was not much concerned with politics, Williams surely
must have identified himself with those under attack in Ingersoll's
famous speech on the nature of the Democratic Party:

> Recollect that the Democratic party did all the things of
> which I have told you. . . . Recollect that this Demo-

> cratic party was false to the Union . . . recollect that
> the Democratic party was false to [273] your country when
> your husbands, your brothers, your fathers, and your
> sons were lying in the prison pens of the South, with
> no covering but the clouds, with no bed but the frozen
> earth, with no food except such as worms had refused
> to eat, and with no friends except Insanity and Death.[12]

Both as a Southerner, who remembered from childhood that Union
soldiers had fared better than his family, and as a banker, anxious
to establish the South as a full partner in the nation, Williams
would have been forced to object to Ingersoll's waving of the "bloody
shirt."

His reaction to this and similar attacks by Ingersoll was not,
however, a typical Southern reaction. Although Williams was a de-
fender of Jefferson Davis,[13] whose pardon Ingersoll had helped to
block, the Southern writer did not react like a Confederate die-hard.
Although Williams believed in the maintenance of the status quo for
Negroes,[14] he did not become a reactionary like the Texas icono-
clast William Brann, who suggested that a day should be taken off
to kill each member of "that accursed race that declines to leave
the country."[15] Although Williams believed in the usefulness of the
church, he did not attack those who disa[274]greed, as did the Georgia
minister, Sam Jones, who called Ingersoll "the devil's dynamo."[16]

Rather, as The Atheist shows, Williams looked past "the
poses" of the Illinois agnostic to what he considered to be the heart
of the man himself. The Atheist was dedicated to Ingersoll, but it
is more than a play written for a man. The hero of the play, mod-
eled after Ingersoll, is a man whose tongue cuts against every man's
beliefs, but whose purse is open to every man's needs. Ingersoll
himself might be describing his own paradoxical position when the
hero speaks, "I came to be a thing abhorred, though loved." And
the Lady's judgment of the Atheist's life, "Thou preached no standard, save by acts, all good . . . Thy way was everywhere bestrewn
with blessings . . . By all those, who, despite thy branded name,
Knew thee a messenger of God," is similar to those made about Ingersoll. The Rochester (New York) Democrat, for example, once
wrote of Ingersoll: "Robert G. Ingersoll is not orthodox in theory,
but we should like to see a better Christian in practice."[17]

Extending Christian charity even to those opposed to Christianity is not, of course, new; but it was unique in nineteenth-century American drama.   In casting The Atheist in the form of the old morality play, Williams was, moreover, making minor theater history, for his use of the form anticipated both the revival of Everyman in New York in the late 1890's and the modern use of the form in such plays as T. S. Eliot's Murder in the Cathedral, Leonid Andreyev's The Life of Man, and Irwin Shaw's Bury the Dead.   The significance of Williams' use of the morality play is not limited to the resurrection of a literary form, however, but is [275] a measure of the dramatist's respect for Ingersoll.   Williams is apparently suggesting that in a living religion in which dogma and the practice are wedded, it is the whole man and not merely his statements on dogma that must be judged.   In arriving at such a conclusion, Williams did not have to look beyond his model, Ingersoll, whose life and actions often reminded antagonistic ministers of their own lack of Christian charity.

What influenced Williams to select Ingersoll as his hero is difficult to determine.   Certainly it was not a politic choice for a Southern businessman; perhaps the removal of the play's dedication to Ingersoll was due to the author's second thoughts on the social wisdom of such a dedication.   Williams was undoubtedly influenced by Ingersoll's reputation among "respectable" people.   The two men, moreover, had many mutual friends.   Ingersoll, for example, was a friend and legal advisor of Lawrence Barrett, the actor, whose funeral oration he delivered. [18]   Barrett was one of the first professional theater people to help Williams in his playwriting, and at the time of the actor's death in 1891, Williams was at work on a romantic play, Dante, which Barrett had intended to act in and produce.   Julia Marlowe, the actress, was a close friend of the Ingersolls, [19] and she, too, had helped Williams in his professional theater career.   Williams was a man of intense loyalty to his friends and could not have helped but feel kindly toward those who aided his friends.

What probably most influenced Williams to look upon Ingersoll as a kind of "unorthodox saint, " however, was neither Ingersoll's

reputation as a public orator nor his reputation as a protector of
the arts. It was rather the reputa[276]tion which the Illinois lawyer had
made as a family man. Williams, himself, placed his literary interests ahead of his business interests, just as Ingersoll placed his
"public duties" ahead of his legal practice; but both men placed
their families ahead of all else. It is interesting to note that both
had families made up largely of women.

The Atheist is not so much a play about religious dogma as
it is a play about the religious fervor of man's love for woman,
and as such it reflects the personal views of both its author and the
man whose life suggested its hero. It might, in fact, be looked
upon as a religious-poetic drama of the symbolic life of Robert
Green Ingersoll. The language used throughout the play reflects
both Ingersoll's philosophy and diction; and the salvation of the hero
through the love of a good woman is, obviously, Williams' reading
of the salvation of Ingersoll.

The failure of historians and biographers to note the play and
its relationship to Ingersoll is not strange. Williams first published
The Atheist as a separate play, and it had only a limited edition in
New Orleans. Later, when it was republished in Williams' volume
of verse The Dream of Art and Other Poems, the dedication to Ingersoll was dropped, and the play itself was glossed over. In ex-
amining reviews of Williams' book, for example, I could find only
one that even mentioned the play. The copy of the play which follows is based on the edition in The Dream of Art and Other Poems, [20]
with slight changes in punctuation to make easier reading. [277]

Notes

1. I am indebted to C.H. Cramer's Royal Bob: The Life of Rob-
    ert G. Ingersoll (New York, 1952) for this interpretation of
    Ingersoll.

2. Espy Williams (1852-1908) was the author of over thirty plays
    which were produced throughout America and in England. Al-
    though he achieved considerable popularity around the turn of
    the century, when he had as many as eight plays being produced
    at the same time, he has been largely forgotten for the last
    half-century. Recently, however, his daughter turned over to
    the University of Southwestern Louisiana library, a con-
    siderable number of his manuscripts, including the original

copies of many of his plays, printed copies of others, a diary, letters, and notes. This collection, including the manuscript of The Atheist, forms the basis of the present study, and unless otherwise noted, all the information concerning Williams is based on this material. [269]

3. In making this claim for Williams, The Daily (New Orleans) Picayune, of Aug. 29, 1908, lists one qualification. Williams, it is argued, is unquestionably first unless one includes Henry Guy Charleton in the southern ranks, and "if Henry Guy Charleton is classed as a Southerner, Mr. Williams ranks unquestionably with him and with the principal playwrights of his day in the American Republic."

4. Harry T. Peck, What Is Good English? and Other Essays (New York, 1899), 235. [270]

5. Cramer, Royal Bob, 16. Cramer points out that when Ingersoll had been a Democrat, the Republican press had attacked him as a "poor, miserable, whiskey-soaked, tobacco-bedaubed, illiterate, blasphemous, red-faced atheist."

6. For an account of Whitman's basic disagreement with Ingersoll's scientific stand, see Richard Maurice Bucke, Thomas B. Harned and Horace L. Traubel, eds., The Complete Writings of Walt Whitman (New York, 1902), IV: 38-40. For a summary of Whitman's political position, see the Introduction, ibid., I: xxx-xxxii.

7. Quoted in Cramer, Royal Bob, 125.

8. Ibid., 65, 72, 261, 265.

9. Albert Bigelow Paine, ed., Mark Twain's Letters (New York, 1917), II: 682. [271]

10. On July 23, 1896, according to an Associated Press story from Philadelphia, Williams opened the session of the United States League of Local Building and Loan Associations with an address, "The Safeguard of American Finances." In the address, Williams forecast that the time was not far distant when "the bonded debt of the United States will be held, not by foreign capitalists, but by the American citizen." The Daily (New Orleans) Picayune, July 24, 1896, ran the complete text of the speech.

11. The handwritten single draft of this play, Marlowe: The Buried Name, was published by the University of Kentucky Press in its Modern Language Microcard Series A. [272]

12. Robert G. Ingersoll, Fifty Great Selections . . . (C. P. Farrell, comp.; New York, 1920), 172-73. Among other things, Ingersoll also accused the Democratic Party in the South of attempting to spread smallpox and yellow fever in New York and of

burning an orphan asylum; ibid., 160.

13. In The Dream of Art and Other Poems (New York, 1892), the same volume in which The Atheist was published, he wrote a poem to Davis (p. 20) which in part was a challenge to Ingersoll, the partisan Republican: "Oh ye whose wanton, fruitless hatred still/ Sought to destroy his peace of life . . . ."

14. In Ollamus: King of Utopiana, a comic opera written by Williams in 1894 and produced in New Orleans, a Negro character is taken to Utopia by a "liberal" as a part of a plan to stir up trouble in Paradise. In revising the opera in 1901, however, under the title of The Royal Joke, which was produced by the Metropolitan English Opera Company, Williams dropped the Negro character--a deletion perhaps suggestive of a change in attitude.

15. Quoted in Cramer, Royal Bob, 95. [274]

16. Quit Your Meanness: Sermons and Sayings of Rev. Sam P. Jones of Georgia (Cincinnati, 1886).

17. Quoted in Cramer, Royal Bob, 144. [275]

18. Ibid., 151.

19. Ibid., 254-55. [276]

20. The only extant copy of the first edition of The Atheist, published some time after 1890 but before 1892, is in the New York Public Library. Less than a dozen copies of the second edition, a part of The Dream of Art and Other Poems, are known to exist. [277]

A Southerner's Tribute

<u>The Atheist</u>

A Modern Masque

by Espy Williams

Scene: Christmas Eve--The Atheist's Chambers, overlooking the
city, The Atheist alone.

Chorus of Devils, In Hell.

Thou unvanquished, though defeated, Spirit infinite of light,

Still in every bosom seated, Throned in never yielding might;

Fallen, still of Heaven's greatest, Thou too wear'st a mar-
tyr's crown,

And Time's earliest and latest vie to echo thy renown.

The Atheist: The usurper, the victorious, self-appointed Lord of
all,

Boasts no victory so glorious, as the battle of thy fall:

For of angels thou wert brightest, for thy works most splen-
did shone,

For thy votaries' hearts were lightest, and thy priests were
full thine own.

His be then the boasted glory, Thine the glory of the gain,

His the far re-echoed story, Thine, the silent, secret reign!

Though of earth all kind adore Him, praise as good the woes
he gave,

Every cringing soul before Him is in secret thy sworn slave.

And this is life, a little while to feel

Kind Nature's sweets, then be resolved in nothing!

Lost even in an unseen respiration,

Less than the echo of a whispered sigh;

And while we live, live only to acquire

A growing sense of our own littleness,

Till we become a jest unto ourselves,

A wreck, self-ridiculed and self-despised.

Our span of being is a little more

Than the bright butterfly's--our happiness

Much less--and that the only difference.

All that has beautiful being, and the sense [278]

To feel and to enjoy, can boast more bliss

Than man, who boasts the power of thought,

And calls himself the lord of earthly kind.

Why should not man then rather be a beast

And grovel in contentment, than be thus

Winged with the aspirations of a god

To soar, however high, to discontent?

(Church bells heard ringing through the city.)

The bells, for midnight Mass. Alas, poor man,

Whose final, only consolation is a myth

Wrought deftly from his own conceit and pride;

A tale of superstition told so oft

It hath become the semblance of a truth

Inwrought indelibly into himself.

(As he pours out wine in a glass, there enters, unseen, one shrouded in a priest's gown and cowl, who, as he is about to drink, speaks.)

The Priest: Drink not, save from the chalice of His blood!

The Atheist: (Starting, putting down the glass.) How came ye,
    priest? and whence? and wherefore? speak.

The Priest: By that straight path that leads to those who need,
    From One who wills ye good, perchance for good.

The Atheist: (Laughing.) A thousand times I have heard such like
        words,
    And still a thousand times been left unchanged.
    Your tests, your arguments, I have heard all,
    Yes, preached them to myself with will attent,
    Yet ever to their condemnation: all.
    There is no God, who, merciful, condemns:

No righteous One, who makes but to destroy.
From nothing, from a never-dying law
We come, and thence to nothing we return;
And they go first who violate that law
And suffer its unfailing execution.
This much alone man knows.   Priests know not more. [279]

A Voice: (Passing in the street below, singing:)
Once in the life of every heart, pure, steadfast, strangely
bright,
The star of Bethlehem shines out upon its lonely night;
And, startled from its shepherd watch, the sleepy soul en-
thrills
With a new life, about to be, the new-born end of ills.

The Priest: "Once in the life of every heart . . . ."   And thine?
You pause.   You turn away.

The Atheist: Question not, priest.
The deeds entombed within the past are dust,
Like ashes of dead men, unlike themselves,
And no one seeks in them their living likeness.

A Maiden: (Singing) Deep in the ocean's deep the purest pearls
are found;
Deep in the dark earth's keep the richest gems abound;
But deeper hidden than these, and priceless far above,
Deep in the heart's sweet mysteries, lies hid the jewel, love.

The Priest: Love only lives within celestial soil;
And he who loves bears heaven within his breast,
Although in ignorance.

The Atheist: Priest, once I too
Thought love an attribute divine, and lent
To mortals to make sordid life more sweet,

And tempt them heavenward by foretaste of heaven.
But I was new to life then, and I loved.
'Twas like a dream of childhood's peaceful sleep,
Full of bright stranger beauties.   There still lives
Within my heart the memory of its sunshine,
But there, too, lives the greater memory still,
Of the black thunder-cloud that wrought its ruin.
We had been raised together, boy and girl.
And all our childhood whims grew counterparts,
Until our years were ripe for flower and fruit.
Then she . . . she was shut out from life, from joy,
Within a convent's wall, while I went forth [280]
Into the busy, battling world of men,
To gain man's heritage of strife and scar.
When next we met, I was a bearded man,
And she . . . . I had seen many fair, and some
Accounted beautiful above the rest.
But she excelled them all.   Something there seemed
About her that bespoke not earth, but heaven,
And won my mad idolatry at sight.
'Twas then my dream of love was; and it lasted
Until your God--yes, your God--stepped between us;
Weighed me, and found me wanting in the scale
Of cant, hypocrisy, pretense to things
Which truth and manhood could not dare profess,
Yet which His priesthood held for blind belief,
For faith unquestioned, from a thoughtless crowd.
'Twas then my dream fled, for she had been won
By such as you, whose subtle mastery
Poisoned her heart against me, till at last
I came to be a thing abhorred, though loved,
An evil spirit doomed to lasting hell,
Unless, good, simple soul, her prayers could save me,
Her life of cloistered penitence wash out
My sins.   So much I trusted, loved her then,
That even I was shaken, and in fear

        Half-doubted for myself. But time and facts
        Dispelled all doubts and fears. Her life was wrecked,
        Full-freighted with youth's bountiful desires,
        Upon the rocks of blind, fanatic faith.
        Her life was lost, her womanhood discarded,
        Her end and place in nature unfulfilled,
        Her very being a self-created void.

The Priest: No, not so. For behold . . . . (Throws off the robe
and cowl and discovers a beautiful woman.)

The Atheist: (Starting up.) Is this enchantment?
        Thou, thou of whom I have been speaking, here? [281]

The Lady: Yes, here in flesh and blood, in womanhood.
        Here from the nunnery to be thy bride,
        Nay, more than that, thy guiding, saving angel,
        To lead thee to a knowledge of thyself,
        And show thee how, despite thy scoffs,
        Thy vaunted infidelity to faith,
        Thou art at heart a very child of God.
        Speak not. Hear Me. Within the convent walls
        My life passed idly day by day in prayer
        For thee, and all was lost in thoughts of thee.
        Think not that there, though shut up from the world,
        The world can enter not to those who seek it.
        So, every day, something I heard of thee:
        Heard of thy jeers and scoffs at things called holy,
        Thy unrepentant sacrilege, and most
        Thy shameless jests on such as I was there.
        But, too, I heard, how all thy deeds to man
        Were fraught with greatest good; how in thy life
        Thou preached no standard, save by acts, all good;
        How, singled from thy kind as a lost soul,
        Doomed by the Church to its eternal hell,
        Instead of shunnings, curses, and damnations,

Thy way was everywhere bestrewn with blessings,
The fruits of thy own sowing, lavished on thee
By all those, who, despite thy branded name,
Knew thee a messenger of God, of Him
Whose life is love, whose love is still to do.
What was I then compared with thee? Nothing.
In all my days of prayer, not one stood forth
Crowned with a living act of good, not one
For sorrow eased, for trouble comforted.
Then in my heart, the star of Bethlehem
Rose steadfast, pure, and strangely bright, and in
My soul I felt the quickening of new life;
And, led as were the shepherds on that night
Of old, I followed till the star stood still
Above thy threshold, here above my head.

The Atheist: Has thou then broken faith, forsworn thy vows,
    To seek, to follow me, the branded one?

The Lady: I have forsworn no vows. The Church that took them,
    True to its aim, its purpose still for best
    Returns me to the world and to myself.
    Nor have I broken, have I lost my faith,
    But have gained greater faith, the faith to do.
(Voices of children passing, heard singing Christmas carols.)

Chorus of Devils in Hell

Like a dream forever lost in the caverns of sleep,
Like a jewel far tossed in the depths of the deep,
Like an arrow's lost flight, Like a meteor's lost light,
Each hope that ye cherish, Be it born but to perish.
Like a rock rent asunder by an earthquake's thunder,
Like a ship storm-driven in darkness rock-riven,
Like the cleft semi-note in a murdered bird's throat,
Like music death-hushed, Like a diamond crushed,
May your hearts with fine pain, Be tortured in twain.

                         The End

V.   The Biographical Sketch
The Playwrights

Even as historical artifacts and relics, many of the forty thousand "lost" plays of provincial America were not at the time of their composition, and have not become, worth publication. Almost any playwright of this period, however, the failures as well as the successes, is of historical interest. Many of the playwrights were men of some social importance in their communities--bankers, judges, doctors, teachers, Army scouts.

In the three articles selected here as examples of ways of writing about the playwrights, the playwrights selected are as varied as the treatments of them. The first article, "J. W. Crawford: Poet-Scout of the Black Hills, " is a conventional documented essay about the New Mexican Army scout playwright, Capt. Jack, and the emphasis is placed upon the historical interest of the man for a region of particular concern to a regional journal. The second, "Ernest J. Whisler--Arizona's Lost Playwright, " is an informal essay about a businessman playwright, and the emphasis is placed upon the academic interest in the man for a regional teachers' journal. The third article, "Felix Voorhies--Judge-Playwright-Actor-Writer, " is a popular account of a state judge playwright, and the emphasis is placed on the man as representative of the area in which a regional, popular magazine is published.

1.   "J. W. Crawford: Poet-Scout of the Black Hills"
(Reprinted from South Dakota Review, II [Spring, 1965], 40-47.)

In 1876 William F. Cody (Buffalo Bill), then in his fifth year as a touring actor, broke off the run of one of his autobiographical melodramas to return to the Dakotas. The United States was in a front-page war with the Sioux; and a man who was building a repu-

110

tation as a frontier scout had to be a part of that war, for a variety of reasons. [1]

He had, in the first place, earned a reputation as a competent army scout, and he might well have judged that his skills were now needed. He had, moreover, spent five years on the stage, giving his audience a first-hand view of the owner of that reputation. Now he had to prove again that the stage actor was also the real-life performer. The eyes of his audience had, at any rate, moved from the Buffalo Bill of Scouts of the Plains and Life on the Border to the front-page melodrama of the Indian war; and if Buffalo Bill were to live, Cody needed to keep his dramas associated with the new events on the border. He needed not only personal association with the new war, but he needed to bring part of that war back to the stage.

From his first appearance as an actor, Cody had seen the necessity of supporting his Buffalo Bill characterization with "real" frontier characters. Wild Bill Hickock and Texas Jack Omohundro had been part of his company, but Wild Bill had quit, and Texas Jack, it would seem, was always a shadowy figure, better known as a stage character than as a "historical" character. [40]

Cody returned to the border with a grand entrance--dressed in his stage costume; and this entrance caused some comment. But the death of Custer required more than a costume. Later in the summer, Cody found in his hand-to-hand fight with Yellow Hand the ideal sort of an action to use in building the image of the hero, and he had this event dramatized for a new "autobiographical melodrama," The Right Red Hand, with which he toured during the season of 1876-77.

When he first received the news of the battle at the Little Big Horn, however, Cody was not able to take a "first scalp for Custer." Rather he sent a telegram to one of the popular border figures, John Wallace Crawford, "The Poet Scout of the Black Hills": "Have you heard of the death of our brave Custer?"[2] Seemingly the purpose of the wire was to make it clear that the "avenging hero" had arrived on the scene and was about to take an heroic action. Crawford must have seemed to Cody to be a good character

to play a supporting role to him as the confidant of the hero.
Everything about his public character to that time suggested such a
role.

Crawford, born in Ireland in 1847, had moved to Pennsylvania
at the outbreak of the Civil War. For a short time he worked in
the mines, but then shortly before his sixteenth birthday he enlisted
in the Union Army. His entire performance in the Civil War was
pictured by him as that of the "pathetic boy volunteer." He was
young and small for his age; and he was, moreover, unable to read
or write until a Sister of Mercy "taught him his letters" while he
was recuperating from combat wounds--an episode that he used as
a "pathetic tale" on many occasions. After the war, he settled in
Pennsylvania; but shortly after his marriage in 1869, he moved
west to find employment as a scout. [3] He was one of the first European settlers in the Dakotas and made something of a reputation
for himself as a responsible civilian scout, story-teller, and tee-
totaler. Cody, in fact, had first been impressed with Crawford
after the Poet Scout delivered a full bottle of whiskey to him. "Capt.
Jack was one of the very few teetotal scouts I ever met," Cody
wrote. [4]

He had, also, worked at his writing and had developed into a
mildly successful sentimental poet. In the summer of 1876, he a-
chieved some national attention when he carried a dispatch for [41] the
New York Herald almost four hundred miles through Indian territory. [5]

Obviously, a man who carried messages, wrote poetry, and
left a man's whiskey alone was born to be a supporting character,
from Cody's point of view. Crawford's answer to his telegram
should, however, have warned Buffalo Bill that Captain Jack had
notions of his own about playing the role of the hero.

As soon as Crawford received Cody's wire, he "immediately
wrote the following verses" and sent them "to Mr. Cody in answer
to his dispatch . . ." His answer--a poetic tribute to Custer--ex-
pressed, in some seventy-two lines, not only his regret for the
death of Custer, but also commented upon his own sensitivity, the
innate corruption of all Indians, the necessity of civilian volunteers

to win the war, the baseness of peacemongers, "Quakers" back
East, and his association with the "other" heroes of the war--Cus-
ter, of course, Cody, General Carr, and Sheridan, whom he ad-
dressed as "Phil, old boy."

The poem opens with Crawford's confession of his sensitive
nature:[6]

> Did I hear the news from Custer?
> Well, I reckon I did, old pard;
> It came like a streak of lightin',
> And, you bet, it hit me hard.
> I ain't no hand to blubber,
> And the briny ain't run for years;
> But chawk me down for a lubber,
> If I didn't shed regular tears.

Crawford, who spent the entire Civil War as a private, gives
a brief account of this service, suggesting that he and Custer served together in the same battles, not merely the same war.

> I served with him [Custer] in the army,
> In the darkest days of the [Civil] war;
> And I reckon ye know his record,
> For he was our guiding star.
> And the boys who gathered round him
> To charge in the early morn,
> War just like the brave who perished
> With him on the Little Horn.

Although Cody in his first "autobiography," published in 1879,
reprinted this poem, [7] Crawford's answer must have proved some-[42]
what of a surprise.   Capt. Jack was known throughout the Black
Hills as a competent scout, but even more than a man of action,
he was known as a soft-spoken man with a sentimental, romantic
affection for nature, a teller of pathetic tales.   In poem after poem
about the Dakota scene, Crawford expressed a conventional love for
nature in Shelley-like verse.   "By the Lake," for example, opens
with these lines:

> My heart is just dancing with rapture
> To the music that springs from the soul,
> As I revel in Nature's seclusion . . .

Instead of affecting the "pard's" and "reckon's" of the western frontiersman, Crawford made a point of speaking and writing a "pure"
language.   In fact, in one of his poems, "Musing," he defended his
right to poetic feelings, even though he had no formal education:

Is there no poetic beauty
In these simple songs of mine?
Must a man be bred in college
Ere he dares to form a rhyme?[8]

Crawford, in fact, until that summer of 1876, had worked constantly to create the image of the gentle, sentimental poet of the Black Hills; and he had, in fact, during those first years of the 1870's, begun the habit of signing himself, "Capt. Jack, The Poet Scout."[9] It was this character of Crawford that Cody hoped to bring into his theatrical company; and in the fall of 1876, Crawford left the Dakotas to travel with Cody in a "co-starring role" as the Poet Scout of the Black Hills.

At the beginning of that 1876-77 season, Crawford held to the pose of the Poet Scout, appearing as a supporting character in the melodramas about Buffalo Bill and reading his poetry. Before long, however, Cody gave him the leading role in Life on the Border. The part had been written for Cody and the character is named Buffalo Bill, but when Crawford took over the role, the character's name was changed to Capt. Jack. This "Capt. Jack," however, has none of the characteristics of the Poet Scout.[10]

At the end of the season, in the summer of 1877, Crawford was accidentally wounded during a performance of The Right Red Hand in Virginia City, Nevada.[11] Crawford, playing the role of Yellow Hand, maintained that Cody had stabbed and shot him [43] while drunk, but the Virginia City newspapers reported that Crawford's wound had been accidentally self-inflicted when the Poet Scout discharged his weapon by mistake before his revolver had cleared his holster. Whatever is the fact of the matter, however, when the Buffalo Bill show disbanded for the summer, Crawford was left behind in Virginia City, wounded and penniless.

Some of Crawford's friends held a theatrical benefit for him, and he was given six hundred dollars. During his convalescence, Crawford and a Sam Smith, the author of a successful comedy, Struck Oil, collaborated on a "western melodrama," Fonda; Or the Trapper's Daughter. This play is autobiographical in that the hero, named Capt. Jack Crawford, is a poet-philosopher and has a reputation as a scout-hunter. Crawford, however, seeking an audience

in the Far West, turned from his Black Hills materials and set the
scene of the play in Utah.   The play deals, not with Black Hills
scouts, but rather with a wagon train of California-born settlers;
and the Mormons, not the Indians, are the villains.

Fonda had a short run in California, and Crawford was offered an opportunity to take his company to Australia, but he was unable to raise the expense money.   Instead he took a job scouting
for the army in the New Mexico-Arizona Indian wars in the late
1870's and 1880's.   Crawford now changed his "public pose" from
the "Poet of the Black Hills" to the "Poet of the Sunshine State,"
the man who discovered a philosophy of life in the southwest "whar
the hand of God is seen."

As far as his role as the first "poet-playwright of Dakota"
was concerned, Crawford seemed, for a time, to be finished.   During his New Mexico years, he gave accounts to the press about his
exploits in the southwestern Indian campaigns.   Once he had written
about his associations with Custer, Wild Bill, Calamity Jane, and
California Joe; now he told of his encounters with Billy the Kid,
Victorio, and Geronimo.   No longer were the Black Hills the best
evidence of "God's handiwork"; now it was the New Mexican mountain scene.   During his dozen years in New Mexico, he toured the
country lecturing on the evils of drink, the moral virtues of the
"real West," and the opportunities to be found in New Mexico.

Then suddenly he returned to his Black Hills adventures.   In
1886 he copyrighted a three-act melodrama, first titled Tat; The
Veteran's Daughter and later The Mighty Truth, a frontier drama [44]
set in the Dakotas of the 1870's.   The leading character--the poet
scout--is now named Jack Wallace (Wallace was Crawford's mother's
name); but, as in Fonda, he is still called Capt. Jack.   This character is an odd combination of the Buffalo Bill character of Life on
the Border and the "sensitive poet of nature" hero of Fonda, and in
typical melodramatic fashion, he overcomes the old villains of his
Dakota days--Indians and Indian agents.

The Mighty Truth is the kind of play that should have succeeded well during the days that Crawford was playing Yellow Hand to
Cody's Buffalo Bill in the Right Red Hand; but seemingly, by the

mid-1880's, the war against the Sioux had become, for his audience, ancient history. Although the play was copyrighted in 1886, in 1900 --when Crawford returned from a gold-searching adventure in the Yukon--so little attention had been paid to it that he was able to announce the play as a new one simply by changing the title; and seemingly those who saw the play in Chicago and San Francisco were unaware of the similarity.

This play was Crawford's main dramatic fare for the first seven years of the twentieth century, and during these years, he gave far more time to his lecturing than to his drama. The character that he created on the lecture platform, however--that of honest Capt. Jack, the Poet Scout of New Mexico--was to serve as the basis for his next and last play. In 1907 Crawford and a Marie Madison collaborated on Colonel Bob. In this play, the Capt. Jack character, now called Col. Bob, seems never to have heard of the Dakotas. He is an eastern-born youth who "finds himself" in the "wild grandeur" of New Mexico; after an adventure in Alaska, he finds wealth in New Mexico and returns to the East to preach his doctrine of salvation through contact with "honest nature," that found in the hills of the "Sunshine State."

Crawford's inconstant career as the "Poet of the Black Hills" suggests, it seems to me, some of the problems in the creation of a permanent frontier literature in the nineteenth century. In the main, those on the frontier who became the literary spokesmen for the "new land" were opportunists, seeing in the new land a chance to win victories in terms of the older civilizations they had left. Crawford, for example, was descended from Scottish people, and although he had not lived in Scotland, yet he equated [45] the "new land" with old Scotland, even to the extent of using the diction of Robert Burns in describing it.

Crawford, moreover, and the other new settler-poets brought a hunger with them, a hunger not merely for land and wealth, but for position. Dislocated from an older civilization, they made attachments to the new land that they expressed in the language of the promoter, not the native. By hindsight, there is something almost ridiculously insincere about Crawford's insistence that each "new

land" he "discovered"--Pennsylvania, the Black Hills, Colorado,
California, New Mexico, the Yukon--was the "finest spot" on earth
and his "native home"; but the settler by the act of moving heart
and belongings to the frontier is forced to defend his migration with
passion.

Crawford--like Mark Twain and Bret Harte to lesser degrees
--was corrupted by the dream of "sudden wealth. " He saw those
about him act out the Horatio Alger story, and he concluded that
anything which does not produce immediate wealth is not worth having.   Such a doctrine may settle a broad wilderness in record time,
but it leads to a shallowness of view.   Crawford, like the miners,
saw in the frontier only that which could be taken away from the
land and sold for a profit in the older civilizations.

It is not a mere coincidence that Crawford, the "Poet of the
Black Hills, " the "Singer of the Sunshine State, " the "Poet Scout, "
should spend the last ten years of his life touring the East and die
in Brooklyn, nor that Twain should join the Boston society, nor that
Harte should move to England.   What saved Twain was that he was
native to the Mississippi, not that he discovered Nevada.   And
Crawford was native only to the roaming generation.

Crawford's claim to the title of "Poet of the Black Hills" is
valid enough historically; but as far as one may judge by his poetry
and his one play about the Dakota territory, Capt. Jack saw the
Black Hill country only as a painted background, a stage property,
for the histrionics of the Poet Scout.   He was, more properly, a
poet in the Black Hills, but not of them.

Notes

1.   A full account of Cody's stage career is given in Henry Black-
     man Sell [46] and Victor Weybright's Buffalo Bill and the Wild
     West (New York: Oxford University Press, 1955).

2.   Cody's telegram and Crawford's poetic reply are given in Cap-
     tain Jack Crawford's The Poet Scout: A Book of Song and
     Story (New York: Funk & Wagnalls, 1886), pp. 106-108.

3.   Leigh Irvine's "Biographical Sketch, " The Poet Scout, pp. v-
     xiv, is the most complete published account of Crawford's
     early career.

4. William F. Cody, The Life of Hon. William F. Cody, Known
    as Buffalo Bill: The Famous Hunter, Scout and Guide: An
    Autobiography (Hartford, Conn.: Frank E. Bliss, 1879), p.
    349.

5. Irvine, "Biographical Sketch," p. xii. Crawford's ride was
    from Rosebud to Little Big Horn to Fort Laramie, and he made
    the trip in less than four days. The New York Herald paid him
    $722.75 for the service.

6. Poet Scout, p. 106.

7. Cody, Life of Hon. William F. Cody, p. 348. Cody dropped
    the poem and all references to Crawford from later editions of
    the biography, probably as a result of a feud between the two
    men.

8. Poet Scout, p. 115.

9. Captain Charles King, Campaigning with Crook and Stories of
    Army Life (New York: Harper & Brothers, 1890), in comment-
    ing on the special qualities of the "great scouts" (p. 112),
    writes only this of Crawford: "We . . . listened to 'Captain
    Jack' Crawford's yarns and rhymes in many a bivouac in the
    Northwest."

10. The only extant copy of Life on the Border, to my knowledge,
    is that owned by Mrs. Buford Richardson, Socorro, New Mex-
    ico, a descendant of Crawford. An edition of it is now in pro-
    gress. This copy is signed by Cody as a presentation to Craw-
    ford, and the part of Buffalo Bill is crossed out and that of
    Capt. Jack written in. The change, however, is little more
    than a change in names. One change, however, does suggest a
    basic difference in their public roles. Cody as Buffalo Bill has
    one piece of dialogue that deals with the observation that while
    a man cannot have too many mothers, he should not have more
    than one father. Crawford changed the word father to mother-
    in-law. (Editor's Note: Life on the Border was published in
    1965 by the Pioneer Drama Service, Cody, Wyoming.)

11. See my "When the Curtains Rise, Scouts Fall Out," Southern
    Speech Journal, XXIX (Spring, 1964), 175-86, for a complete
    account of Crawford's quarrel with Cody over this "accident."[47]

2. "Ernest J. Whisler--Arizona's Lost Playwright"

(Reprinted from Arizona Teacher, LII [May, 1964], 19-20.)

Arizona has always been a popular setting for American dra-
ma. Buffalo Bill's press agent, John Burke, even called himself
"Arizona John" to cash in on the popularity, although as many of
Burke's enemies pointed out, he never got southwest of Denver.

Such titles as Augustus Thomas's Arizona (1899); W. F. Mann's
Arizona Bandit (1906); Frances Morris's Arizona Bess (1892); Cath-
erine Davy's Arizona Girl Bandit (1907); Roy Foster's Arizona Incident (1900); Harry Lacy's Arizona Jim, and Jacob B. Rue's Arizona Stampede (1913) attest to the popularity of the state as a setting for drama, but also suggest that the American playwright saw
Arizona largely as a "wild and woolly domain. "

Most of the playwrights who liked the word Arizona in their
titles knew the state only from the geography books. Thomas, the
most famous of the American playwrights using the title, and Lacy
were New Yorkers; Mann was a Baltimore resident; Foster was a
Chicago playwright, and Rue was from New Jersey, for examples.

Nor did Arizona receive much better treatment from those
with closer associations. Miss Morris, for example, was a Colorado Springs girl when she wrote the rip-snorting Arizona Bess,
and "the unkindest cut of all" came from an Arizona-New Mexico
Indian Scout, Capt. Jack Crawford. Crawford, who scouted for
General Crook in the Victorio and Geronimo campaigns, finally
made his home in New Mexico. Here he wrote a play, Colonel
Bob, which has a young heroine from Arizona, but her father took
her "east to New Mexico to civilize her. "

Arizona had few playwrights during the early years to "protect" her from the fast-gun, melodramatic writers. From 1882,
when Frederick Stanford, a temporary resident of Tombstone, wrote
the first Arizona play, The Stinger; or, The Arizona Carnival, until World War I, only twenty Arizona residents copyrighted plays.

And even most of these were more interested in the myth of
the frontier bloody battleground than in the drama of its emerging
civilization. Edwin Baker, a Nogales playwright, for example,
wrote about The Finish of Pete. Ernest Sutherland Bates of Tucson

wrote about The Children of the Mesa. Harrison Conrad of Flag-
staff found his ideal woman in Bronco Kate. Ernest Lamson turned to the Arizona mountains for his melodramatic Found in the
Rockies; or Cave Creek.

The Most Successful

Perhaps fortunately for Arizona, the most successful playwright was Ernest J. Whisler. Unfortunately, Whisler wrote for
the amateur theater so his plays were unknown to turn-of-the-century audiences except through the school and community amateur
stage. But with his plays, he was ranked as one of "the best for
the amateur theater."

Although most of Whisler's drama would still be good academic and community theater fare, especially for an Arizona audience
interested in its dramatic history, Whisler is practically unknown
today.

He was, however, the only Arizona playwright to be both published and produced and yet even some of his published plays have
just about disappeared. His plays, like At the Postern Gate, published by the Penn Company in 1902; Lexington, [19] published by
T. S. Denison Company in 1912; and A Trick Dollar, published by
Denison in 1902, have now become "rare book" items. The only
known extant copy of A Trick Dollar, for example, is in the "rare
book" collection of the University of Illinois Library, a library
noted for its "special collections."

By some trick of fate, however, three of Whisler's plays--
Tommy's Bride, Private Tutor, and Alias Brown, all published by
the Walter H. Baker Company of Boston--are still on the public
market; at least they were a year ago. And they were still selling
at their turn-of-the-century prices: thirty-five cents for Tommy's
Bride, seventy-five cents for Private Tutor, and twenty-five cents
for Alias Brown. The University of Illinois Library sets one hundred dollars as the value of its sole copy of A Trick Dollar, and
even at this price the book is not for sale.

Agents at the Baker Company said they had not received or-
ders for any of Whisler's plays in almost a half century, and they

were mildly surprised to find that they still have some copies in
stock. None of the plays is any longer covered by copyright, and
there hasn't been a single reissue in the last fifty years.

From Back East

Whisler, seemingly, was originally from "back East," a fairly common origin for Arizonans at the turn of the century. His
first two plays, both copyrighted in 1902--At the Postern Gate and
Robin Adair--were written when Whisler was a resident of Rochester, Penn. With the success of these plays--he sold At the Postern Gate to the Penn Company--Whisler moved west, as far as
Chicago, where in October, 1902, he copyrighted A Trick Dollar.

Chicago may have just been a change-of-trains for Whisler,
for after 1902, all of his plays were written from Tucson, Arizona.
In 1907, he wrote The Private Tutor; in 1910, The Sacred Lion; in
1913, The Smoking Set, and in 1914, Alias Brown, all copyrighted
from Tucson. In 1912, his Trick Dollar was copyrighted by the
Denison Company from Chicago, but seemingly Whisler wrote it in
Tucson.

Whisler is the only known Arizona playwright to use the southwestern setting for social comedies. Two of his plays--Lexington
and Robin Adair--are romances, but mostly Whisler was interested
in catching the current social foibles in the farce. When he uses
the southwestern setting, Phoenix and points west, it is with a complete lack of self-consciousness of the Western Bad Man image.

His Alias Brown, for example, is set in Reno, Nevada, but
Whisler's Nevada is the twentieth-century version, not the Zane
Gray one. The play opens with a "barroom quartet" singing "Oh,
Gee, I'm glad I'm free . . . . He's got his divorce, hurrah!
Hurrah!" It closes with the Reno hotel clerk, Vincent Allgood, ex-
plaining to the young lovers: "I'm sorry to disappoint you, but I've
telephoned all over the city, and there's not a minister in Reno
who is familiar with the wedding service."

Another of Whisler's "still available plays" is set at Clear-
field College, presumably in Arizona. But it is not the Arizona of
Girl Bandit or Bronco Kate. Whisler's play, The Private Tutor,

deals with a college student, Fred Spencer, who is about to be expelled from college for "having a good time." His father, an oil millionaire, and his socially conscious mother will withdraw him from school unless he can trick them.

Unfortunately he is exposed, and as the play ends, he needs to find work: "I can lead a cotillion, I can roller skate, and I can play 'Home Sweet Home' on the piano with one finger . . . ," he summarizes. Fortunately, however, he doesn't have to go into politics, as a friend suggests. Fred has "learned his lesson" and he will start "at the bottom" in his father's oil wells.

Tricks and romance, oil wealth and divorce--this is the "stuff of life" that Whisler found for his dramas in old Arizona. His view of Arizona was probably a strange one for Easterners who saw the state as the land of Geronimo and the Cisco Kid, but a lot of Arizona old-timers today would probably find his characters and settings a lot closer to what they remember of Arizona as a territory. [20]

3. "Felix Voorhies--Judge-Playwright-Actor-Writer"
(Reprinted from Southwest Magazine, II
[February, 1960], 3, 24.)

"And next only to New Orleans is Southwest Louisiana." That
is the verdict of America's judges of beauty and interest, in a recent article on "The U.S.A. as a Touristland" in The Saturday Review.

New Orleans, itself, was ranked fifth among "America's most
interesting spots," right behind Washington, D.C., New York, San
Francisco, and the Grand Canyon. And in Louisiana, only Southwest Louisiana was ranked with New Orleans as a leading "beauty
spot." In fact, Howard K. Smith, one of the judges, ranked the
Bayou Teche area even ahead of New Orleans for "a kind of rural
beauty not found anywhere else."

It is not, of course, only the "rural beauty" that has drawn
the approval of visitors here. It's food and coffee, grace and
charm, tolerance and humor. It is, in brief, all of the things that
made Felix Voorhies (1839-1919), gentleman, judge, playwright, author and wit, both a symbol of this area and a unique kind of artist
in the development of American literature.

Judge Voorhies

Felix Voorhies was born in St. Martinville on January 1, 1839;
and although his education and his legislative duties took him out of
the area from time to time, it was in the world of St. Martinville,
Breaux Bridge and Lafayette that he made his contributions to a
way of life that has made this area of Louisiana one of the most
comfortable places in the United States to live.

Mr. Voorhies was, of course, an example of the "dedicated
public servant." He was a judge, the son of a judge, the brother
of a judge--Albert, who in 1870 edited the Revised Civil Code of
Louisiana--and he dedicated one of his plays to another judge.
Voorhies can also be viewed as an important, if minor, figure in
the American local color movement for his book, Acadian Reminis-
cences, published in 1907.

The C. C. C.

But it was as the founder of the C. C. C. --the Chocolate, Coffee, and Cake Club, an amateur theater society--that he best set
an example of what life has to offer for a cultivated person living
in "Little Paris, " as St. Martinville was known in the last century.

Judge Voorhies not only was the stimulus for an atmosphere
that made possible active amateur French theatricals in St. Martinville, Breaux Bridge, and Lafayette; he was also the area's leading
playwright and director and an accomplished amateur actor.   But
strangely enough even with these theatrical activities, Judge Voorhies was not concerned with using the area as a launching program
for a career into "bigger things. " As he saw the American theater
in his age--a show of broad burlesques, melodrama, and sentimental comedy--to write for the amateur theaters of southwest Louisiana was to work with the best in cultivated America.

The Voorhies family came to America originally from Holland
--where they were the Van Voorhees; but early in America's colo-
nial history, the family married into families of Acadian and French
ancestry and became a part of the history of the French-Acadians
in America.   There is a popular legend, for example, that Felix's
grandmother on his mother's side, the Widow Borda, was the [3]
person who gave shelter and protection to "Evangeline. "

As a playwright, always a gentlemanly avocation for him,
Judge Voorhies brought to the area's stage a sophistication and wit
that looked to the past drama of Moliere for examples and forecast
the future drama of Somerset Maugham and Noel Coward.   In fact,
one of Voorhies' twenty-one plays, Petite Fille et Grand'mère,
written by him about the turn of the century, has the same plot and
tone as Maugham's The Circle, considered by many critics to be
the most urbane English drama of the twentieth century.

It is a kind of paradox, in fact, that of all Louisiana's nineteenth-century playwrights--and many of them were much better
known than Voorhies--his plays are probably the only ones that today's Evangeline Country would find pleasure in viewing.   For example, one play which the Judge wrote in French in 1873 and then
translated into English in 1889, "All Husbands Are Alike, " deals

with the problem of a husband who feels that marriage has lost its excitement. In fact, the husband tells his wife, "After six years of married life, my dear little wife, what could we say to each other." His wife, who apparently is as modern as today's "Advice to the Lovelorn," uses a ruse to make her husband think he is in danger of losing her. And the play ends with this comment by the husband: "Love without a passing cloud grows monotonous, and a little jealousy is a spring seasoning to married life."

The Self-Critic

Although a lawyer himself, one of Voorhies' principal targets for satire was the lawyer; and although a learned man, he also found much to ridicule in the professor. Yet, today, except for the concern of a professional scholar, Miss Marcella Frances Schertz, who wrote her thesis about him in 1940, his plays, and the delightful relics of his age, would now be forgotten. The Judge kept manuscripts, but only a few of his plays were ever published, and one has been republished in the past half-century. In fact, if Judge Voorhies were to view the scene today, he would probably conclude, "My plays are as dead as the amateur theater movement in southwest Louisiana." And then he would probably smile and add, "But the charm is still here--the coffee, chocolate, and cake. And where these are, eventually there will be good amateur theater again." [24]

VI.   Some Literary Criticism:
The Plays

Even if all the plays are not worth editions, often they contain elements that are critically and historically interesting. For
the three articles in this chapter, I took plays by a New Orleans
playwright, Espy Williams, and examined them for what they suggested about subjects in theatre and cultural history. The first,
"Williams' Dante: The Death of Nineteenth-Century Heroic Drama, "
is concerned with the historical development of a kind of play. The
second, "Classical Tragedy in the Province Theater, " examines another of Williams' plays as evidence of a kind of theatre taste in
America at a particular time. The third, "The Life and Death of
a Louisiana Play: Espy Williams' 'Unorna', " is an examination of
a play and its stage history to suggest certain cultural truths about
the American stage at the turn of the century. For articles of
this nature, regional journals in the area in which the playwright
lived are normally the most likely markets; but such studies have
a general interest beyond any one area, and all three of these ar-
ticles--and not just one--could have easily been published in national journals as well as in regional ones.

1.   "Williams' Dante: The Death of Nineteenth-
Century Heroic Drama"
(Reprinted from The Southern Speech Journal, XXV
[Summer, 1960], 255-263.)

A typed manuscript of a Southern play, Dante and Beatrice,
by Espy Williams (1852-1908) has recently been discovered. [1] It is
a slight manuscript of thirty-seven pages, and the title page de-
scribes it as a "Florentine Romance in Three Acts. " The alternate
title, Dante, is given on the first page of the play itself. Another
copy of this play, this one titled Dante, is in the copyright office of

the Library of Congress, where it was placed by the author in 1893.
These are the only two extant copies of the play; and, apparently,
although the play was advertised for production as late as 1898, [2]
about eight years after its first composition, the play was never
published nor produced.

Dante and Beatrice or Dante is a highly heroic treatment of
the Dante-Beatrice story. Williams makes use of the historic-leg-
endary material by treating the affair between Dante and Beatrice
as a conflict of love and honor. In the play, Dante is kept from
marrying his beloved Beatrice because of the political aspirations
of her father, Folco Portinari, and the plotting of Dante's enemy
and rival, Corso Donati. Beatrice escapes dishonor--marrying a
man she does not love--by joining a convent; and then she escapes
convent life in death. The play is written in pseudo-Elizabethan
blank verse that can best be sampled in Dante's final speech of the
play, a speech in honor of the dead Beatrice:

> Dante: 'Tis her guiltless spirit
> Has been recalled to its celestial home,
> From its sad banishment upon this earth.
> O Beatrice,--my life's eternal saint! [255]
> Thy love hath purified my soul on earth,
> And hallowed it with a celestial passion,
> Whose mystery hath lifted me above
> The reach of mortal sense, and crowned my life
> With the supernal halo of its greatness.
>
> (During the above the nuns have kneeled in rear
> of Dante and begin singing the "Miserere.")

Curtain.

The play belongs to the tradition of the nineteenth-century
heroic drama that Harlan Hatcher calls "romantic" and John Gass-
ner "neo-romantic"; and since, with the occasional exception of such
plays in this tradition as Rostand's Cyrano de Bergerac, our own
age has been content to neglect them, there would be little sense in
calling attention to this particular example, Dante, except for an
odd fact of American theatrical history. Dante, although the fact
has never been noted publicly before, is the play that the American
actor, Lawrence Barrett, commissioned, apparently in the hopes
that with such a starring vehicle he could finally achieve his life-

long ambition to surpass Edwin Booth and become "America's greatest tragedian. " Dante is, thus, a play that contains those elements
that the nineteenth-century tragedians thought were best for theater;
and as such it should probably be given a little more attention than
it has thus far received.

I

In 1890, when Williams first started on Dante, he was still a
relatively unknown playwright. He had written a number of full-
length dramas--Eugene Aram (1874), Merry Merrick (1873), Parrhasius (1879), Prince Carlos (1875), Queen Mary (1875), and Witchcraft (1886). He had also written at least one one-act play, Morbid
Versus Quick, and a great deal of occasional poetry. [3] Several of
these plays had been produced in New Orleans; the poetry had been
published in the New Orleans newspapers and such national publications as The Mercury and Godey's Ladies Magazine; some of the
plays had been printed privately at Williams' [256] own expense; and Eugene Aram had been run serially in The South Atlantic Magazine.
Except for such slight attention, however, Williams, in spite of almost twenty years of rather serious effort, had been unable to get
any sort of a professional hearing. Even in the late 1880's, Alcée
Fortier, in his Louisiana Studies, could afford only a couple of sen-
tences to Williams in his survey of the literature of the state. Williams' reputation by 1890 was scarcely such as should have engaged
the attention of so prominent an actor as Barrett.

In 1875, however, when Williams, then twenty-two, was trying
to interest someone in Eugene Aram, he had asked Barrett to read
that play. Barrett did and complimented Williams on the work and
suggested he do further work. During the fifteen years between
their first meeting and 1890, Barrett had been in and out of New
Orleans, and apparently a friendship had grown between the "almost
great" actor and the would-be playwright.

In 1890, another actor, Robert Mantell, found a copy of Williams' play, Parrhasius;[4] and he was so impressed with it that he
purchased the stage rights from Williams for $3,000. Williams,
at this time, was a successful financier, but this sale was the first
"important" money he had ever received for his writing. Apparent-

ly the sale impressed Barrett, perhaps because Mantell belonged to
the new school of actors who were challenging the authority of such
actors as Barrett and Booth. Barrett told Williams not to expect
too much from Parrhasius on the stage, for it was "too gruesome
for modern taste"; but the sale seems to have suggested to Barrett
that Williams might be the playwright who could write the starring
vehicle he needed. It was at this time, at any rate, that Barrett
commissioned Williams to write Dante for him.

II

Lawrence Barrett, more than anything else in life, wanted to
be America's greatest actor. As far as popularity and profit were
indications, moreover, he could have claimed that he was second [257]
only to Edwin Booth when he and Booth made their famous tours in
the last years of the 1880's. [5]

As early as 1857, when he was only nineteen years old, Barrett was on the professional stage as one of the minor characters
in Richard III. Edwin Booth made his professional debut in this
same production; Booth played Richard, a role given to him largely
because of the reputation of his famous father. Booth was aware
that the other actors resented his inherited favorable position; and,
seemingly, although he had the good sense not to show it, Barrett
was among the resentful. Barrett and Booth, however, were con-
genial with one another; and in 1870, when Booth was putting together an "all-star" company, he selected Barrett to join him. Barrett had by this time established himself as a good actor, but Booth
was not impressed with Barrett's talents. In fact, Booth complained that "all those half-baked stars such as Barrett . . . require
$300 a week." Yet he recognized that however short Barrett fell
of being the popular star of the age, he was a competent actor.
He concluded his complaint, "If we can make these damned idiots
[Barrett and Edwin Adams] pull together, I don't care what we pay
them."

Barrett did star with Booth's company. He was, for example,
Leontes in Booth's production of The Winter's Tale; and Booth
seems to have been satisfied with his acting. But Barrett was not
an actor who drew great crowds or who built a personal following;

nor was he an actor who could successfully parade as a member of the "royal family" of the American theater, a role that Booth obviously gloried in. Barrett, in fact, lived in an atmosphere of sneers and condescension. Booth was forever making a point of insuring that Barrett's feelings were not slighted by social oversights, and at the same time a body of stories was growing up about Barrett's social background. One such story had it that Barrett's mother took in washing to support her family. Another story circulated at that time was that Barrett's father was an Irish immigrant named Brannigan, who had come to America to escape starvation. Barrett had simply taken the English name to hide his ancestry. [258]

Whether it was Barrett's failure to draw crowds or his questioned ancestry, Booth finally decided that Barrett as a star was not good business, and he suggested that he be cast in supporting roles. Barrett refused and instead went to New Orleans where he could pick his own roles. Even though he starred in New Orleans, Barrett was well aware that New Orleans was not New York and that he would never achieve national prominence there. In 1872, therefore, when Booth decided to produce the historical play, <u>Marlborough</u>, Barrett wrote to him and asked for the leading role. From general remarks that Booth had earlier made, Barrett assumed that Booth had promised him such a part.

Booth wrote Barrett, however, that his name would not draw crowds. He commented, moreover, that Barrett did not have the right appearance to play the aristocratic English duke. He offered Barrett a lesser role. Barrett was angry. "I shall not accept the humble role you allocate to me," he wrote Booth. "If <u>you</u> really stand at the head of my profession then <u>you</u> are only my compeer . . . and when Time gives his judgment, I may not after all be so far behind your illustrious self . . . ."

Barrett's opinion that he and Booth were equal rivals for the title of "America's greatest actor" became a standing joke of the acting profession. Once when Booth was giving a performance, a man named Mark Grey shot at Booth because he thought the actor was sneering at him when he said, "Mark where she stands." It was Grey's idea that Booth sneered when he said Mark. Grey was caught and put in an asylum, and during the course of an interview with a newspaper reporter, he remarked, "Besides Booth is not so great an actor as Barrett." Joseph Jefferson, another famous actor of that age, wrote to Booth, "It is an interesting theme in the future of the stage that the only man who thought Barrett was better than Booth turned out to be a lunatic."

The quarrel between Booth and Barrett lasted for seven years. In 1880, Barrett wrote and asked Booth for a reconciliation, and Booth agreed. He was still of the belief that Barrett was arrogant, but he was leaving for a season in London and seems to have been willing to end the quarrel. He invited Barrett to a farewell breakfast his friends were having for him at Delmonico's, and later he reported that Barrett had insisted that he be seated "above the salt. "[259]

Booth's season in England had been planned to prove that he, and not Henry Irving, was the greatest Shakespearian actor. London audiences, however, refused to agree; and until Irving suggested that they appear together, Booth had a very cold reception. Booth was very sensitive to rebuffs, and he even complained that Queen Victoria was too much of a "snob" to come to see him. This cold English reception, however, seems to have made Booth more democratic, more in love with his homeland, and more fond of his friends. When he returned to America in 1885, he went to visit Barrett and his family, who were then living in Cohasset, Massachusetts. He was much impressed with the happiness of Barrett's home life, but he discovered that Barrett still had one desire above all others--to be the greatest actor in America. Booth wrote of him, "Barrett said intensely that he would be willing to act without making money for fifty years if by then he would be considered the head of his profession." During the same visit, Barrett suggested to Booth, who hated business, that they tour together as co-stars. Barrett offered to handle the business arrangements, and Booth was to have the top billing. Booth agreed.

III

The several seasons in which Booth and Barrett toured the country as co-stars have gone down in theater history as the most

successful in America. Business, other commitments, and illness
frequently turned the team into a single star; but when the two appeared, they consistently played to full houses and at double fares.
Eleanor Ruggles, Booth's biographer, points to the reason for their
success: "Booth and Barrett appealed to the conservative, well-to-
do elements in every community, which could safely bring its young
daughters and give the girls the satin programs for their memory
books. " The other actors complained, of course, that the Booth-
Barrett team was unfair competition.

The critics complained, too, but on different grounds. The
New York Press, for example, complained about the sameness of
the bill. "A clock-beating art is held out to us, " the reviewer reported. "Mr. Booth as Iago, Mr. Barrett as Othello. Mr. Booth
as Othello, Mr. Barrett as Iago. Tick, tick, tick. " The Kansas
City Star pointed out that although the pair were making money,
"they are for the present nearly worn out. " Nym Crinkle, the
critic, was [260] savage in his attacks. Once he reported, "Nowhere
but at a public funeral and a public performance of Shakespeare do
we parade the relics of departed youth. "

Booth was frequently ill and more frequently simply disinter-
ested, and it became obvious that he was ready to leave the stage
whenever he could do so gracefully. Nym Crinkle called attention
to the fact that although on occasion Booth could act, he seldom
wanted to do so. Barrett was ill, too, with a glandular trouble;
but since his illness resulted in disfiguring bumps on his face, it
was viewed as more of a threat to his stage appearance than to his
life.

Barrett, however, seems to have realized that although his
present arrangement with Booth was making money and giving him
popularity, he could not long count on Booth. Obviously, he was
planning the next step in his theatrical career--a step that called
for a new play, solely his property, that would give him an opportunity to display his acting skill.

IV

Barrett's disfiguring illness became so severe that he finally
was forced to leave the company and go to Germany for the waters.

While in Europe, however, he spent some of his time looking for a starring vehicle for himself. He went to England and saw Tennyson about starring in the poet's play, Becket. Tennyson had written the play for Irving in 1878, but the play had been judged unfit for the stage; and Irving seems to have had doubts about performing it. [6] In fact, according to a program note for a 1905 production of Becket, the play was "Adapted for the stage by Henry Irving." Barrett did not get Becket. Tennyson either had decided that he wanted no one other than his favorite actor, Irving, to do it, or Barrett had the same reservations about the play and had decided that it was not the play he needed.

Whatever the reason, Barrett did not return with Becket, but rather when he returned to the United States, he asked Espy Williams to write him a play about Dante. Williams wrote a draft of the play, probably the one titled Dante and Beatrice. Barrett then made suggestions, and after further rewriting, Barrett decided that the play, probably now titled Dante, was the drama that would [261] give him the opportunity to prove he was "the greatest actor of the age."

Dante and Beatrice is obviously constructed for an actor who wishes to display his varied talents. Each of the three acts opens with "lesser" characters explaining the action and preparing for the entrance of Dante. The exposition scene in Act I takes only one of the twelve pages; in Act II five of the twelve pages are given to exposition, but these five pages are largely given to Beatrice; and in Act III, the exposition scene takes only two pages. The rest of the play belongs to Dante. Each of the curtain lines closing the separate acts gives the scene entirely to Dante, who shares it only with the "body" of Beatrice. The third act and the play end with Beatrice's dead body serving as a prop for Dante's funeral oration. The first act ends with Dante "letting fall his sword, and opening wide his arms to Beatrice," who "falls into his arms," while he shouts, "Banished from Florence, but not from Paradise." The second act closes with "Beatrice fainted with Nina supporting her," while Dante shouts his exit line, "We all shall meet again!" Dante is obviously a play written for an actor who wants to know for whom the audience is applauding.

The last season, 1890-91, of the Booth-Barrett tour showed
that the two actors could not long continue as a team. Booth had
been out of the company from December until March; and, although
they were still successful, box office sales had fallen enough to
worry Booth. He knew that Barrett was enthusiastic about a new
play, and he seems to have been willing to ring the curtain down on
his acting career and leave the stage to Barrett.

The necessity of formally ending their contract never came,
however. In March, 1891, Booth and Barrett were ending their
season. On March 18, they were doing Richelieu with Booth in the
starring role and Barrett playing the youthful, romantic Du Mauprat.
Barrett was ill when they arrived at the theater, but he insisted on
performing. During the third act, when his business was just about
over, he whispered to Booth, "I can't go on." He made his exit,
and the last few lines of his part were taken by another actor. He
was in bed the next day, and when Booth went to visit him at the
Windsor, Barrett told him not to come near him. "My disease may
be infectious," he told Booth. "You must be very careful." On the
next day, March 20, Booth inquired of Theodore Bromley, the stage
manager, the state of Barrett's health. He was told that Barrett
"had gone." Barrett was dead. [262]

V

Espy Williams in New Orleans heard about Barrett's death and
put the manuscript of Dante and Beatrice away. Sometime later he
reworked the material, but obviously a play written for an actor in
the Booth-Irving-Barrett tradition needed a Booth, Irving, or Barrett. It is ironic, in fact, that a decade later, Henry Irving, the
only one of the trio still on the stage, thought that a play about
Dante would be his salvation. In the late 1890's, Irving was in difficult financial circumstances, and he hoped that another tour of the
United States would repair his fortunes. He feared, however, that
his repertory was too small. The rising playwrights in England,
like Shaw, were not writing plays that "met his requirements. He,
therefore, had to apply to Victorien Sardou . . . who readily fell
into Irving's suggestion for a drama with Dante as the central figure." Sardou's play picks up the legend of Dante's life at the point

at which Williams' play ends; and Beatrice appears only as "The
Spirit" in Sardou's play. Dante, moreover, is no longer the youthful lover.

Sardou's Dante was produced on April 30, 1903, at the Drury
Lane Theatre. It was judged a poor play, but Irving's powers as
"producer and player" were proved to have been "unimpaired at the
age of sixty-five." Irving, in spite of the poor returns on the play,
was convinced that Dante was a success, a "triumph," and he took
it to New York where it was a "dismal failure." Irving never returned to America.

Barrett's desires for a Dante role and Irving's satisfaction
with Sardou's play, even in the face of failure, are not unusual; nor
was Williams' failure to find another actor for his play, nor Irving's
failure with Sardou's play. Both Dante plays belong to the age of
Barrett, Booth, and Irving, the era of heroic romantics, an era
that died with Ibsen; and while the faithful followers of the old actors were still willing to applaud the ghosts of their old heroes,
they were unwilling to tolerate playwrights who wished to prolong
that age. It is, therefore, not surprising that Williams' Dante, a
tailor-written play for that age, now remains a museum piece, existing only in two copies. Williams wrote a nineteenth-century heroic drama just in time for it to be tossed into the casket in which
the genre itself was being buried. [263]

Notes

1. For detailed accounts of Williams' career see "A Shakespeare
   Idol in America," The Mississippi Quarterly, XII (Spring, 1959),
   67-74; "Bright American Minds, British Brains, and Southern
   Drama," Southern Speech Journal, XXIV (Spring, 1959), 129-134;
   and "A Southerner's Tribute to Illinois' Pagan Prophet," Journal
   of the Illinois Historical Society, LI (Autumn, 1958), 368-383.

2. Dante was advertised as available for production in Williams'
   The Husband (New Orleans, 1898). [255]

3. See "Espy Williams: New Orleans Playwright," Bulletin of the
   Louisiana Library Association, XXI (Winter, 1959), 137-139, for
   a bibliography of Williams' works. [256]

4. This play is now available in a micro-card edition. Espy Williams: Parrhasius: A Southerner Returns to the Classics, edit-

ed with an introduction (Lexington: University of Kentucky Press, 1958, Series A, Modern Language Series, No. 26). [257]

5. The account of the relationship between Booth and Barrett is more complete in Eleanor Ruggles, Prince of Players: Edwin Booth (New York: W. W. Norton & Company, Inc., 1953). The details in this article are taken from that study. [258]

6. The Life of Henry Irving, II (New York, 1908). All the details of Irving's interest in Becket and Dante are taken from this study. [261]

2. "Classical Tragedy in the Province Theater"
(Reprinted from American Quarterly, XIII
[Fall, 1961], 410-413.)

The two nineteenth-century productions of Sophocles' tragedies
(Antigone in 1845 and Oedipus in 1882) in New York could, as Miss
Alexander[1] has pointed out, "hardly be considered a success." The
criticism of the New York World--". . . the blind and bloody
Oedipus is exceedingly repulsive, view it as one may."--justifies
her conclusion, moreover, that "The tragic vision of Sophocles was
far too distant from the viewpoint of New York in 1882 . . . to be
received with enthusiasm by a wide public."

A second conclusion, that "Only a few literary sophisticates
[college boys and professors] were ready to do it honor," is perhaps in need of qualification.   Seemingly, if one may judge from
the reception given a pseudo-classical tragedy of ancient Greek life,
Parrhasius,[2] Sophocles would have fared far better if his Oedipus
had been presented in any of the province theaters of New Orleans,
Memphis, San Francisco or St. Louis than it did in its New York
production.   The failure of what was apparently a most interesting
production of Oedipus in 1882 contrasted with the successes of Parrhasius in the province theaters of the 1890's suggests that the theater-goers of interior America were much more ready for classical
drama than were the New Yorkers.

Parrhasius was written in 1878 by a young New Orleanian,
Espy Williams (1852-1908),[3] and produced by an amateur group in
New Orleans that year.   The city was at that time a favorite one
with American actors, and Williams had an acquaintance with many
of them.

Earlier, in 1874, he had written a tragedy, Eugene Aram,
based on the novel by Bulwer-Lytton; and Lawrence Barrett, the
actor, had looked at it for Williams[4] and commented that while the
play had "great literary quality," it lacked "construction" and would
not be successful on the [410] stage.   Williams complained to his diary
that this judgment showed a want of taste and was evidence of a
serious weakness in the American theater.   He and Barrett, however, became and remained friends throughout their lives.[5]

After the New Orleans production of Parrhasius, [6] Barrett told
Williams that although the play was interesting, it was "too gruesome" to succeed on a modern stage. Williams, nonetheless, had
the play published at his own expense, but offered it as a poem:
Parrhasius: or, Thriftless Ambition: A Dramatic Poem. [7] Williams'
treatment of the play as a "dramatic poem" suggests that he was
perhaps influenced by Milton's Samson Agonistes. However, although a few years earlier he had complained about the difficulty in
reading Aristotle, [8] it is obvious from a reading of Parrhasius that
his main influence was Greek tragedy. The play is, in fact, an
imitation of the drama of Sophocles.

The New York Mirror editors who complained of the Oedipus
production, "If Mr. Cazauran should write, and Manager Palmer
produce a piece with a plot like this . . ., it is probable Anthony
Comstock would close up the theater as a disorderly house . . .," [9]
would have been even more horrified with the plot of Parrhasius.
The protagonist, Parrhasius, is a painter with two overwhelming
passions, his art and his wife, Lydia. He is, as the play opens,
in the midst of an interesting art experiment. He wishes to paint
"pure agony." To achieve this purpose, he needs a model who ex-
presses "pure agony." He, therefore, buys a noble slave, tears
out his tongue, and has the man tortured so that he may paint his
features in the moment of agony. The tearing out of the tongue
serves a double purpose. On the one hand, it prevents the noble
slave from interrupting the work with his screams; and, on the
other hand, it heightens the agony. The conclusion is not altogether
happy. The slave dies, and then it develops that he is Damon,
Lydia's lost father. Lydia, when she discovers her husband's crime
and her father's end, reacts in a way that would have pleased the
editors of the Mirror. She dies of shocked horror. [411]

The play in all of its mechanical details, except for a chorus,
is an imitation of classical tragedy. The plot is borrowed from
Greek legend; there are only a few characters, a single action, a
single scene and a "noble hero" who falls through the sin of hybris.
Admittedly, a theater-goer might be deeply moved by any Greek
tragedy and yet be horrified and dismayed by Parrhasius. It is un-

likely, however, that anyone who approved of Parrhasius would object to Oedipus in any of the terms expressed in the reviews of the
1882 production in New York. The complaints about the "school
book" quality of Sophocles' verse and the lack of decorum in the
plot of Oedipus would hardly have been satisfied by the pedestrian
blank verse of Parrhasius. The torture of the "noble slave," Damon, moreover, takes place on stage in Williams' play. It is, in
fact, the central action of the play.

In the early 1890s, a copy of the 1879 edition of Parrhasius
found its way into the hands of Robert Mantell, the Shakespearian
actor. In 1892, G. P. Putnam's Sons published a collection of Williams' poetry, A Dream of Art and Other Poems. The Boston
Transcript gave the book a favorable review, and Mantell, who was
then playing Boston, saw the review and associated the name of the
poet with the author of Parrhasius. He wrote to the Transcript for
Williams' address and later wrote to Williams asking for the stage
rights to the play.[10] Mantell eventually bought the play for
$3,000[11] and produced it in the province theaters across the nation
as the principal offering in his repertoire.

The reviewers, seemingly, were impressed with the productions of Parrhasius in the province theaters. The reviewer for the
San Francisco Examiner called it, "A powerful piece of dramatic
writing; it is the work of genius." The San Francisco Chronicle
called it, "The strongest tragic scene in modern drama. One of the
most important contributions to our dramatic literature in years."
The Memphis Appeal reviewer declared, "The play is the best work
of native origin that has been seen here in a decade." The Kansas
City Journal reviewer reported, "The conception and treatment are
magnificent."[12] [412]

In a letter to Williams, accompanying the contract, Mantell indicated his belief in the seriousness of the play. He wrote, "I begin my season early--July 10 at Salt Lake City and work out to the
coast; then south through Texas. Will play in New Orleans about
Sept. 10. I hope to have the play in pretty good shape at that time.
I have been having some nice drops painted, about seven in number,
to take with me to give it a good chance for success. The cos-

tumes will also be very fine, and I am picking out my people more
for 'Parrhasius' than for any other of my plays.   I intend to intro-
duce a Grecian ballet of dancing girls and flute players into one of
the scenes as a feature of the performance. "[13]

So successful was Parrhasius in its single-act classical form,
in fact, that in 1893 Williams did three-act and four-act versions
of it, altering its classical structure to an Elizabethan form and
adding a happy ending. [14]

Whether audiences who were drawn to Parrhasius because of
its classical structure were indifferent to the Elizabethan versions
or whether Mantell simply tired of the play after a few seasons is
not known; but the play was removed from his repertoire after a
few years.   During its few years of "province glory," however,
Parrhasius demonstrated that a taste for classical tragedy existed
in the nineteenth century in America, perhaps exclusively in the
province theaters.   In this connection it is interesting to note that
when American drama and theater became respectful of the "classical heritage," it was the province-born men of letters like T.S.
Eliot, Tennessee Williams and Robinson Jeffers who made the best
use of it, not the New York-theater-trained playwrights. [413]

Notes

1.   Doris M. Alexander, "Oedipus in Victorian New York," Amer-
     ican Quarterly, XII (Fall, 1960), 417-21.

2.   Espy Williams' Parrhasius: A Southerner Returns to the Clas-
     ics (Lexington: University of Kentucky Press, 1958), Kentucky
     Microcards, Series A, No. 26.

3.   See "A Southerner's Tribute to Illinois' 'Pagan Prophet'," Jour-
     nal of the Illinois Historical Society, LI (Autumn, 1958), 268-
     73, for a short account of the playwright.

4.   The details of Williams' relationships with New Orleans actors
     during the 1870s are recorded in a diary he kept during 1874-
     75. [410]

5.   A poem dedicated to Barrett, "Lawrence Barrett," is in Wil-
     liams' A Dream of Art and Other Poems (New York, 1892).
     See, also, "Williams' Dante: The Death of Nineteenth-Century
     Heroic Drama," Southern Speech Journal, XXV (Summer, 1960),
     255-63.

6. Parrhasius was produced first in 1878, but as late as 1889, it was still being given amateur productions in New Orleans. According to programs of the play, the Women's Social Industrial Association gave one performance at Grunewald Opera House in New Orleans on March 1, 1889. For this performance, Parrhasius formed the second half of a two-part program. The first part was "Vocal and Instrumental Music." On April 4 of that year, a second performance was given. For this performance, a farce by Williams, Morbid Vs. Quick, formed the first half of the program.

7. (New Orleans: Southern Publishing Company, 1879), 26 pp.

8. Aristotle was "too airy," Williams recorded in his diary in 1874.

9. Alexander, "Oedipus in Victorian New York," p. 419. [411]

10. The letter to the Boston Transcript was forwarded to Williams and is now in the library of the University of Southwestern Louisiana. It reads: "My dear Sir, I have found myself so interested in the little tragedy, 'Parrhasius,' that I wish to know something of the author. Can you put me on the track? Even his address would be a help. I regret that in the rush of many duties I have been unable to say in print all that I felt concerning this fine work, but hope to find the opportunity soon." It is signed Robert Mantell and dated May 21, 1892.

11. New Orleans Daily Picayune, June 14, 1892.

12. These reviews, and others, were reprinted as part of an advertisement for Parrhasius in 1898. Espy Williams, The Husband (New Orleans, 1898). The play, at that time, was being offered for general professional and amateur production. [412]

13. The letter to Williams was printed in the New Orleans Daily Picayune, June 14, 1892, as a part of the story announcing the sale of the play.

14. The author's typed manuscripts of both the three-act and four-act versions are in the library of the University of Southwestern Louisiana. They are titled: Parrhasius: A Tragedy in Three Acts, "Founded Upon the Author's One Act Tragedy of the Same Name," dated 1893, 41 pp.; and Parrhasius: A Classic Tragedy in Four Acts, dated July 28, 1893, 75 pp. [413]

3.   "The Life and Death of a Louisiana Play:

Espy Williams' 'Unorna'"

(Reprinted from Louisiana History, V

[Spring, 1964], 143-160.)

It is a commonplace of literary criticism that little drama
produced in America before World War I is of much value, even as
social history.   In writing of the season of 1898-99, for example,
John Chapman and Garrison P. Sherwood not only make no claims
for the plays of that year as literature ("The final season before
the turn of the century was not . . . an important one in the history of the drama"), but they also comment that even in the history
of the theatre the season "was lively enough, " but not important. [1]
No better demonstration exists, in fact, of the low opinion that historians hold of the uses of America's drama for historical purposes
than the two centuries of neglect shown America's first English-
language play.   This play, Androboros, written in 1714 by, or at
least in cooperation with, the Governor of New York, Robert Hunter,
deals with a political-military-religious quarrel of that time; and it
has yet to be used in any critical analysis of that quarrel. [2]

The reasons for the poor reputation of American drama in the
eighteenth and nineteenth centuries are well known.   The [143] corrupting influences of the "star system, " the indifference of producer and
audience to literary values, and the generally low state of dramatic
literature throughout the Western world contributed to produce plays
devoid of meaning and artistic finish.   The stars wanted plays that
offered them opportunities to display their speaking ability; [3] the
audiences wanted entertainment through escape; the producers wanted
to get rich providing this escape; and the then-current European drama offered no good example to the American theater.   Thus the
governing idea of what theater should be militated against American
playwrights' creating a drama of much value either to the historian
or the aesthete.

The playwright, too, has been blamed.   On the one hand, writers of genuine merit, like Mark Twain, Henry James, W. D. Howells,
and G. W. Cable, who attempted to write for the stage and failed,
have been blamed for their inability to learn stagecraft.   And writ-

ers who by their popular successes demonstrated their knowledge of stagecraft have been blamed for lacking literary talent. Even a superficial examination of the theater conditions under which the playwrights had to work, however, demonstrates that until these conditions were changed, the modern drama of Chekhov, Shaw, and Ibsen could not be born.

When the Southern historian in search of new sources for an understanding of life in the South during the eighteenth and nineteenth centuries turns to drama (if he ever does), the results are dismal; and he is likely to conclude that the South itself was the wrong environment for producing a drama of any worth. [4] Even for the Southern historian with no concern for the drama, the assumption is there: something [144] in the nature of the Old South opposed the creation of a Southern dramatic literature.

An examination of the stage history of one Louisiana play which toured the South at the beginning of the twentieth century, however, suggests that even a "dedicated" playwright, one who was not only concerned with literary values and stagecraft, but willing also to make compromises with current production practices, found the American theatrical scene an impossible one.

The playwright was Espy Williams (1852-1908), [5] and the play was Unorna, [6] a romantic supernatural melodrama that made a Southern tour in the fall of 1902 and died for unusual reasons on Thanksgiving Day in Memphis, Tennessee, just at the peak of its popularity. Its "life and death" suggest that American theater practice was not merely indifferent to literary value and stagecraft, but that actors and producers alike looked upon the playwright as a natural enemy and upon the play as an obstacle that had to be overcome for them to be successful as actors and producers.

Espy Williams was born in New Orleans on January 30, 1852, of parents originally from Ohio and Pennsylvania. His father, trained for the law in Ohio, worked as an engineer and school teacher in Carrollton, then a separate township outside New Orleans. Obviously a man with considerable cultural [145] interests, he not only wrote a history of Carrollton, but seems also to have served as a guide and critic for his son while Espy was learning to

write drama and poetry. Although not Southern-born nor in sympathy with slave-holding, the Williams family were loyal to their a-
dopted home; and as a result of this loyalty, at the end of the war
and reconstruction, they found themselves in somewhat straitened
circumstances. Espy, named for his maternal grandfather, Professor Espy of the Franklin Institute, was forced by these circumstances to end his formal schooling in 1868, one semester short of
graduation from a New Orleans high school, to enter business. As
a New Orleans financier, he was successful; and at the time of his
death in the summer of 1908, he was chairman of the board of a
New Orleans home building and loan company.

Williams made his living as a banker; however, the theater
from first to last was his chief interest. In writing of his contri-
bution to letters after his death, the New Orleans Daily Picayune
(August 29, 1908) called him "The South's Leading Dramatist" and
summed up the rewards of his literary life: "Mr. Williams realized a fact made plain throughout the South that literary work, however successful, offers no large pecuniary rewards, and he did
much of his composition and study in the intervals of an active
business career."

At the age of sixteen, Williams wrote his first play, a verse
tragedy, The Burned Forest. When his father told him it was
"wretched verse," Espy destroyed the play and began studying again.
He copied all of Shakespeare's Hamlet and Home's Douglas for the
sole purpose of strengthening his facility with blank verse. During
1874 and 1875, Williams kept a diary;[7] and, although this was an
important period in the [146] establishment of his business career, the
diary records nothing but his literary interests and his desire to
write something of importance. During that period, for example,
Williams wrote a tragedy, Eugene Aram,[8] which he had printed at
his own expense to distribute to actors, writers, and directors.
Lawrence Barrett, the Shakespearian actor, read Aram and advised
Williams that although the play was "good literature," it needed
strengthening in "construction." Williams accepted the advice, but
he complained to his diary that this lack of concern with literary
values was a serious fault of the theater.[9] Author Eliza Ann Dupuy

also read the play and told Williams it was "excellent literature, "
but that he would have no financial success unless he were more
"sensational. " Although, as the play Unorna demonstrates, Williams
later became more "sensational, " at the time he complained that
except for her one novel, The Huguenot Exiles, the rest of Mrs.
Dupuy's works were artistic betrayals and that, while her suggestions were probably "sound commercial advice, " he hoped for something more than the kind of success she advocated.

During the 1890's, in such plays as A Cavalier of France, [10]
Dante, [11] and Unorna, Williams seemingly deserted his own critical
standards for popular success. At the end of his life, however, he
was still trying to write a play which would be worthy of literary
immortality. In the summer of 1908, while in constant pain and
aware that he was dying, he spent his last weeks composing a tragedy, Marlowe: The Buried Name, a "Shakespearian tragedy, " which
he hoped would win for him the "blue ribbon" in literature. [12] [147]

In 1900, however, Williams seems to have been more concerned with immediate popular success than with everlasting glory.
This was the year he started on Unorna, and already he had enjoyed
several commercial successes. One play, Parrhasius, [13] which he
wrote first, in 1879, on the single-act structure of Greek classical
tragedy, had proved so successful when Robert Mantell toured A-
merica with it in the mid-1890's that Williams turned the one-act
classical version into three-act and four-act melodramatic imitations
of Elizabethan drama. Although most of his successes were in the
province theaters of St. Louis, Memphis, Kansas City, San Francisco, and the smaller towns of the United States and Canada, one,
A Cavalier of France, had a New York production with Louis James
in the lead. Another, The Husband, had its debut in the Park Theater in Philadelphia. Several had London performances. In the
1890's, too, Williams explored the possibilities of American comic
opera and wrote the libretto for one, Ollamus, later retitled The
Royal Joke. An imitation of Gilbert and Sullivan with the then-current American scene as its background, this play had two runs in
New Orleans and later played in St. Louis. [14]

Although most of his drama was written in imitation of other

playwrights--Shakespeare, Schiller, Tennyson, Bulwer-Lytton, and
Sardou--Williams seems to have been motivated by only two desires: to write the best dramatic literature of which he was capa-
ble and to obtain a stage hearing for his plays. From 1874 when
he wrote Eugene Aram until 1893 (when Lawrence Barrett died before he could star in Dante, a play Williams had written especially
for him), he did his most original work.

Parrhasius, for example, anticipates by almost half a century
the modern revival of stage interest in classical themes and forms,
which have strongly influenced such playwrights as [148] O'Neill, Anou-
ilh, Giraudoux, Cocteau, Sartre, and Tennessee Williams. The Clair-
voyant, [15] set in New Orleans, is an early attempt at "local color"
in the drama, although the failure of his friend, George Washington
Cable, to write a successful play using "local color" should have
discouraged Williams if he had been seeking only commercial success. The Atheist, a one-act play which appeared in his volume of
verse, The Dream of Art and Other Poems, [16] is unusual for its
age in both plot and structure and is closer both to the medieval
play Everyman and Eliot's Murder in the Cathedral than to the
conventional melodrama of its own age.

With the commercial stage successes of such plays as A Cavalier of France, however, Williams evidently decided, after twenty
years of struggling for attention, that to get the stage hearing he
wanted, he had to write the kind of plays actors and producers
wanted. The decade of the late 1890's and early 1900's was a period for Williams of "stage pieces, " plays based on popular novels,
a period of melodramatic, escape literature.

As a reviewer for the Memphis Appeal (November 3, 1902)
pointed out, "To be popular as a dramatist now it is necessary [for
the playwright] to climb through the window of a publishing house. "
It was thus natural that Williams in his desire "to be popular"
should turn to the novels of F. Marion Crawford, the greatest "ro-
mancer" of the age. In two dozen novels, Crawford had not only
made himself one of America's most popular writers, but he was
also one of the five most popular American writers in Europe.

Williams' selection of Crawford's The Witch of Prague, however, is difficult to understand, especially in terms of what the playwright did with it for his play, Unorna. The play bears only a slight resemblance to the novel in plot and none at all in form, and in several striking particulars the play is [149] in basic disagreement with the novel as to its attitude toward experience. Crawford's novel is pseudo-mysterious; Williams' play is almost prosaically realistic. The two works, moreover, stand opposed on social attitudes. The Witch of Prague, for example, is openly anti-Semitic. Crawford attributes to the Jews all of the stock vices: greed, cruelty, and cowardice. Unorna, on the other hand, is pro-Jewish. Williams attributes to them all the stock virtues: generosity, compassion, and courage. In The Witch of Prague, the villain is Jewish, and with his Jewish followers, he is the great threat to the heroine and to the well-being of the city. In Unorna, the villain, Kafka, is a Christian; and the Jews of the city are the people who succeed in saving the heroine from the violence of a Christian mob.

Possibly the novel was suggested to Williams by Clarence Brune, [17] the producer, who hoped that the play would make a star of his wife, Minnie Tittle Brune. The Witch of Prague seems to have been selected because of the character of Unorna, the "Witch of Prague." Crawford, of course, was selected for the value of his literary reputation, and the Brunes did what they could to suggest that Crawford had used Mrs. Brune as his inspiration for the leading character. A reviewer for the San Antonio (Texas) Express (November 7, 1902), for example, reported to his readers, "It is said that Marion Crawford on seeing her [Mrs. Brune] play 'Fedora' [by Sardou] at once concluded that she was especially fitted for the role of Unorna. . . ." Other newspaper accounts reported that Crawford was deeply impressed by her talent and knew that "she was born" to play the part.

Although it is quite obvious that the Brunes were responsible for the stories associating Mrs. Brune with Crawford, they seem to have been successful in convincing the novelist that they knew nothing about the origin of such stories. In a letter to Williams, dated October 11, 1902, and sent to the playwright in New Orleans

from Crawford at "Villa Crawford, [150] Sant Agnello of Sorrento," the
novelist commented both on these stories and on the relative contributions of both writers to the play. Since many of the reviews
suggest that the play was essentially Crawford's work, the novelist's denial is worth quoting in its entirety:

> Dear Mr. Williams,
>
>   I was ill when I received your cable & am even now
> obliged to dictate my letters, though there is nothing seri-
> ous the matter with me except neuralgia.
>
>   I am delighted to hear that the production of "Unorna"
> at Norfolk was pronounced a success & I heartily congrat-
> ulate you upon this result with the sincere hope that it may
> be permanent. I have seen a curious note in the Dramatic
> Mirror to the effect that Mrs. Brune had spent most of the
> summer with me in order to complete the play. As I am
> sure this could not have come from any statement of hers,
> I shall not take the trouble to contradict it. I wish it had
> been in my power to be of more use as a collaborator, but
> I have been more overworked than ever this year, & after
> all I am very glad that you should get the sole credit for
> what is altogether yours.
>
>   I sail for New York in a few days & if you are there
> during the winter it would be a great pleasure to have a
> long talk with you. If the Brunes give the play anywhere
> in the East, pray tell them to let me know as I should like
> to see it.
>
>   With warm greetings,
>   Always yours faithfully,
>   F. Marion Crawford[18]

Obviously, Crawford's only association with the play, Unorna,
was in authoring the novel, The Witch of Prague, upon which the
play was based; and when one considers the looseness of the relationship between the novel and the play, one can quite agree with
Crawford that Williams "should get the sole credit for what is altogether" his.

    It is difficult to determine just what the Brunes did or did not do about many aspects of the production and the [151] publicity surrounding it. It was generally recognized by the press, and occasionally resented, that Mrs. Brune had employed an overly ambitious press agent. A reviewer for the Richmond (Virginia) Dispatch (September 24, 1902) liked Mrs. Brune's performance but advised ". . . it would be well for her ambitious press agent to let her stand upon the pedestal of her own merits, upon her own individuality. She is not Bernhardt."

Mrs. Brune was even more ambitious than her press agent, and this too was generally recognized by the press. Even a sympathetic reviewer for the Memphis News (November 28, 1902), in reporting her illness, began his sick-bed "sob story" with the description, "An ambitious young woman. . . ." Minnie Tittle was a performer in the nineteenth-century tradition of "the old trooper." Born in San Francisco, the third girl in a family of three actresses, she made her first appearance, according to the Galveston (Texas) News (November 9, 1902), at the age of four in The Lights of London. Thereafter, except for four years of formal schooling, she was constantly on the stage. At first she played comic roles in such plays as Editha's Burglar and A Trip to Chinatown, but after her marriage to Clarence Brune, she turned to tragedy.

Her first leading tragic role was with Frederick Warde as Lenora in The Lion's Mouth, a romantic melodrama, produced by Brune. Thereafter she played only "serious" roles, principally the heroic feminine leads in the plays of Shakespeare and Sardou. Although her press agent claimed that she was even then "The American Bernhardt" and that the role of the witch in Unorna was an advance for her only in that this was the first part written especially for her, she was in 1902 still a relatively unknown actress. Williams himself, in an interview with the New Orleans Item (June 21, 1902), defended the choice of Mrs. Brune for the leading role in these words: "While Mrs. Brune is not yet very well known just at present, she is destined to become so because she has a magnetic personality." Earlier in the same story, presumably on information given by Williams, the Item reporter gave the lie to the story that made Williams a mere stage mechanic: [152]

The play was submitted to Mr. and Mrs. Brune some time
ago for any suggestions that they could make on the play itself, or any of its characters.   They read it over carefully,
and aside from a few minor changes Mr. Williams' work was
left as he had written it.   It was stated that Mr. Williams
had dramatized Mr. Crawford's book with the famous author's
assistance, but this is not a fact.   He told Mr. Williams that
the ideas were Crawford's, but the work was that of Mr.
Williams.

Obviously the work of divorcing Williams from his play had already
progressed far enough to bring forth objections from the New Orleans playwright.

Presumably Mrs. Brune was very anxious to gain recognition
as a star even before her performance on the stage in Unorna, but
it was as the star of Unorna that she clearly intended to establish
her reputation.   According to the original plan, the play was to
open in New York in the fall of 1902.   The Brunes, after spending
the summer in Europe, decided, however, that a promotional tour
of the South would aid both the star and the play.   This tour was
planned, not merely as a series of try-outs to polish the play for
its New York opening, but as a campaign to arouse national interest,
principally in Mrs. Brune.   Throughout the tour the press agents
for the play sent releases to the local papers to encourage attendance, worked consistently to keep the New York papers informed of
the state of the tour, and planted stories about the star, such
stories as those that had brought objections from Williams and
Crawford.

The play itself is unusual enough to have attracted attention
from audiences that then reverenced the novels of H. Rider Haggard
and Crawford and were later to make The Green Goddess a long-
time box office success.   It deals with hypnotism, black magic,
cobra music, pagan dancers, and a climactic Christian miracle.
These elements were advertised for the play and generally were
well received.   The reviewer for the Birmingham (Alabama) Ledger
(October 17, 1902) was not unusual in her observation of these elements, except in her objections to them.   "It is, " she wrote of the
play, "almost [153] as creepy as H. Rider Haggard's work, notably 'She'
. . . .   It is horribly Indian, clothed as it is in an atmosphere

of weirdness, wild unnatural love, and religion. " The reviewer
concluded that, "It cannot truthfully be said that a play of the character of last night's was pleasant. It was entertaining and interesting, but the impression it left on those who saw it was horrible.
It seemed like a dream that several potations of absinthe might ex-
cite. "

The strenuous schedule set for the company in its Southern
tour was even more of a nightmare than the Birmingham reviewer
found the play to be. It opened on September 22, 1902, at the
Academy of Music in Norfolk, Virginia, and by the time it closed
in Jackson, Tennessee, the last of November, the play had been
performed in nine states--from Virginia through the Carolinas to
Florida, from Georgia through southern Tennessee to Alabama,
from Louisiana throughout Texas to Memphis--usually stopping at
all the larger towns and cities for one or two performances.

Judging from the reviews in the local press at each of these
stops, the response was favorable. Mrs. Brune received the most
attention. The reviewer for the Norfolk (Virginia) Landmark (September 23, 1902) claimed that she "justly won . . . the soubriquet
of the American Bernhardt. " The Richmond Virginia Pilot (September 23, 1902) commented, "Her work of last night would alone
stamp her as one of America's leading emotional actresses. . . ."
The Richmond News (September 24, 1902) seemed impressed by
everything about the play and its star. Of Mrs. Brune, the reviewer wrote, "Her best point is her figure. A oneness of control
enables her to evoke all shades of emotion by a mere pressure of
the cerebral switch-board. " The Charlotte (North Carolina) Daily
Observer (October 1, 1902) complimented the local management for
selecting a play which "showed discriminating taste and much wisdom. " The Charleston (South Carolina) Evening Post (October 2,
1902) called the play "the event of the season. " Even when the
crowds were thin, as they were at the November 4 performance in
Galveston, [154] Texas, the reviewers defended the play and decried the
lack of taste of the town. The reviewer for the Galveston (Texas)
Daily News (November 5, 1902) complained, "The very name of F.
Marion Crawford, the towering giant in American literature, should

be sufficient to fill a house wherever people are supposed to be
educated and know anything of literature, but there were only a few
who could answer present. "

An examination of the reviews, in fact, leads to only one
conclusion. Almost everyone liked the play because it was "new, "
"different, " "exciting, " and "weird"; and everyone was pleased with
Mrs. Brune's performance. If the Brunes had been merely looking
for a play that would "earn its way" in New York and on the road,
the Southern tour should have proved the worth of Unorna. The
New York Morning Telegraph (September 23, 1902), for example,
apparently assumed that New York theater-goers would agree with
the verdict of the Southern audiences; it reported that Unorna and
Mrs. Brune received nine curtain calls at the end of the first act
alone in the Norfolk opening. Other New York papers recorded the
progress of the play throughout its tour. Obviously, however, a
successful play was not the principal desire of the Brunes. The
play itself was simply to be the means to an end; the end was Mrs.
Brune's professional reputation. Unorna was intended to prove that
Mrs. Brune was "the American Bernhardt"; but, unlike Bernhardt,
Mrs. Brune seemingly did not intend to demonstrate her claim with
a Hamlet.

Many promotional devices were used to call attention to the
play, but, apparently, only as a means of bringing the audience to
see Mrs. Brune. Unorna opened in Norfolk at an evening performance; that afternoon a single performance was given by Clarence
Brune's company at the Royal Princess Theatre in London. Brune
did not follow that London premiere with a run of the play, but the
expense of preparing a cast for a single performance was "justified"
under the heading of promotion. A release which appeared in the
Virginia Pilot (September 22, 1902) showed Brune's reasoning: "Ow-
ing to the difference of time between London and Nor[155]folk both performances will occur at the same time. Afternoon there is night
here. " Quite obviously, in Brune's opinion, a play having simulta-
neous openings on two continents was an important play.

Once the importance of the play was established, however, the
intent seems to have been to center the attention of the audience on

Mrs. Brune. Williams' authorship of the play was given little attention. In spite of Crawford's very generous statement that Williams deserved sole credit for a work that was altogether his, the
programs and press releases suggested that the New Orleans playwright was little more than a stage mechanic, "an adaptor." A-
gain and again he is given credit for being "clever" while Mrs.
Brune and Crawford are called "geniuses." Crawford, of course,
already had achieved "fame"; hence he was viewed as no threat to
Mrs. Brune. Crawford, moreover, was in Italy at the time of the
tour, but Williams had joined the company in Norfolk and had remained with it until the play reached New Orleans. Crawford's
reputation also had value in giving prestige to Mrs. Brune by association, but Williams was still an unknown to the major theater
world.

The attempt to transfer Crawford's reputation to Mrs. Brune
seemingly was effective, if somewhat obvious. According to "planted stories," Crawford had written the play for Mrs. Brune; her
theatrical genius was thus the real source of the play. It was suggested, moreover, that Mrs. Brune was not merely playing a role;
she was the "wild, mysterious" Witch of Prague, Unorna. The reviewer for the Age-Herald of Birmingham, Alabama (October 17,
1902), for example, was told that the "oriental furnishings [used in
the setting of the play] are genuine and highly regarded by Mrs.
Brune," information presumably intended to convey the notion that
the furnishings were her personal property and hence evidence of
her mysterious background. This attempt to associate Mrs. Brune
and the character, Unorna, in the public mind had good precedent
in American theater history. Booth had established that he was
Hamlet, Joe Jefferson that he was Rip Van Winkle, James O'Neill
that he was the Count of Monte [156] Cristo. It has, in fact, frequently
been pointed out that an actor could achieve "great fame" in a play
recognized to be of little value. [19]

The future for the play seemed clear. Mrs. Brune and
Unorna had both attracted attention, and Mrs. Brune was Unorna.
When the company reached Memphis on Thanksgiving Day, Novem-
ber 27, 1902, however, Mrs. Brune fell ill with typhoid fever, and

it was announced fifteen minutes before curtain time that she would
be unable to go on.   An actress who had been playing a supporting
role, Mrs. Isabel Pengra Spencer, was selected to take Mrs.
Brune's place, although Mrs. Spencer had had only two rehearsals.
Throughout the tour, all the reviews had emphasized that the play
was a personal triumph for Mrs. Brune.   "Along the Atlantic sea-
board and in the South," the Memphis Appeal reported, "she has
won the best approval, and she looked forward to the approval of
this city, expecting here to make the test that was to launch her
into the larger cities of the East."

Obviously, without Mrs. Brune, there should have been no
"approval."   Her absence from the cast, however, had only a small
effect upon the response which Memphis theater-goers gave Unorna.
Only seven people asked for their money back for the afternoon performance, reported the Appeal.   And all seven were "visitors to
Memphis," according to the Memphis News.   The audiences for
both the afternoon and evening performances were described by the
Appeal as being "large and enthusiastic."   The Appeal reviewer
pointed out, moreover, that "The story [the play] is not literally
copied" from Crawford's novel.   Although he credited Crawford with
contributing more of the dialogue than the novelist actually had, his
calling attention to the play as the work of the playwright, and not
of the actress and novelist, indicates that in Memphis, at least, the
audience was concerned with the play as a play--not merely as a
vehicle for a star or as an adaptation of a novel. [157]

Mrs. Spencer's performance, in spite of her lack of prepara-
tion, was not a disappointment to the Memphis audiences.   After "a
nervous first act," the Appeal reviewer concluded, "The performance given was one of high artistic quality."   It was, in fact, "a
remarkable one.   As an evidence of approval she was given five
curtain calls. . . ."   The play in its Memphis performances seemed to have passed "the test" that would "launch" it "into the larger
cities of the East."   Unorna, even without Mrs. Brune, was "good
box office."

In a performance scheduled for Jackson, Tennessee, the next
day, Mrs. Spencer again played the role of Unorna.   Following the

Jackson performance, however, the play was not taken to New York as originally planned, but suddenly disappeared, never to be revived. After having proved itself under all sorts of conditions and after having created a mild national interest, Unorna was dropped by the Brunes, both the star and the producer. Presumably, if Unorna could succeed without Mrs. Brune, it was not the star-making material that the Brunes sought. Not only did Unorna fail to have its New York opening, but Clarence Brune, who owned the copyright and who had invested fairly heavily in the production, did not even apply for copyright protection. [20]

There is no record of Williams' feelings concerning either the play or the Southern tour after Memphis. His "log" of the journey of Unorna ends abruptly with the account of the Memphis performances. Although Williams had had previous associations with Clarence Brune in the production of his plays, [21] after Unorna he wrote no more plays at Brune's suggestion. He did, however, write one more play based on a novel by F. Marion Crawford, Madame de Maintenon, "A Comedy of Manners in Four Acts, Originally by F. Marion Crawford, and Amended, Reconstructed, and Modified by Espy Williams. "[22] Although he was still interested in drama [158] suggested by novels, "the life and death" of Unorna apparently discouraged Williams from ever again working intimately with the producer and the "star. " [159]

Notes

1. John Chapman and Garrison P. Sherwood, The Best Plays of 1894-1899 (New York, 1955), 65.

2. A study by Richard Bienvenu, University of Colorado, urging that greater attention be paid to Androboros because of its historical worth, has been accepted for publication by the New York State Historical Society. [143]

3. See Paul T. Nolan, "Williams' Dante: The Death of Nineteenth-Century Heroic Drama, " Southern Speech Journal, XXV (Summer, 1960), 255-63, for an account of the effect of the "star system" on one of Williams' plays.

4. It is worth noting that no existing anthology of Southern literature yet includes a play, although in the past few decades such Southern playwrights as Tennessee Williams, Carson McCullers,

and Lillian Hellman have produced plays judged to be of genuine merit. [144]

5. For accounts of Williams' life and works see the following ar-
    ticles by Paul T. Nolan: "Espy Williams: New Orleans Play-
    wright," Bulletin of the Louisiana Library Association, XXI
    (Winter, 1958), 137-39; "A Southerner's Tribute to Illinois'
    'Pagan Prophet'," Journal of the Illinois Historical Society, LI
    (Autumn, 1958), 268-83; "Bright American Minds, British
    Brains, and Southern Drama," Southern Speech Journal, XXIV
    (Spring, 1959), 129-34; "A Shakespeare Idol in America," Mis-
    sissippi Quarterly, XII (Spring, 1959), 64-74; and "The Case
    for Louisiana Drama," Southwestern Louisiana Journal, IV (Jan-
    uary, 1960), 35-43.

6. Although this play was never published, a typed copy exists in
    the Williams Collection of the library of the University of South-
    western Louisiana in Lafayette. It is titled, "Unorna: A Dra-
    matic Creation by F. Marion Crawford, Prepared for the Stage
    by Espy Williams." It is dated, "Opening Date Sept. 22, 1902,"
    and bears the subtitle, "The Witch of Prague." Williams kept
    a "log" of the Southern tour of the play--press notices, manu-
    scripts with production notes, and letters; these items are also
    in the Williams Collection. [145]

7. In addition to the few standard sources of biographical informa-
    tion concerning Williams' life--Who's Who in America, Alcée
    Fortier's Louisiana Studies (New Orleans, 1894), and newspaper
    clippings--the author is also in the debt of Mrs. Phillips Ende-
    cott Osgood, the playwright's daughter, both for specific person-
    al material concerning her father's life and career and for per-
    mission to use letters, a diary, and other private papers be-
    longing to her late father. Williams kept a personal-literary
    diary during 1874-75; the original is in the Williams Collection
    in the University of Southwestern Louisiana library. See Paul
    T. Nolan (ed.), "Journal of a Young Southern Playwright: Espy
    Williams of New Orleans, 1874-75," Louisiana Studies, I (Fall,
    1962), 30-50; (Winter, 1962), 33-54. [146]

8. Eugene Aram (New Orleans, 1874), "Printed, but not published,"
    Amos S. Collins, Printer.

9. For a detailed account of Williams' relations with Barrett see
    Nolan, "Williams' Dante: The Death of Nineteenth-Century
    Heroic Drama."

10. This play, with a critical introduction, is included in Paul T.
    Nolan, The Selected Works of Espy Williams: Southern Play-
    wright (Lexington, University of Kentucky Press, 1960, Ken-
    tucky Microcards, Series A, No. 45).

11. See Nolan, "Williams' Dante: The Death of Nineteenth-Century
    Heroic Drama."

12. For an edition of the play with an explanatory introduction see
    Paul T. Nolan, Marlowe: The Buried Name, A Romantic Mel-
    odrama by Espy Williams (Lexington, University of Kentucky
    Press, 1960, Kentucky Microcards, Series A, No. 31). [147]

13. For an edition of the play with an explanatory introduction see
    Paul T. Nolan, Espy Williams: Parrhasius: A Southerner Re-
    turns to the Classics (Lexington, University of Kentucky Press,
    1958, Kentucky Microcards, Series A, No. 26).

14. An edition of Ollamus with an introduction is included in Nolan,
    Selected Works of Espy Williams. [148]

15. This play is in Nolan, Selected Works of Espy Williams.

16. See Nolan, "A Southerner's Tribute to Illinois' 'Pagan Proph-
    et'," 268-74, for an account of Williams' use of the morality
    drama in The Atheist. The Dream of Art and Other Poems
    was published by Putnam (New York) in 1892. [149]

17. For an account of Williams' association with Clarence Brune as
    a producer see Nolan, "Bright American Minds, British Brains,
    and Southern Drama." [150]

18. This letter is in the Williams Collection of the University of
    Southwestern Louisiana library. The underscores are added
    for emphasis. [151]

19. See Nolan, "Williams' Dante: The Death of Nineteenth-Century
    Heroic Drama," for an instance of "role-making" in Williams'
    earlier association with an actor. [157]

20. At least, Dramatic Compositions Copyrighted in the United
    States from 1870 to 1916 (Washington, D.C., 1918) makes no
    mention of the play.

21. See Nolan, "Bright American Minds, British Brains, and South-
    ern Drama."

22. Williams' typed script of this play, the only known extant copy,
    is in the Williams Collection of the University of Southwestern
    Louisiana library. It is a [158] typed manuscript with inked addi-
    tions and is dated "March 17, 1903." Apparently, the play was
    never produced. Although Williams lived until 1908, the only
    other full-length play he seems to have worked on after 1903
    was Marlowe: The Buried Name, a handwritten copy of which
    is in the University of Southwestern Louisiana collection. This
    last play was never completed. [159]

The Feature Approach
The Popular Article

Generally speaking, popular articles--those appearing in Sunday supplements and general magazines--are seldom considered as part of the academic publishing world. Such articles, however, have two uses. For one, they are an outlet for well-researched articles; and, secondly, they are the means of research. One certain way to uncover new materials about a regional writer is to write a popular article about him for a magazine in his region. As the result of various popular articles I have written, I have received unpublished manuscripts, letters, journals, clippings, photographs, programs, and personal recollections of the various playwrights on whom I have been working.

For this chapter, I have selected four popular articles. The first, which is slightly more academic in tone for it was intended for an education journal, concerns New Mexican playwrights. The other three, which appeared in the state capitol Sunday supplement magazine of Louisiana, concern Louisiana plays. These articles differ from the traditional documented research essay in only two obvious ways. First, all documentation must be internal, and it is only generally indicated. And, secondly, the tone is breezy, informal, chatty.

1. "From Shakespeare to Nagel"
(Reprinted from New Mexico School Review,
XLII [March, 1963], 14-15.)

A history professor once told me that there were only two histories he liked to teach: the history of his own neighborhood and the history of the world. "Everything else is too much or too little."

Teachers of literature--especially of dramatic literature--often

158

feel the same way, and perhaps in no other aspect of our public
school teaching does the distance between too much and too little
seem so far as in our educating our students in the drama.

In our English classes, the bias is all in favor of too much.
Shakespeare's plays occupy a position in our schools second only
to the Pledge of Allegiance. No student, it is assumed, and with
justice, can be considered educated in any sense of the word unless he has been exposed to at least two or three of Shakespeare's
plays, usually Julius Caesar, Macbeth, and As You Like It. Various English teachers would, if they could, add other Shakespeare
plays to the list and include the works of other too much playwrights: Sophocles, Moliere, Congreve, Ibsen, and, perhaps, Eugene O'Neill.

In our drama-on-stage programs, however, it is the feeling
among the school directors that Shakespeare and Company are far
too much for the high school student. It is true, of course, that
occasionally an exceptional director like George B. Nason of Sandia
High School in Albuquerque will produce Shakespeare successfully.
But even with such a director, the result is viewed more as an experiment than as a usual part of the education-in-drama program.
Mr. Nason, in writing about his production of Julius Caesar in the
October, 1962, issue of Dramatics, described the work as an over-
coming of "the problems of producing Shakespeare in high school."

Mr. Nason, moreover, is not a usual high school director.
A list of the favorite plays for 1961-62, as selected by high school
directors, shows that they feel the "best" plays for the high school
theater are those that are near in time and place, modern American plays. The favorites with directors last year, for example,
were in this order: Our Town (80), Ask Any Girl (74), You Can't
Take It With You (67), Curious Savage (65), Arsenic and Old Lace
(60), Diary of Anne Frank (54), Night of January 16th (48), Our
Hearts Were Young and Gay (37), The Man Who Came to Dinner
(35), and Oklahoma! (33).

Among these favorites, Moliere's The Doctor in Spite of Himself ranks fortieth, Sophocles' Antigone ranks forty-sixth, and
Shakespeare's A Midsummer Night's Dream ranks fifty-fifth, right

behind Gramercy Ghost. These three are the only ones of the Eng-
lish-classroom playwrights in the first sixty. Obviously the too
much playwrights, in spite of their monopoly in the classroom, are
not doing too well on the school stage.

There are, of course, good reasons for Shakespeare's ranking
first in the classroom and fifty-fifth on the stage, while a play like
Time Out for Ginger will never be mentioned in class but ranked
eleventh in performance. On the one hand, students must be
taught to understand that great drama contains truths that require
concentration. On the other hand, students must know, without
argument, that drama is here and now as well as there and yester-
day, and that it offers immediate pleasure as well as lasting profit.
Mr. Nason shows rare insight when he announces that he plans to
make Shakespeare a regular part of the theater program at Sandia
High School and a great deal of common sense when he blends into
the best the nearest. His production of Julius Caesar, for example,
included a "sacrificial dance" choreographed by a senior student
there at Sandia.

This paper is not intended to be simply an argument that the
drama activities, in classroom and on stage, must be a combination of the best in world theater and the most popular in American
theater. It should be both of these, but also should be something
more.

Our Town is, for the purposes of pleasing the student, probably a better play for the high school theater than Hamlet or Oedipus. It is closer in time and in place because Wilder is closer in
time and in place than are a sixteenth-century English playwright
and a pre-Christian Greek. Our Town as a play, of course, is
also closer in language and in problems to the high school student.
Yet, even without these qualities, the simple knowledge that Wilder
lives in our time and clime is a conditioning for the student to expect a personal understanding, the kind of understanding that he is
surprised to find in Shakespeare and Sophocles.

There is, however, another writer of drama who is even
closer to the New Mexican student than the American playwright.
He is the New Mexican playwright. When one thinks of a state

playwright, he usually thinks of the man who writes the historical
pageant. But every state has others--men and women who are
playwrights and residents of the state. Some of these playwrights
write about their immediate environment as Shakespeare did about
his England in Henry IV. Some write about times and places beyond the state's history and border; [14] but, as with Shakespeare's
Hamlet, something of the immediate environment and time forms
their dramas. A New Mexican playwright who makes Ancient
Greece his setting gives his audience a New Mexican's Ancient
Greece.

The educational advantages of making people familiar with
their immediate culture have long been recognized. "What Shakespeare did three centuries ago is beyond us in time and in understanding; but what the playwright in Las Vegas or Albuquerque or
San Marcial did fifty years ago or last week we can do, too, and
we surely understand, for he saw life from our hill." Thus runs
the argument. This attitude toward drama, toward any art, is a
necessity if an environment is to produce citizens who are either
to practice or understand the arts.

New Mexico, it is true, had relatively few playwrights before
World War I. Only five New Mexicans, for example, copyrighted
plays from the state between 1870 and 1916. Only two of these--
Captain Jack Crawford, the "Poet Scout," and Davis Risdon of Gal-
lup--wrote plays that are still extant.

But New Mexico since World War I has become one of the
favorite locations, not only for artists, but for writers of all de-
scriptions, including playwrights. Such plays as Maxwell Anderson's
Night Over Taos (1932), Margaret Larkin's El Cristo (1926), and
Thomas Wood Stevens' Coronado Entrada (1928) are, without question, part of the drama of New Mexico.

But there are others, too--playwrights who sit in New Mexican towns, looking at New Mexican scenes, seeing with New Mexican eyes--who are sometimes only vaguely aware that the plays
they are producing always owe, at least in part, something to the
location in which they were written. They consider that they write
for the stage, and they consider their location a mere accident of

place as far as their plays are concerned. From the playwright's
point of view such an attitude is probably all to the good; plays
written from a consciously Greek point of view or English point of
view or New Mexican point of view are likely to be little more than
self-conscious bids to tourists.

From the point of view of the people of any locality, however,
it is lamentable that the playwright's native ties are unknown.
Shakespeare writes a better play for the English than for the French,
and a New Mexico resident writes a better play for New Mexico
than he does for Florida. It should follow thus that plays written
by New Mexicans which have proved successful elsewhere will have
something extra when produced at home, be more successful.

It is true, at the present time, that it is difficult for the New
Mexican stage director to find the New Mexicans who write for the
national theater--the Broadway stage, the national play-publishing
houses. New Mexico playwrights do exist, however; they are worth
hunting out, and they are worth discovering at home.

Lyda Nagel is one such playwright, the only New Mexican
resident to publish plays with Baker's Company since the end of
World War II. (Other publishing companies, I am sure, can pro-
vide their lists of New Mexican playwrights, but I selected Baker's
Company largely because it is a popular one with high school directors.)

While Miss Nagel was a resident of Albuquerque, she had
eight one-act plays published by Baker's Company: Women Who
Wait (1941), Strictly Feminine: Five One-Act Plays for Women
(1949), A Touch of Lilac (1950), and A Debt to Pay (1951). All of
these plays, written for all-women casts, have already demonstrated
their stage-worthiness. Women Who Wait, for example, won first
place when it was presented at the annual one-act play contest of
the Los Angeles District of the California Federation of Women's
Clubs.

When one considers the talent and training necessary to create
worthy plays, moreover, one is aware of the need for each state to
take special care of its own. Miss Nagel, now Mrs. A. Ray Tidwell of Ventura, California, has been working with theater since she

was a child. She wrote her first full-length play at the age of
thirteen. In her academic training at Mt. Vernon Seminary in
Washington, D. C., and at the University of Southern California,
she majored in languages, drama, and writing. She holds both the
B.A. and M.A. from the University of Southern California and has
done additional graduate work at the University of Arizona, a school
she selected because of her "deep love for the desert of the Southwest."

During the 1940's she taught in Quito, Ecuador, and traveled
about South America. In Bolivia, she met her husband, A. Ray
Tidwell, a native of New Mexico, and after her marriage in 1946,
she lived in New Mexico until moving to California in 1960.

In addition to her published plays, Miss Nagel has also written some as yet unpublished dramas for the Summerhouse Theatre
in Albuquerque, Los Angeles City College, and Whittier College.
Among these unpublished plays is "a play of modern New Mexico,"
Leave Only Pride.

None of Miss Nagel's available one-act plays is consciously
set in New Mexico, but most of them carry an almost visible mark
that will say to high school students, "This author has seen my immediate world."

This article does not suggest that any high school should build
its entire drama program, even its entire theater program, on the
plays of state residents. It does suggest, however, that for the
best learning experience, the in-state playwright needs to be a part
of that program. Shakespeare, Sophocles, Thornton Wilder, and
Lyda Nagel are pretty good bases from which the New Mexico teacher in the classroom and the teacher on the stage can say, "This is
what drama is. Think about it and feel comfortable with it. It is
yours." [15]

2.   "Playwright Judge Howe Poked Fun at Antebellum Eden"
     (Reprinted from Sunday Advocate [Baton Rouge, La.]
                 Magazine, March 12, 1961, 3E.)

The intention of the nation to spend the next four years com-
memorating the hundredth anniversary of the Civil War has already
been criticized.   Dave Garroway, the star of the television Today
show, for example, recently editorialized that reliving the events
of the bloodiest war in our history, day-by-day, is likely to have
as its main result the opening of old wounds and the refiring of old
hatreds.

"Let the dead stay buried," he argues.

Strangely enough, Mr. Garroway would receive some support--
even in the strangest places.   But probably the strangest of his al-
lies, if he were still alive, would be William Wirt Howe, Louisiana
Supreme Court judge, Civil War veteran, and historian.

At first glance W. W. Howe would seem to be in the first
ranks of those who proclaim that in antebellum America, "Men were
men, women were ladies, and the whole country was a blooming
Eden."

Howe was a major at the end of the Civil War, after having
spent four years in combat service.   During forty-two years in public life in Louisiana, from 1865 to 1907, he held a number of Louisiana's highest official and social offices.

He was judge of the Criminal Court of New Orleans from 1865
to 1868.   In 1868, he was appointed justice to the state Supreme
Court and served there until 1872.   From 1900 until 1917, he was
United States District Attorney for the eastern division of Louisiana.

Howe was also a national authority on civil law, the author of
"Studies in Civil Law," published in 1896.   He lectured before the
law students of St. Louis, the University of Pennsylvania, and Yale
University.

Among his many social service honors, he could list the
presidency of the Louisiana Historical Society, the presidency of
the New Orleans Art Association, and the presidency of the New
Orleans civil service board.

He was the author of many historical articles, including a

study published in 1889, "Municipal Government of New Orleans, "
a work "written to promote better city government. "

He was, also, a member and treasurer of the University of
Louisiana (now Tulane University) board of administration and a
member of both the New Orleans Chamber of Commerce and the
Board of Trade.

He was elected president of the American Bar Association in
1898, and he was a vestryman of Christ Church Cathedral in New
Orleans.

Finally, during the Civil War he was the adjutant general on
the staff of Gen. Lee.

A man with such qualifications would seem almost to have
been born to lament the passing of the old ways and days.

But Howe was born in Canandaigua, N. Y., the son of the
principal of the Canandaigua Academy. He was, also, educated in
western New York, at Hamilton College, from which he graduated
Phi Beta Kappa and valedictorian of his class in 1853.

He moved southward for his legal studies, to St. Louis. But
once they were completed, he returned to New York City to practice law.

Although he was in New York when the war broke out, he enlisted in the 7th Kansas Cavalry as a lieutenant, and the Gen. Lee
under whom he served was Gen. A. L. Lee, not the Southern hero,
Robert E.

At the end of the war he went to New Orleans, where he held
a military appointment as judge of the criminal court, and his appointment to the Louisiana Supreme Court was made by the federal-
ly-appointed governor, H. C. Warmouth.

Although Judge Howe owed his jurist appointments to the fed-
eral government and to two Republican presidents, McKinley and T.
Roosevelt, he was not a "carpetbagger." The fact that he was
elected president of the Louisiana Historical Society to succeed
the venerable Charles Gayarre is, of course, ample proof of that.

He was, all of his contemporaries agreed, a man with a great
deal of tact, a man who sympathized with the "Southern condition. "
In 1882, when a new edition of Martin's "The History of Louisiana, "

was published, Howe was invited to submit a "Memoir of the Author," a task he performed with good humor, respect, and grace.

Judge Howe was not a man to openly challenge the views of his native-born neighbors and friends. Yet he had a respect for the law as an instrument not only of justice, but of Christian charity.

The questions that should be asked of a lawyer after his death are these, he wrote: ". . . what was his influence in developing in fair and fruitful forms the jurisprudence of his country; what old abuse did he destroy, what new and needed reform did he construct; did he, like Tribonian, convert the laws of an empire which had been a wilderness into a garden; did he, like Domat, trace the civil law in its natural order as it flows from those two great commands of love to God and love to man . . . ?"

Seemingly he saw in the idealizing of the past, the antebellum days, a danger to the future. Being a Unionist in the South, he apparently knew the futility (and bad manners) of openly challenging his associates. But being Judge Howe, he had to give his warning in his own way.

The way he apparently used was through a play, "The Late Lamented," which Alcée Fortier, the father of Louisiana literary history, pronounced "a very good comedy."

In plot outline, "The Late Lamented" seems innocent enough of preaching intent. Mrs. Billington, the lovely young heroine, has built a mausoleum in her garden, in memory of her late husband, Major Bagatelle, "the late lamented." And she proclaims to her present husband, the Colonel, that her late husband was "a hero who had but one fault and that was that he was mortal."

Mrs. Billington's idealization of her "late lamented" is imitated by her maid, Mary. The maid is being pursued by the colonel's gardner, John Poole, but Mary tells him frankly, "Do you expect me to wear pink flowers for you? Oh, he was a man." The man is her former lover, James Barber, the late Major Bagatelle's orderly and, like the major, supposed to have been killed in the Battle of Pea Ridge.

Unfortunately for the ladies, James Barber returns and announces that Major Bagatelle is still alive, the captive of the Indians.

Faced with the return of their two old lovers, Mrs. Billington and Mary now remember their faults. James Barber is a drunken lout, and Mrs. Billington now admits a few faults in "the late lamented" other than his mortality.

She admits to the Colonel: "I married Major Bagatelle. He was very handsome. I thought his soul must be as beautiful as his face. I opened my heart to him as frankly as a flower opens to the sun. I gave myself to him without reserve, staking my whole life on that single card. I lost. I was deceived. He was faithless and shallow. That he squandered my fortune was nothing, but that he scorned my love, so lavished on him, was terrible."

She even asks Col. Billington--now not really her legal husband--to run away to Mexico with her.

The play ends happily, of course. James Barber is a liar and the Major is really dead. He died when "a stray shell exploded near him, and a fragment struck him in the small of his back. The wound was not at first thought dangerous, but the genial habits of the Major were adverse to the progress of cure." The Major was, as his wife finally admits, a man much interested in the bottle.

The easy moral of the play is simple: happiness comes only when one lives in the present.

The comedy apparently was intended as an allegory for the nation, a reminder that the past always looks better than it was.

Howe did not, of course, burlesque the South. He set his play in a "villa on the Hudson River" and no mention is made as to whether the Major was a Union or Confederate soldier.

Some things which Howe obviously considered "the real Southern values" were praised. Attention is called, for example, to the "crape myrtle . . . that the Colonel brought . . . from Natchez" and to "the fine chestnut mare . . . daughter of Lexington."

But the myth-making of both North and South that those who lived in antebellum America were all heroes is sharply rapped.

Howe evidently intended the play to "laugh the myth-makers" into good sense. He not only wrote the play for this purpose--the

only dramatic work he ever wrote--but he also had the play copyrighted and published, at his own expense, in 1878.

There is no record of the play's ever having been produced,
and although in the printed version it seems to have pleased Howe's
associates, it was hardly a best seller. So few copies exist, in
fact, that one may find one today only in the rare-book rooms of
college and university libraries.

The failure of the play to gain for itself a place in the history of American drama and satire is probably due to its subtlety.

When one is poking fun at something as large and fundamental
as a people's myth-making, he perhaps needs to outrage his readers
with another "Modest Proposal, " not amuse them with so indirect a
bit of subtle criticism as Howe's "The Late Lamented. "

3. "Louisiana Playwright Struggled with Shakespeare,
Marlowe and Fame"
(Reprinted from Sunday Advocate [Baton Rouge, La.]
Magazine, January 7, 1962, 3E.)

The Louisiana summer of 1908 was hot and long. In north
Louisiana, farmers looked over the red hills and hoped for rain.
In Baton Rouge, it was almost too hot to argue about the coming
fall election between William H. Taft, Republican, and William
Jennings Bryan, Democrat. It was a hot world, but a peaceful one.
The first world war was still a half dozen years off, and the big
news was that Judge Landis had fined Standard Oil twenty-nine mil-
lion dollars.

Down in New Orleans, Louisiana's most successful playwright,
Espy Williams, was dying. As he lay confined in his bedroom, with
blinds drawn and the ceiling fan slowly whirling, there was no question in his mind that this was his last hot summer.   On August 27,
he would die.

After his death the state papers would lament his passing
under captions reading, "The South's Leading Dramatist." And although a young Shreveport playwright, Lee Arthur, was then making
a big hit on Broadway, there was little question that Espy Williams
was still the most successful playwright in the state.

He had written over thirty plays. Some--like "A Cavalier of
France," "The Husband," "Parrhasius"--had been successful on the
big city stages. "A Cavalier of France," for example, had run
for two weeks in New York with Louis James in the lead.   "The
Husband" had debuted in the Park Theatre in Philadelphia with Robert Mantell in the lead.

His plays, in fact, were being produced in Canada, the United
States, and England; and some of the best-known actors in the A-
merican theater were asking him to write for them.

Lawrence Barrett, an actor second only to Booth in popularity,
had asked Williams to write a play for him. Williams wrote the
play, "Dante," and Barrett was getting it ready for a nationwide
tour when the actor died.

Robert Mantell, who bought his first commercial success,

"Parrhasius," liked that play so well that after touring with it in a one-act version, he commissioned Williams to make three-act and four-act versions, too.

Minnie Tittle Brune, a rising young "American Bernhardt" at the turn of the century, wanted Williams' plays. Her husband, Clarence Brune, was an actor-producer; and he bought at least one of Williams' plays, "Unorna," for her; and then he bought a second, "The Emperor's Double," for himself. The first play he scheduled for a New York run after a Southern tour, and the second he planned to use for a season in London.

By 1900, Williams had at least twenty-five plays in production: tragedies, comedies, farces, and even a musical, "Ollamus."

The last several years of Williams' life--the years after 1900--were filled with professional disappointments for the playwright.

Minnie Tittle Brune touring with "Unorna," for example, was successful in every town from Virginia through Texas to Memphis. When she arrived in Memphis, however, she fell ill of the fever. Memphis was to be the last try-out for Williams' play. Next stop was to be Broadway. But with the star's illness, her producer-husband dropped the play. And it was on Thanksgiving Day, 1902, that the play closed.

About the same time Williams dramatized a novel by a New Orleans friend, Mrs. E.M. Davis. He gave the play the same title as the novel, "The Wire Cutters." But after the play was finished and ready to go into rehearsal, a pirated version, "Hearts of Gold," opened in New York and was even brought to the Dauphine Theater in New Orleans for a run. Mrs. Davis sued for copyright infringement, and the authors of "Hearts of Gold" made a few superficial changes. But its success ended any hopes for a production of Williams' play.

The play Williams wrote for Brune, "The Emperor's Double," was all set for a London audience. But then Brune decided that no English audience would see a play in which Napoleon was the hero. Williams suggested that Washington, Philip Sheridan, or Oliver Cromwell be used in Napoleon's place. Brune decided the British of 1900 were just as opposed to the Revolutionary hero as their grandparents back in 1776 had been and that they wouldn't know who Cromwell or Sheridan was.

In spite of such disappointments, Williams, however, kept working. It was during these last years that Williams wrote "Madame de Maintenon" (1903), "Don Carlos" (1905), "John Wentworth's Wife, " and "The Scarlet Camelia, " and he probably did a translation of Baus' "A New Play. " But seemingly the same bad luck that had dogged his steps with "Unorna, " "The Wire Cutters, " and "The Emperor's Double" worked against these plays, too. There is no evidence that any of them was ever produced.

As a New Orleans editorial writer commented at the time of Williams' death, the Louisiana playwright had early recognized that the financial rewards of literature were slim.

He had started writing in 1868, at the age of sixteen, and 1892 was probably the first year in which he made more money on his writing than it cost him. But money evidently meant little to Williams as a writer, except as a standard of success. As a successful New Orleans financier, he not only could afford to write without profit, but he also spent his money to write. Half a dozen of his plays were printed by him for free distribution: "Parrhasius, " "Morbid Versus Quick, " "Eugene Aram, " "Witchcraft, " "The A- theist, " and "Don Carlos. "

But fame was the spur that drove him. In a journal he kept in 1874-75, Williams told himself that he would write until the world acknowledged that he had created something of value.

"I shall yet make myself a place among those whose names are in the mouths of living men long after they have been taken from this Earth. I know not why, but I feel it--and the feeling is not one of Egotism or Vanity. I have felt it all my life--and I shall feel it until this end shall be accomplished. "

Although he had some successes, by 1908 Williams knew that he had not yet made that place for himself. And he knew he was dying.

At the beginning of this century Bernard Shaw, then an upstart young critic and playwright, argued that " . . . there is one prize that is always open to competition, one blue ribbon that always carries the highest critical rank with it.   To win, you must write the best book of your generation on Shakespeare. " Shaw's own entry was his one-act play,   "The Dark Lady of the Sonnets, " and clearly by "best" Shaw meant the book with the most controversial interpretation of Shakespeare.

Williams' entry was a three-act heroic melodrama, "Marlowe: The Buried Name. " Williams' theory was that Christopher Marlowe was the real author of those plays now attributed to William Shakespeare.

Williams kept a calendar of his progress. He started the play on June 7, 1908.   He finished the first act on June 17 and finished revising it on June 20.   He started Act II on June 22, finished the rough draft on July 15 and the revision on July 19.   He finished only the first draft of Act III, and the date of its completion, the last date he recorded, was July 25.   He had planned an epilogue to follow the play, but he never got to this.

In early August, Williams recognized that the play was finished as far as he was concerned.   It still needed minor corrections, a rewrite of Act III, and the final epilogue, but Williams realized that he would never make them.

He did want one performance, however; and he had one.   He gave it himself.   He called his wife and three daughters into his sickroom to listen to his reading of it.

"The memory of that reading, " his youngest daughter Eunice (now Mrs. Phillips Endecott Osgood, a novelist living in Summit, N.J.) says, "has remained forever fresh.   My father, thin and drawn from a long and painful illness, yet so courageously attempting to divert his mind from his pain with this last work--an old-fashioned lap board across his armchair . . . that day just two weeks before his death, when he read the complete manuscript to my mother, myself, and two sisters. "

When the playwright died, his wife attempted to settle both his financial affairs and his literary one.

Mrs. Williams was, according to her daughter, "completely ignorant of business methods and with anything to do with the market

for theatrical works. She had been very proud of my father's successes but didn't share his enjoyment of what was then considered
the 'bohemian' atmosphere of writers and theater. "

An agent friend asked to examine one of the unpublished manuscripts, perhaps of a play called "The Social Rebel. " At least,
all that remains of that play is the knowledge of its title. Mrs.
Williams consented and gave him the manuscript, but when she
wrote later and inquired about it, the agent denied he had ever
heard of the play.

Mrs. Williams then bundled together all of the manuscripts,
including "Marlowe: The Buried Name, " and put them in storage.
Sometime later, the family sold "Kirkwood, " the New Orleans home
at 921 South Carrollton. The eldest daughter took her father's manuscripts to Cincinnati with her. Here they remained for many
years unopened. When the eldest daughter died, the manuscripts
were sent to Mrs. Osgood in New Jersey. And a few years ago,
she gave them to the library at the University of Southwestern
Louisiana in Lafayette.

Last year the University of Kentucky Press released a micro-
card edition of "Marlowe: The Buried Name" for the general use
of scholars in American literature and history. And in the past few
years others of Williams' plays have been published in scholarly
journals and micro-carded for academic use. In this respect, Williams' name has found a place for itself in "the mouths of living
men. " It is to be doubted, however, if this was the fame that Williams pursued so diligently from early manhood to his deathbed.

There is little chance that "Marlowe: The Buried Name" will
ever challenge "Cat on a Hot Tin Roof" in the modern theater. If
the play had been produced in 1908, however, the catchiness of the
theory might have made the play a controversial curio. A Life
magazine article of a few years ago sparked a general public argument when it reported the same theory Williams used in the play.
Paradoxically, Williams did not share Shakespeare's fame, but
rather his hero's fate. Like Marlowe, Williams has become a
"buried name. "

4. "Louisiana's First Play Champions 'Human Rights'"

(Reprinted from Sunday Advocate [Baton Rouge, La.]

Magazine, January 8, 1961, 1E.)

Three years from now, in 1964, Louisiana will celebrate the
150th anniversary of the production of its first home-written play,
a classical tragedy, "Poucha-Houmma," by Louis Paul Balthazar
Le Blanc de Villeneufve.

In many respects, "Poucha-Houmma" is exactly the kind of
first play that one would expect in a state which began its civilized
existence as a French colony. The play was written in French and
imitates the neo-classic style of the great French tragic playwrights,
Racine and Corneille. It is a play, like those of the French heroic
period, that abounds in heroic characters, noble sentiments, and
bombastic speeches. Every character in the play seems eager to
die for his beliefs and always with a "It is a far, far greater thing
I do" speech.

What makes the play unusual, however, is not that it is Louisiana's first play, nor even that it was the first play of a man in
his seventies. It is rather, as Alcée Fortier pointed out in his
"Louisiana Studies" in 1894, that Louisiana began its dramatic tradition with a plea for "human rights" for the rejected people of
Louisiana.

De Villeneufve's intention in writing "Poucha-Houmma" was
"to demonstrate that nobility is not a matter of race, but rather a
matter of personal qualities possible to the natives whom many
Louisianians had treated as barbaric semi-slaves."

It is the Indians, notably the Choctaws of the Mississippi Delta
region, whom de Villeneufve defends. His Indians are copper-skin-
ned Romans, speaking in a style known only to the heroic drama.
But the episode that de Villeneufve dramatizes was taken from a
scene of real life in Louisiana.

The play deals with the sacrifice of Poucha-Houmma, chief of
the Houmma nation, and, as de Villeneufve treats of it, the play becomes a combination of "Julius Caesar" and "A Tale of Two Cities."

"Poucha-Houmma" is a five-act verse tragedy set in an Indian
village on the banks of the Mississippi River in the fall of the year

1751. It opens with an Indian "thanksgiving" by Poucha: "The earth, under your eyes had displayed her presents. To your Benefactor present them an offering. May he gladly accept your pious sacrifice."

The thanksgiving, however, is interrupted. Poucha's son, Cala-be, has killed a member of a neighboring tribe, and, according to tribal agreements, he must now himself be sacrificed. Poucha, however, sends the boy away; and when the members of the neighboring tribe come for revenge, he offers himself in substitute.

Cala-be, in the meantime, returns to pay for his crime, but he arrives too late to save his father. As the curtain falls, he is told by his uncle that his father has satisfied his enemies, but that he, Cala-be, now has an eternal obligation to his people and to justice:

"Tell him especially that ever just and fair He must lead the nation to proud prosperity. This dreadful memory, this gory sacrifice Will be the punishment of your act, Cala-be. Keep well the memory of the crime, of the pain, And of the great duties your father left to you."

De Villeneufve's characterization of the Louisiana Indians as brave, formal, civilized people, "more the antique Romans than the eighteenth-century Indians," was not, of course, a popular one in the state. Laws existed barring the Indians from legal and social participation in the affairs of their native land.

But de Villeneufve had been for too long intimately connected with the history of the state and the Indians to be openly challenged.

He had come to Louisiana sometime around 1750 as a Commandant to serve as the government agent among the Indians in the Opelousas district, a post he held from 1752 to 1758. It was shortly after his arrival here that he heard the story of Poucha-Houmma, the chief who sacrificed himself to save his son's life. He had been present when the French officer who had investigated the incident made his report to the governor, Vaudreuil.

The Indians had early engaged his sympathies, and he sought to present their cause in the earliest literature composed in Louisiana. In 1753, for example, he wrote an epic poem, "La Fete

du Petit Ble" (The Feast of the Young Corn), part of which he a-
gain used in his tragedy, "Poucha-Houmma." This poem has the
distinction of being the first literary work composed in Louisiana.

Although de Villeneufve left France at the time that Rousseau
was preaching his "social equality" theories, the French Commandant was not a democratic revolutionist. As the play shows, he
preferred a paternal and enlightened despotism to all forms of government, and he had a distrust of the common people of all races.
His plea was not for human equality, but rather it was for the recognition of human virtue wherever it appeared.

The play, seemingly, had little effect in changing public opinion in Louisiana concerning the rights of the Indians. It was produced at the French Theater in New Orleans and later published,
but it had neither a long run on the stage nor great sales as a
book. In fact, so few copies have survived that one may now find
a copy only in the rare-book rooms of the university libraries.
There has, moreover, never been a second edition of the work, although now a one-act version of the play for high school production
has been prepared by Mrs. Katherine Finley in her "Selected One-
Act Plays by Louisiana Writers." The play was translated for the
edition by Mrs. Alex Allain, whose husband is one of the descendants of the author, de Villeneufve.

If de Villeneufve failed to bring about a change in public opinion about Indians, his play, at least, started a policy of antibigotry
in Louisiana drama that has run pretty consistently from 1714 to
the present.

Over and over again, Louisiana playwrights have taken their
stand with the ostracized group. Espy Williams in his melodrama,
"The Witch of Prague," for example, turned an anti-Jewish novel
into a pro-Jewish play in 1910. New Orleans-born Lillian Hellman,
in such plays as "The Little Foxes," has over and over again been
the champion of the legal and social exiles. Shreveport-born Arthur Lee Kahn, in such plays as "We-Uns of Tennessee," took up
the defense of the poor people of the South, "the pore white trash,"
against the prejudices of the whole nation.

None of these, however, was perhaps quite as eloquent as was

Louisiana's first playwright, de Villeneufve, who used the most
stately of all dramatic forms to insist that the "lowly savages" of
Louisiana were not only entitled to human consideration, but should
by rights deserve the admiration of all who respect "human greatness."

VIII.   By-Products of Research
Related Materials

Almost a by-product of research done in the "lost" play manuscripts of provincial America is the related material that comes
to the researcher--letters, journals, and the like. Sometimes
these related materials are of more interest than the plays themselves, and they may be made public either as editions or as the
basis of critical articles. The three selected for this chapter all
came to me from relatives of the playwrights after they had read
various articles that I had written. The first two articles are essentially editions of letters written by or to the playwright. The
third article is largely based on a journal kept by a playwright.

1.   "Bright American Minds, British Brains and
Southern Drama: A Letter and an Introduction"
(Reprinted from The Southern Speech Journal, XXIV
[Spring, 1959], 129-134.)

For the serious student of theater, American drama begins
with Eugene O'Neill, the post-World War I period, and the art theater. Such a statement sums up general critical thinking today, and
no amount of research or re-investigation is likely to change the
verdict that prior to World War I American drama, as literature,
was wretched and Southern drama was non-existent. Plays, of
course, were being written by Americans, including Southerners.
Between 1870 and 1916, American playwrights were copyrighting
their wares at the rate of over a thousand plays a year.

A reading of most of these plays, however, is likely to bring
nothing but discomfort to the dramatic aesthete, but the ideational
historian will find in the plots, characters, and language of these
plays much that is still forming the content of our better drama today. What is different between the postwar and the prewar drama

178

is not a matter of the skills of the playwright, but rather a matter of the intent of the playwright, as this was formed by the opinions of the dramatic dictators--the producers, directors, and actors.

A letter, written September 24, 1902, from such a producer-director-actor dictator, Clarence Brune, to Espy Williams, [1] gives insight into some of the reasons why it was difficult for American playwrights, especially Southern ones, to write as well as they could, let alone as well as they should. This letter, but recently come to light among the late playwright's effects, is, of course, not unique in the attitude it reveals; but it is perhaps more frank than most. As Williams was a native Southerner who intended to remain in the South, Brune probably felt that he was in a position [129] to be more demanding than he would have been with a New York playwright, who might have shopped elsewhere.

On April 5, 1901, Williams, one of New Orleans' most successful financiers as well as the state's most successful playwright, wrote the last speech of a play upon which he had been working since 1899:

Nap: Greater than a soldier, you shall wear a soldier's honors to the grave!

(Kneels--placing the cross upon the Baron's breast--as--

Curtain)

The End

He signed the manuscript and dated it: "New Orleans, La., April 5th, 1901. Espy Williams, P.O. Box 1250."

Williams, then at the high point of his dramatic career, had not yet decided on a title for this romantic play about Napoleon. He listed four "provisional" names: The Guest of Holdstein, The Emperor's Double, The Baron's Last Love, and Baron Holdstein. It was finally under his second choice, The Emperor's Double, that he sold the play to Brune.

What happened to the play after the sale to Brune has long been forgotten, unrecorded by even those few faithfuls of the history of American drama before World War I. Arthur Hobson Quinn, Allan G. Halline, Thomas H. Dickinson, and George Odell do not even mention the playwright in any of their studies. Even John S. Ken-

dall fails to record his existence in his study, The Golden Age of
New Orleans Theater. Williams, of course, is mentioned frequently
in such records as Who's Who, the Best Plays series, and Alcée
Fortier's Louisiana Studies. But nowhere, except in the private
correspondence of the playwright and in the manuscripts left among
his effects, is there any record of the play, The Emperor's Double.
Clarence Brune has been forgotten even more completely than Williams.

In 1901, however, those interested in the "rise of Southern
Literature" were looking to the combination of Williams and Brune
for the start of a nationally known, Southern-written drama. By
that year, Williams had written over twenty-five plays, a number
of which had received respectable attention on the American stage.
A one-act play [130] written in 1879, Parrhasius, had caught the attention of the Shakespearian actor, Robert Mantell, when it was published in 1892. Mantell bought the stage rights for $3,000, and
Williams expanded it into three and four-act versions which Mantell
made a part of his repertoire. Another play, The Cup of Bitter-
ness, was renamed The Husband and also played by Mantell from
Philadelphia to San Francisco. Lawrence Barrett, probably the
best-known "Southern" actor-producer in America, was collaborating
with Williams on a romantic tragedy, Dante, at the time of his
death in 1891. Walker Whiteside toured both England and the United
States with Williams' The Man in Black. A Cavalier in France had
a week's run in New York with Louis James' company and proved
very successful in "western tours. " A comic opera, first titled
Ollamus (and set in Utopia), then renamed A Royal Joke (and set on
Mars), was hailed in New Orleans as "the birth of Southern opera"
when it was produced there by the Metropolitan English Opera Company in 1901.

During the first decade of the twentieth century, at least ten
of Williams' plays were being produced simultaneously in theaters
in America: in Boston, Philadelphia, Houston, Dallas, New Orleans, Memphis, Seattle, Kansas City, San Antonio, San Francisco.
It was, in fact, with no more than normal exaggeration that The
Daily (New Orleans) Picayune editorialized on his passing, August

28, 1908, under a headline titled, "The South's Leading Dramatist."

Of Clarence Brune far less is known today. According to the records of <u>Dramatic Compositions Copyrighted in the United States from 1870-1916</u>, he was the author of one play: <u>A Parted Fellowship; or The Curate of Belmont</u>, registered in 1891 as a comedy drama in four acts. There is no record that this play was ever produced or that Brune ever wrote another; but his association with the theater thereafter was as actor, director, and producer. Sometime before he began his association with Williams, Brune had married a young California actress, Minnie Tittle, who was then being advertised by her press agents as "The American Bernhardt." In 1902 she starred in <u>Unorna</u>, a play which Williams had written from F. Marion Crawford's novel, <u>The Witch of Prague</u>, and which Brune produced, although he was in London at the time it opened.

<u>Unorna</u> was Williams' biggest disappointment of the year. It opened in Norfolk, Virginia, Sept. 22, 1902, and both the play and Minnie received enthusiastic reviews. Then it travelled on a circuit [131] that was to take it from Virginia, to Florida, through Texas, and to Memphis. It was shown successfully in Richmond, Lynchburg, Roanoke, Columbia, Charleston, Jacksonville, Birmingham, Montgomery, Houston, San Antonio, and Dallas. Plans were being made for a New York opening in December. On Thanksgiving Day, 1902, however, the day the play was to open in Memphis, Mrs. Brune was "confined to her bed in the Gayoso Hotel" with malaria. For reasons now forgotten, this was the end of the stage history of <u>Unorna</u>.

At the time of its opening, however, Brune in London attempted to give the publicity men an assist. On the evening that the play opened in Virginia, he gave a single performance in the afternoon in London. The differences in time between Virginia and London then gave the press agents a legal excuse to advertise the play as opening simultaneously on two continents.

Brune, as every piece of evidence shows, was interested in the prestige that a London run gave to a play. The one play he mentions in his letter as being in his London repertoire of 1902, <u>The Fatal Wedding</u>, by Theodore Kremer, ran for eight perform-

ances in New York at the Grand Opera House, opening October 28,
1901. This, seemingly, was the extent of New York's interest.
Brune, himself, speaks ill of it, although he took the leading role.
In its New York run, it boasted, among other attractions, an ac-
tress named "Little Cora Quinten" and "Gertrude Haynes with her
Choir Celestial including Master James Byrnes and 25 choir boys."

    At the time he wrote this letter, Brune had more than a nor-
mal interest in Williams. He envisioned a theatrical empire for
himself by the simple method of prestige advertising. As his purchase of Williams' play and the changes he intended to make in it
and the purchase of The Fatal Wedding show, Brune was but little
concerned with either literary or theatrical quality. He considered
English audiences stupid, but he considered himself shrewd enough
to adapt any play to satisfy their debased tastes. Moreover, he
believed that any play that succeeded in London could not fail in
the United States. He had purchased several of Williams' plays,
some of which, seemingly, he never produced; and in this letter he
indicates pretty frankly how he intended to force them to success.
Moreover, at this time, Brune's wife was a guest of the New Orleans playwright while she was preparing for the Unorna role.

    From Brune's point of view, Williams' new play, The Emper-
or's [132] Double, was going to offer some difficulty in England. The
play, like Shaw's Man of Destiny, deals with the French emperor,
Napoleon, whom of course (from Brune's point of view) no Britain
would ever accept as a hero. As a matter of fact, the real hero
of the play is Baron Holdstein, the Emperor's double who gives his
life to save Napoleon's. Brune's letter makes it quite clear that
this would never do. Seemingly Brune had stated these same objections earlier, for Williams seems to have suggested three alter-
nates for his "revolutionary conqueror": George Washington; the
Union general, Phillip Sheridan; and Oliver Cromwell.

    To these suggestions, the producer wrote the following letter:

                                              Sept. 24, 1902

My dear Mr. Williams,

    I wrote you last night in re "Emperor's Double" & tonight I
receive yours of the 13th inst. about it. Your proposition is satis-

factory enough except the first clause as to territory--You know my
only object in producing any play in England particularly with myself in the bill is the good it will do me in the States later.   You
don't imagine I am in The Fatal Wedding for the good it does me
in London.   Although it gives me a standing here the great benefit
is the advertising I get in the States out of it--And as I shall undoubtedly return to the States next year or year after I would not
produce any piece to which I did not have the American rights.
Without the American rights I wouldn't take the risk on the production here of any play if I were given the English rights for nothing
free of royalty.

I do not agree with you about making either Cromwell, Washington or Sheridan the leading part.   In the first place the Baron is
the leading part & his double whoever he should be as small a part
as consistent.   I had in mind the substitution of the Duke of Wellington for Napoleon--Nelson has been done here by Forbes Robert-
son but I believe Wellington has not though I am not absolutely positive.

The only one you mention that I think might do at all would
be Cromwell but that is a rather hazy period in the average British
mind.   His [sic] would not accept Washington & would not know
whom you were talking of if you used Sheridan.--You are accustomed to the bright American Mind but if you were here a short
time you would see that the English brain must be handled in an [133]
entirely different way and I should rather take chances on Napoleon
& the German Baron than have you attempt to rewrite it giving it
an English atmosphere.   I know you will not take this statement
particularly to yourself for I would be fearful of any author who had
not had this opportunity of experimenting with English Audiences.
Take my word for it they're a queer lot.   I don't believe a great
majority of them think at all or if they do it's a half hour behind
time--I had to change line after line & situation after situation in
"The Fatal Wedding. "   If they'd gotten it as it was done in America it would have been all over before they knew what was going on.
--Being an American it is rather difficult for me, but I had pur-
posely witnessed quite a number of Suburban Melodramatic produc-

tions so I rehearsed the Company to give it to them as they were accustomed.   I simply mention these things to let you know some of the difficulties one gets up against.

You know also the difficulties attending changes suggested by correspondence.   It was even difficult when you were with us--If you conclude to let me have the Emperor's Double I would suggest the characters remain as they are (which I am frightened to death of in England & consequently would feel that I had an unnecessary burden in the unpopularity of the characters or allow me to change or have changed as I think best.   I favor Wellington--It could be arranged that you only appear as author.   [That Williams appear as the only author.]

I haven't thought out a good title but it could be easily determined later.

I would like to know definitely whether you will let me have it or not on receipt of this--As it is getting late--pantomine season commences in Dec. & then dramatic business is at a standstill practically until late Feb. which season is not good until the last of April.

I will ask you to cable me "Yes" or "No" on receipt of this & if yes you can send on Contract giving me until say May 15th to produce.   You can follow the Unorna Contract.   I would hope to do it in Nov. unless the other piece with which I will probably open the Royal Court is a sufficient success to keep it on.

With best wishes I am

> Yours
>
> Brune

P.S.

Take care of Mrs. Brune in N.O. [134]

Notes

1. A collection of over thirty of Williams' plays, a diary, clippings, and this letter was deposited with the University of Southwestern Louisiana library in February by Mrs. Phillips Endecott Osgood, the playwright's daughter.   These materials are the basis for most of the information in this article. [129]

2. "When the Curtains Rise, Scouts Fall Out"

(Reprinted from The Southern Speech Journal, XXIX

[Spring, 1964], 175-186.)

The western scout as stage hero has a long history in American theater, dating at least back to 1831, when James K. Paulding's Lion of the West introduced a Philadelphia audience to the romantic American frontiersman, Col. Nimrod Wildfire. Not until the 1870's, however, did the scout become a standard figure in American drama. Augustin Daly's Horizon in 1871, based on Bret Harte's stories, and Frank Murdock's Davy Crockett in 1872 proved--seemingly forever--that buckskin and gunsmoke are the proper ingredients for box office success. Other events of the 1870's, outside the theater, also turned America's eyes toward the western scout--the dime novels of Ned Buntline and Prentiss Ingraham and the Indian wars.

The wars against the Indians in the 1870's were probably the most popular the United States ever fought. They had all the right ingredients--opportunities for personal valor, colorful personalities, and the certainty of a victory that would come without risk or expense to the taxpayer. The defeat of Custer in 1876, moreover, gave a sense of moral righteousness to the entire series of western invasions. It was Valley Forge, the Alamo, and the firing on Fort Sumter rolled into one. The dime novelists were the popular historians, not only recording the events but bringing to the East a new American hero, the Indian fighter scout.

In late 1871, the scouts of the Indian wars made their first stage appearance.[1] On December 16, before a sell-out crowd in Chicago, Buffalo Bill (William F. Cody), Texas Jack (Omohundro), and Ned Buntline opened in an opus, Scouts of the Plains, a new version of [175] Fred Meader's drama, Buffalo Bill. The performance demonstrated that no matter how weak the acting, if the leading characters were played by "the real thing," commercial success was assured. In the next few years, other "scouts" were added to the cast--John M. Burke, "Arizona John," who later became Buffalo Bill's press agent; Wild Bill Hickok, Indians, and lesser figures.

In 1876, with the Sioux uprising in the Dakotas, Buffalo Bill

left his show to return to the West as a scout. It was during this
summer that he fought Yellow Hand, in the famous "First scalp for
Custer" episode; and it was during this summer, too, that he engaged John Wallace Crawford, the poet-scout, to tour with him during the 1876-77 season.

The events of this theatrical season with Buffalo Bill and the
poet-scout, "Captain Jack," are interesting, both because they throw
light on one aspect of American theatrical history that has received
little attention and because they show the general concern of some
minor authors with the creation of an American drama. Cody, in
his Story of the Wild West and Camp Fire Chats,[2] pays scant attention to this episode in his life and does not even mention Crawford.
Crawford, however, in 1894 wrote a letter to Buffalo Bill in which
he recounts the events of that year, a letter now made public for
the first time.[3] This letter not only gives a good picture of one
aspect of American theatrical life of that period, but it also cor-
rects the belief that the western drama-makers did not take their
work seriously.

The common view of the scout-actor-playwright is probably
best expressed by Buffalo Bill's description of the writing and performance of one of his own plays. "Mr. J. Clinton Hall, manager
of the Rochester Opera House, was very anxious to have me play
an engagement at his theater," Buffalo Bill wrote, "so I agreed to
open the season with him as soon as I got my drama written. . . .
My new drama was arranged for the stage by J. V. Arlington, the
actor. It [176] was a five-act play, without head or tail, and it made no
difference at which act we commenced the performance. Before we
had finished the season several newspaper critics, I have been told,
went crazy in trying to follow the plot. It afforded us, however,
ample opportunity to give a noisy, rattling, gunpowder entertainment, and to present a succession of scenes in the late Indian war,
all of which seemed to give general satisfaction."[4]

Cody's easygoing, tongue-in-cheek manner was, however,
only a manner. The pose of the western scout as a man not much
concerned with art in any of its forms, as a man who looked upon
show business simply as an easy way to make a few dollars, as a

man a little impatient and a great deal amused with drama was, it
would seem, only an affectation.   As Crawford's letter to Cody
demonstrates, when the curtains rise, scouts fall out for the most
basic of all theatrical emotions, professional jealousy.

I

Crawford must have appeared to Cody as a good supporting
character for his frontier plays.   Born in Ireland in 1847, he had
come to America shortly before the outbreak of the Civil War and
before his sixteenth birthday had run away from home to serve with
the 48th Pennsylvania Volunteers.   Wounded twice in action, Crawford was taught to read and write by a Sister of Charity while recuperating from his wounds.   When the war ended, he returned to
his home in Pennsylvania, married in 1869, and then went west to
seek his fortune.   He was one of the early settlers in the Black
Hills and was serving as a civilian scout for various communities
when the war against the Sioux started. [5]

In the summer of 1876 he was a scout for the Army and made
headlines when he carried a dispatch for the New York Herald.
Crawford at the time was making $150 a month by scouting; and
although this was an impressive salary, he had a wife and children
back in Pennsylvania, and many of his friends were making "big [177]
money" in mining and on the stage.   Crawford, moreover, seems
to have fallen in love with the written word, especially his own;
and although he considered himself primarily a poet, he also wished
to be a playwright.

That summer Buffalo Bill was planning two shows for the
coming season, Scouts of the Prairie and Life on the Border, and
he later added The Right Red Hand.   He offered Crawford the "starring role" in Life on the Border, and Crawford accepted.   The play
opened in Rochester, New York, that fall and then went to the
Grand Opera House on West Twenty-third Street in New York.   It
was successful and played later that season at the Bowery Theater
and Hooley's Theater in Brooklyn and then made a tour across the
country, closing in Omaha. [6]

Crawford, a prohibitionist, complained that much of his time
was spent in keeping Cody sober, but he enjoyed the theater.   When

Buffalo Bill returned to his ranch in North Platte, Nebraska, Captain Jack stayed in Omaha to take care of the business. The manager of the Bush Street Theatre in San Francisco wired an offer to Buffalo Bill for his and Captain Jack's appearance; and after a squabble about money, Crawford agreed to go with the show to the West Coast. After a successful run in San Francisco, they went to Virginia City, Nevada, to end the season.

II

The events of the 1876-77 season were bitter ones for Crawford, at least they seemed so eighteen years later when Crawford wrote to Buffalo Bill about the matter. According to his letter, Crawford was shot, cheated, underpaid, and betrayed by Buffalo Bill. Since Cody never mentioned the episode, it is difficult to sift the "exact truth" of the matter from "the rumors"; but the Nevada Territorial Enterprise from June 24, 1877, to July 1, 1877, gave accounts of the occurrences upon which Crawford's complaints were based.

On June 24, the Enterprise announced that "Buffalo Bill, Captain Jack and company will appear at the National Theatre Monday evening, in the five-act Western drama of 'Life on the Border'." On June 26, the Enterprise gave the play a favorable review and announced it would be "repeated this evening." On June 27, the [178] play got another favorable review, and it was announced, "Tonight will be given the 'Red Right Hand,' [sic] which will no doubt crowd the house, as the piece is full of startling situations, with much fun sprinkled all through it."

Although Crawford was occasionally mentioned in the reviews, Buffalo Bill was, both on and off stage, the real hero, "a brave fellow."

The performance of June 29 ended with a catastrophe for Crawford, the "accident" that is the basis for his complaint. In the Enterprise accounts of June 30 and July 1, however, Cody is even here pictured as a hero.

"The play of the 'Right Red Hand' . . . ," the June 30 Enterprise reported, "ended as it was not begun. The last act was in successful progress, and the fight between J. W. Crawford alias Cap-

tain Jack, who impersonated Yellow Hand, and Buffalo Bill was in-
augurated . . . Captain Jack, before mounting his horse, had cocked
his pistol, and placed it in his holster. In attempting to draw
it with his usual dexterity and celerity, it caught, and in the en-
deavor to extricate it was discharged." And "Yellow Hand" Crawford "bit the dust," a victim of his own carelessness.

"After the curtain fell," the Enterprise account continued,
"there was a general rush of Captain Jack's friends for the stage.
It was then ascertained that the discharge had made a deep and
painful wound a little below the left groin. Drs. Bergstein,[8] Grant
and Tufts were soon in attendance, and examination showed that the
wad with which the pistol was loaded entered at the place indicated,
ranged down some four inches and there lodged . . . . The wound
is large, ragged and painful, but not necessarily dangerous . . . ."

"There was [sic] several rumors afloat last evening . . . .
Some said that Buffalo Bill had shot Crawford in the head; others
that the horse had stepped on him. The foregoing, however, are
the facts of the case."

Crawford maintained that Cody had wounded him through his drunk-
en carelessness and later often suggested that a presentation of [179]
the "true facts of the case" would cause a public scandal. It is to
be doubted, however, that even if Cody's public knew and believed
Crawford's account they would have much cared. Cody was the
hero; Crawford was merely a victim of an accident. The Enterprise, for example, ended its account with the assurance that, "This
affair, however much it may be regretted, will not in any way interfere with the matinee at 2 o'clock this afternoon." The July 1
Enterprise reviewed the matinee and reported that the show had
"attracted a large audience, made up principally of women and children. The play, 'Life on the Border,' gave great satisfaction . . .
Buffalo Bill played both his part and that of Captain Jack."

According to Captain Jack, Cody not only wounded him, but
he also left him penniless in Virginia City when the show ended.
One of Crawford's friends later repeated this account publicly:[9] "In
this mock fight Crawford was accidently shot in the groin, through
the carelessness and drunkenness of the man to whom he had been as

Damon to Pythias and the hero-manager even refused to pay the
doctor whom he himself had summoned before leaving the Poet
Scout on his back in a hospital, with just $58.00 all the money he
had on earth. "

According to this story, "Yet Crawford did not complain;" but
he certainly did let his condition be known. To help him, friends
gave a benefit performance from which $600 was realized. During
his convalescence, Crawford and a Sam Smith, the author of a popular melodrama, Struck Oil, collaborated in dramatizing one of
Crawford's Black Hills poems. Titled Fonda; or the Trapper's
Dream, [10] this three-act play was a highly romantic, somewhat autobiographical account of Crawford's early adventures in the Rocky
Mountains. [180]

Crawford got a company together and opened with his new
play at the same theater in San Francisco in which he and Cody had
played a successful six-weeks engagement a few months earlier.
"The play was pronounced a success. He had no money and no manager, yet with a company of fifteen people, made a ten week's tour
through California. "

Alfred Dampier, then the manager of the Theatre Royal in
Melbourne, Australia, offered Crawford a contract to bring Fonda
to Australia; but Crawford first had to raise the money to ship his
company. He asked Cody for help, and after first agreeing to let
him have the money, Cody later told him that he would be unable to
do so.

III

Without money and without prospects, Crawford accepted an
offer from General Hatch, "then fighting Indians with the 'fighting
ninth cavalry' . . . to act as his Chief of Scouts during the Apache
campaign, against old Victorio, Loco, Nana and Geronimo. "

For the next twenty years Crawford was a scout and, after
1886, the custodian of Fort Craig in New Mexico. During this time
he rewrote his play Fonda and wrote another, The Mighty Truth; or
In Clouds or Sunshine. Both plays were frequently presented at the
smaller theaters across America, sometimes with Captain Jack
playing the leading roles. [11] During these years, too, he did a con-

siderable amount of prospecting in the New Mexican hills, frequently having his hopes raised but not realizing much profit. In 1894, he went to Europe in hope of inheriting a fortune from his mother's family, the Wallaces of Scotland; but seemingly his Scottish ancestors were no more generous with their riches than were the New Mexican hills. It was during this trip that he wrote his letter to Cody.

During these twenty years, Crawford published several volumes of poetry, The Poet Scout: A Book of Song and Story, published [181] first in 1879 and then revised in 1886 and 1891, and Camp Fire Sparks in 1893. He became a popular lecturer for the causes of prohibition and the rights of Civil War veterans and proclaimed against the evils of the dime novel and cigarettes. In his plays, poetry, and lectures he presented himself as "Capt. Jack, the Poet Scout," a simple man of the West; and although he seldom mentioned Buffalo Bill by name, except in paying poetic tributes to him, he wrote and spoke often about the "faker" scouts who did all their Indian-killing on stage, and he implied that Cody was the worst of the fakers. He had written a number of poems about Buffalo Bill, based on their Black Hills adventures; and these he continued to republish through the years. The poems, in fact, led the public to believe that Buffalo Bill and Captain Jack were friends.

In January, 1917, Buffalo Bill died, and Crawford, who was himself dying at the time, "got the news that Colonel Cody, with whom he had ridden in many a wild charge against the Sioux, had gone over the great divide. It depressed him. [12]

"'So Bill Cody has gone!, said Captain Jack. 'I guess they will be sounding taps over me pretty soon. Well, when we meet Tall Bull and that tough old codger, Sitting Bull, on the other side and stick up our hands, palms forward, and say, "How, Kola!" there will be a lot to talk about!"[13]

V

If this letter which Crawford wrote to Cody is typical of the conversation between the two scouts, Sitting Bull and Tall Bull probably had little opportunity to say much more than "How, Kola!"; however, the vituperation that Crawford poured into this letter seems

more a matter of style than of any deep hatred. There is no evidence that Crawford even mailed the letter; in fact, Crawford admits that he had written other letters of this nature before and had
been persuaded not to send them.

The Letter

Hotel Metropole

London W. C.

September 19th 1894

W. F. Cody Esq.

Dear Sir,

I am informed that I have been attacked through the press by [182]
small Burk. [14] Say call off your beagles, you can't afford to take
a hand in such business. I am sure you do not want the true story
which I know published. Do you remember when you wired me at
Virginia City when you had left me on my back a stranger and penniless, shot through your drunkeness . . . ? You [said then], "If
you need any money or if I can do anything for you at any time let
me know." Shortly after I did so, because I believed in you . . .;
I thought you really meant what you said in your letter. In spite of
your treatment of me, I believed you were the real genuine hero
Buffalo Bill that Ned Buntline and other writers had glorified (but
that was before I had learned the true story of the killing of Yellow Hand . . .). I wired and asked you to let me have $500 as a
loan to go to Australia where I had an engagement with Mr. Alfred
Dampier . . . . You wrote and asked me to meet you at your
ranch and after the round up you thought you could let me have it.
I went on a fool's errand for when I reached Denver I wired you to
Manchester N. H. You replied "Business is bad, cannot let you
have the money." Yet if you will turn to your books you will see
that you played to over $800 the night before; I happened to have a
good friend with you who wrote me at the time. Now what was
your object in all this? Simply to prevent me from going if possible. Why? Because you knew that if I went, my Pure, Pathetic
and true pictures of our glorious West, which for twenty-five years
you have been libelling with your blood and thunder "red right hand"
dime novel impossibilities, would interfere with your trip to Europe

which you were then contemplating . . . . I can pile up facts
since the 24th of August 1876 when you left your command to fill
theatrical engagements until the time you left me to die in Virginia
City, and even refused to pay the doctor's bill. After begging me
to change from the scout in the last act and do the horseback fight
as Yellow Hand, which the man playing the part refused to do because of your drunkeness, twice in the knife fight you put the point
of your knife into me, once in the knee from which I still suffer. [15] [183]

Before we went to San Francisco and after you had closed
your season in Omaha you went to North Platte, telling me to receive and forward mail or telegrams. This message came from
Managers Bush Street Theatre, W. F. Cody--"For yourself, Captain
Jack and Pictorial printing will share after one thousand dollars. "
I retransmitted this and added--"I leave for Saint Louis tomorrow. "
You wired back--"Wait for my letter. . . ." In it you begged me
to go to Frisco, saying you [would] make salary all right, when I closed
with you at Omaha---Because as a frontier's man I did not ask for
a contract but trusted to your honor? When you said if business
was good you would pay me a good salary, . . . I replied--If not
good you would not owe me a cent. What did you pay me after
clearing over $20,000? The same as you paid your chief property
man--$20 dollars per week and expenses . . . .

Say Bill do you remember [after a performance in Newark,
New Jersey] how you kicked the door of my room next morning,
compelled me to jump out of bed, and swore by all that was good,
bad and indifferent that I was the star. Then you know the Frisco
papers said Crawford can act, but Cody is a stick. . . .

In Frisco I asked you for $100 dollars per week (I get that a
night now); you were making thousands, you allowed me $40. I
told you to fill my place, giving you a week, finally compromised
on $50. . . . I am not and never have posed as a great Scout and
Hero, and Indian killer; and you know I have repeatedly refused to
allow the men who created you a hero to do the same for me. [16]

But understand this, and deny if you can, when you refused
the loan you proffered, I accepted the position of Chief of Scouts
from General Edward Hatch, and in the first three months of the

Victorio campaign. . . . I saw more actual Indian fighting and
took more desperate chances than you ever did. . . . Of course
I do not refer to the Indian fighting you had on the stage and in the
Wild West Show in the last twenty-five years.

. . . . Now why should you claim after Texas Jack died that
you were the only one left and King of them all. And yet you
know that Texas Jack never was a Scout, never saw a hostile and
never fought [184] Indians, except with you on the mimic stage. I am
told that your man Friday, Major? John Burk--another of your
creations, for you have manufactured a lot of longhaired fakes--
has amongst other things said in the press that I want to become
famous through Colonel Cody and that I cannot spell some simple
word in the English language. Now I do not believe Johnny can
create much of a sensation on that score, for it is a well known
fact that I had to make my cross when I enlisted as a boy soldier
at the age of sixteen and while scar-faced Burk was getting his
scars in bar rooms, I was trying to learn at the Front, and while
wounded at the Hospital, so that I could write home to an angel
mother. . . . I had a long letter Johnny wrote me when managing
Texas Jack in '77 in which he roasts a certain fellow who kicked
him out as he did Ned Buntline when he thought he could get along
without him. . . .

Here is another truth that suggests itself on account of Burk's
reference to my bad spelling; he might have added bad grammer
[sic], but you know very well that you yourself never wrote a para-
graph for publication in your life and that you are not in reality the
author of your book or any other dime novel supposed to have been
written about you. I do not claim to have any great amount of literary merit . . . , but I consider at least that I use good straight
American English and Mr. Burk should not throw stones, for the
whole outfit are ensconced in a glass case and a real good statement with backbone and ginger in it would bust the conservatory
and your noses would be all tip-tilted like the petals of a rose.

. . . . For seventeen years newspapers . . . have all been
asking me to tell them about frontier humbugs and dime novel
heroes. I have held my tongue . . . [for] those depending on you

. . . . [But] privately, let me whisper to you I know of nothing
that is honest and true and manly in which you are my superior.
I have written many letters like this to you before . . . , but
when I asked a friend to look over them, as a result of council
they were torn or burned, but there is no one here to counsel me
today, my blood is up and right it should be when I recall some of
your insinuating letters. In one you informed me that my hair had
been forcibly cut from my head. You know you lied when you
wrote that. . . .

    I know of none in all my acquaintances who showed such in-
gratitude as you did for whom I did so much and unselfishly, for
you know I was honest. . . . [185]

    But this long letter will weary you, you are not as robust as
you used to be and I know that you will read it, for every line
must be interesting, especially when you consider all that there is
behind it. . . .

    I have nothing more to say[17] except that if I find you have in-
stigated the attacks on me, it will be my duty to defend my reputation on my return.

Yours truly

[J. W. Crawford]

Late Chief of Scouts

U. S. A. [186]

Notes

1. A full account of Cody's stage career is given in Henry Black-
    man Sell and Victor Weybright's Buffalo Bill and the Wild West
    (New York: Oxford University Press, 1955). [175]

2. (Chicago: Thompson & Thompson, 1902) Of the Virginia City
    episode, Cody wrote only, "Upon leaving San Francisco I
    made a circuit of the interior towns and closed the season at
    Virginia City, Nevada." p. 689. Cody never mentions Craw-
    ford's name in the entire book.

3. Crawford's typed copy of this letter is now in the possession of
    his great-granddaughter, Mrs. Buford Richardson, Socorro, New
    Mexico. I am indebted to Mrs. Richardson for permission to
    use not only this letter, but also for hundreds of other mater-
    ials--letters, unpublished works, and editions of Crawford's
    published poetry. [176]

4. Story of the Wild West, p. 689.

5. The Dictionary of American Biography and the various editions
    of Who's Who in America from 1899 to 1917 give brief ac-
    counts of Crawford's career. The fullest accounts are those
    of Leigh Irvine in Crawford's The Poet Scout: A Book of Song
    and Story (New York: Funk & Wagnalls, 1886) and of John G.
    Scorer in Crawford's Lariattes: A Book of Poems and Recita-
    tions (Sigourney, Iowa: William A. Bell, 1904). [177]

6. Weybright and Sell, Buffalo Bill and the Wild West, p. 127.

7. All of the Enterprise accounts appear on page 3 of the respec-
    tive issues. [178]

8. Henry Bergstein, M.D., who wrote the chapter on "Medical
    History" for Sam P. Davis' History of Nevada (Reno: The
    Elms Publishing Co., 1913), was also a playwright. At least,
    in 1877, he wrote and copyrighted one play, "a drama in 5
    acts," The Philanthropist's Error. Dramatic Compositions
    Copyrighted in the United States from 1870 to 1916 (Washington,
    D.C.: U.S. Printing Office, 1918). [179]

9. This account of the episode was given as an introduction to
    Crawford when he appeared on the lecture platform in the early
    1900's. A copy of the introduction is owned by Mrs. Richard-
    son (see note 3). Cody is never mentioned by name, but is
    called the "Big Mogul," the "star," and a "would-be hero."
    Crawford is quoted as speaking of him as Bill: "Bill busted
    Murphy all to h-ll." Crawford, obviously, supplied all the
    details for the introduction.

10. Crawford is the only author listed on the title page of the play
    filed in the copyright office of the Library of Congress in 1879,
    the only extant copy of the play. An edition of Crawford's
    three frontier plays--prose, autobiographical melodramas, Fonda,
    The Mighty Truth, and Colonel Bob--is now in progress. [180]

11. On March 16, 1880, Texas Jack Omohundro, one of Buffalo
    Bill's original "supporting stars," had the leading role in Craw-
    ford's Fonda, then titled The Trapper's Daughter. Crawford,
    however, received so little attention for his authorship that
    Herschel C. Logan in his Buckskin and Satin: The Life of
    Texas Jack (Harrisburg, Pennsylvania: Stackpole Company,
    1950), p. 180, after an examination of the newspaper accounts
    of the play, assumed that Texas Jack was the author. [181]

12. "The Poet-Scout," Literary Digest, LIV (March 24, 1917), 837.

13. P. 20. [182]

14. "Major" John Burke started as a character actor in repertoire
    theaters. Born in the District of Columbia, he was known as

"Arizona John," although he had never seen Arizona. For
forty years, he was Cody's "partner, manager, friend, and
press agent." Sell and Weybright, Buffalo Bill and the Wild
West, p. 105.

15. This is the only mention of a knife wound that I have found in
any of the accounts of the "accident." [183]

16. Although Crawford was an announced "foe" of the dime novel,
he seems also to have been proud of his associations with the
dime novelists and listed Ned Buntline among his "dear
friends." See my article, "Captain Jack: The Relentless Foe
of the Dime Novel," Dime Novel Round-Up, XXXI (November,
1963), 102-04. [184]

17. Crawford added a "P.S." to this letter, asking Cody to have
the letter published in its entirety. For this edition, the letter
has been somewhat abridged; but the only omissions (and all
are indicated in the text) are those that repeat claims and complaints made elsewhere in this article. [186]

3. "A Shakespeare Idol in America"
(Reprinted from The Mississippi Quarterly, XII
[Spring, 1959], 64-74.)

Shakespeare idolatry in nineteenth-century America was of such magnitude that it would be difficult to exaggerate it. This idolatry has been held responsible for stifling native talent; and it has, in fact, become a mark of a writer's powers that he was able to accept Shakespeare's genius without imitating his style, without becoming an idolator before the Shakespeare idol. In understanding the idol, however, the main concern has been with the effects of the idolatry: the general popularity of Shakespeare in America, the manner in which major writers like Melville and Whitman were able to use Shakespeare without becoming imitators, and the manner in which minor writers were unable to avoid imitation. It is the purpose of this study to look at the idol itself, rather than at the effects of idol worship. It is believed that such a view may lead to a better understanding of the problem of the young nineteenth-century American writer trying to achieve self-expression in a land, as both Hawthorne and James complained, with no established literary tradition of its own, and one in which the high regard for Shakespeare exercised a numbing influence on new writers.

A recently discovered diary of Espy Williams[1] (1852-1908), a Southern playwright and poet, suggested such a study, for Williams' con[64]cept of Shakespeare shows the idol in one of its popular forms and reveals its author as a man struggling with this idol for the right to a clear and private grasp of literary values. Moreover, when Williams' attitude toward Shakespeare is contrasted with that of an eighteenth-century diarist, James Boswell, it not only becomes apparent that Williams' concept of Shakespeare has idolatrous qualities but it also suggests that such an idol is a product of Williams' century and perhaps of his nation also.

The use of these two for the purpose of analyzing an American idol of Shakespeare has much to recommend it. Although the men have little in common, the private journals of each (Williams' diary and Boswell's London Journal, 1762-1763)[2] offer sharply contrasted views of two men in relatively similar positions.

Both Boswell and Williams were young men when they kept their journals, each twenty-two. Both were eager for literary fame. Both felt themselves outside the main literary world, Boswell because he was a Scot in London and Williams because he was a Southerner in post-Civil War America. Thus each probably had more than a normal respect for the common opinions of the age as they were articulated by the established men of letters. Williams, of course, as a playwright was concerned with Shakespeare's reputation not only as a literary leader but also as a stage writer; and many of Williams' comments are concerned with the problems of producing plays. For the purposes of this study, however, beyond a few sweeping suggestions, the effects of Shakespeare's reputation on the writings of the two men has been ignored. It is rather the purpose of this study to suggest the nature of the idol itself than to analyze its effects on literature.

Boswell and Williams, if one may accept the evidence of their journals, view Shakespeare in radically different ways. For Boswell, Shakespeare is a fine writer, but not necessarily the finest in the language; and his merits lie in stirring the "tender" emotions. Such an opinion Boswell thinks worth defending, at least in his journal. Boswell, moreover, looks upon Shakespeare as a playwright in the process of being established and one whose plays are still open to new interpretations. Williams, on the other hand, accepts the common opinion that Shakespeare is the supreme artist, especially in his ability to inspire awe. Moreover, although Williams objects to the claims made for Shakespeare's "god-like" artistry, he paradoxically demands that each production of a Shakespearian play be done in an "orthodox" fashion, as though it were the creation of a god. In general it might be said that Boswell "likes" Shakespeare and wishes him well and that Williams "worships" Shakespeare, but wishes him dethroned. This Shakespeare [65] idol, as seen by one American, is, then, a god-like creator of literature exact and single-purposed in its nature, demanding a single orthodox approach in its presentation, and awe-inspiring in its effects. When such an idol is seen, one may easily understand both the imitations of Shakespeare and the frantic anti-Shakespearian protests of such worshippers as

Williams.

I

For both Boswell and Williams, Shakespeare is a poet of
great merit and deserving of high reputation; but what in Williams
is a resentful concession is for Boswell a happy recognition. Boswell, for example, records a conversation in his Journal (December 25, 1762): Goldsmith: "I am afraid that we will have no good
plays now. The taste of the audience is spoiled by the pantomime
of Shakespeare. The wonderful changes and shiftings." Davies:
"Nay, but you will allow that Shakespeare had great merit?" Goldsmith: "No, I know Shakespeare very well." Then Boswell concludes, "Here I said nothing but thought him a most impudent puppy" (p. 106).

Williams, on the other hand, instead of attacking Shakespeare's
detractors, attacks his worshippers. On January 12, 1874, for example, after reading Moore's Life of Byron, Williams concludes
that there is too much hero-worship in the world. "The last thing
that pleases me in the work," he writes of Moore's biography, "is
that it shows Byron as a man. Great men are not gods, but men.
The world is very apt to cover a man's humanity over with the
mantle of his fame, and worship him in his greatness alone." Williams earlier admits his own "hero-worship" of Byron, but now in
consideration of hero-worship as an abstraction, he turns to Shakespeare and attacks it. "It is a common thing," he writes, "to hear
Byron & Shakespear spoken of, not as men but mythical some-
things known by those names to whom anything was possible in their
hire, simply because they were Byron & Shakespear . . . . They
were men to whom all things were not possible, as, if one will
study closely, their own works show. . . ."

On January 19, 1874, however, Williams, after reading Otway,
pauses to consider the matter of plotting and decides that Otway's
plots are "somewhat unnatural." Again he turns to Shakespeare,
this time for defense of Otway, whom he admires. "For that matter, however," he writes, both in defense of Otway and in support of
the argument that Shakespeare could not do all things, "even many
of Shakespear's plots are not only unnatural, but improbable

and impossible, for instance, 'The Tempest,' 'Midsummer Night's Dream'--The Witches in 'Macbeth' and the Ghost in 'Hamlet'." Williams then concludes, "To be natural, probable, or possible is not always necessary in fiction, except that your costume must be right. Let the story be as impossible as you please--if you dress it the right way, and the dress makes nothing untrue to Nature-- you will pass." [66]

On January 26, 1874, Williams saw a New Orleans production of Bulwer-Lytton's Richelieu. Williams at the time was at work on a play based on Bulwer's novel, Eugene Aram, [3] and thus he was already committed to Bulwer. "The plot itself is a grand thing," he writes, "the most perfect embodiment of an historical character on the English stage. . . ." Again Williams turns to Shakespeare as the natural figure for all comparisons and calls Richelieu "above anything of Shakespear." Shakespeare's reputation, however, forces Williams, even in a private diary, to qualify the judgment. Bulwer is better than Shakespeare in this respect "for the simple reason that Shakespear's historical personages are not true to themselves. In other words--Richard, Macbeth, and Lear are founded upon traditions of these characters, and he has no data to which he is confirmed. Richard is historical only in the events which are wrought in his life as given in the play, for the man himself--he is Shakespear's own creation--and no more the true Richard than any creation of the imagination. This is true of both Lear and Macbeth--nay--even more true in their case as they were far more traditional than Richard." As for Hamlet, Williams writes, "I do not reckon Hamlet among Shakespear's histories as no one does--simply for the reasons cited in the case of Richard etc. Yet Hamlet is a real person in history--whose Father was murdered by a brother and whose mother, a partner in the crime, afterwards wedded the murderer. Shakespear, however, has so far departed from the historical man in this instance as to com- pletely destroy the reality and transform him into fiction."

Williams, time after time, makes such criticisms of Shake- speare that Boswell would have considered him in the same class with Goldsmith, "a most impudent puppy." It is obvious, however,

that Williams, unlike Goldsmith, is an orthodox Shakespeare wor-
shipper.   Others surpass Shakespeare, by Williams' standards,
only in fields, like historical "embodiment, " in which Shakespeare
does not compete.   Shakespeare's limitations, by Williams' standards, like his "unnatural . . . improbable, and impossible" plots,
are limitations so transcended by Shakespeare's practice that Williams uses them to justify similar "limitations" in lesser men like
Otway.

Boswell, in contrast, has no fault to find with Shakespeare or
his plays, but Boswell's criticism lacks the devotion of the "wor-
shipper, " a lack that evidences itself by what Boswell fails to say
and by the context in which he places his comments about Shakespeare.   While Boswell thinks Goldsmith an "impudent puppy" for
not acknowledging Shakespeare's "great merit, " at the same time
he does not even suggest that Shakespeare's methods should be uni-
versal practice.   In fact, Boswell, seemingly, would agree with
Goldsmith that Shakespeare's "panto[67]mime" is having an unfortunate
effect on the drama, if Goldsmith would agree that Shakespeare yet
"had great merit. "

Boswell, moreover, does not surround his comments on
Shakespeare with a tone of reverence, as does Williams.   Williams,
for example, discusses "trivial matters" in his diary, but such dis-
cussions never follow comments on Shakespeare, probably from the
same logic that stops a man from telling funny stories at a funeral.
Boswell, on the other hand, completes a comment on Shakespeare
and immediately starts on an unrelated matter.   On April 13, 1763,
for example, Boswell and Temple saw a performance of Macbeth,
"played by Holland, who played it but poorly and affected us little. "
If Williams had seen such a performance and drawn such a conclusion, the next page or two of his diary would have given an act-by-
act account of the play.   Boswell, however, moves from what for
Williams would have been the sublime Shakespeare to the ridiculous.
"I went home with Temple, " Boswell writes, "and sat till near
twelve, and was very happy, " presumably about other matters than
Shakespeare.   Then he relates an account of his meeting with "a
monstrous big whore in the Strand" and of the adventures that be-

fell him in this "low street debauchery" (pp. 240-241).

II

Williams' "idolatry," however inverted it may at times appear, and Boswell's casual acceptance of Shakespeare as a writer of merit cause the two men to approach the production of a Shakespearian play in different ways.   For Boswell, Shakespeare is an excellent judge of human nature and should be studied for his psychology.   In the Journal for January 11, 1763, for example, Boswell writes of his agreement with Thomas Sheridan's analysis of Garrick's performance of King Henry IV because Sheridan bases his arguments on psychological analysis.

> He [Sheridan] showed to my conviction that Garrick did not play the great scene in the Second Part of King Henry with propriety.   "People," said he, "in this age know when particular lines . . . are well spoke; but they do not study character. . . . For want of a knowledge of this, Mr. Barry acted the distress of Othello, the Moorish warrior whose stubborn soul was hard to bend and that of Castalio, the gentle lover who was all tenderness [in Otway's The Orphan], in the self-same way.   Now Mr. Garrick in that famous scene whines most piteously when he ought to upbraid.   Shakespeare has discovered there a most intimate knowledge of human nature.   He shows you the King worn out with sickness and so weak that he faints.   He has usurped the crown by the force of arms and was convinced that it must be held with spirit.   He saw his son given up to [68] low debauchery.   He was anxious and vexed to think of the anarchy that would insue at his death.   Upon discovering that the Prince had taken the crown from his pillow, and concluding him desirous of his death, he is fired with rage.   He starts up.   He cries, 'Go chide him hither!'   His anger animates him so much that he throws aside his distemper.   Nature furnishes all her strength for one last effort.   He is for the moment renewed.   He is for a moment that spirited Henry the Fourth.   He upbraids him with bitter sarcasm and bold figures.   And then what a beautiful variety is there, when, upon young Harry's contrition, he falls on his neck and melts into parental tenderness."

Boswell's acceptance of Sheridan's argument, "I yielded this point to Sheridan candidly," suggests that for Boswell the question of Shakespearian interpretation is still an open one, one that can be settled by an appeal to a reasonable man's knowledge of human nature.   Moreover, although Boswell agrees, he suggests that this

point of criticism was not one that required such a fervent defense.
Of Sheridan's method of criticism, Boswell concluded, "But he certainly talked too extravagantly." From Boswell's point of view, of
course, an interpretation of Shakespeare was only a literary opinion, not a moral conviction.

In contrast, Williams' criticism is a moral conviction and his
critical statements have the ring of dogmatic pronouncements. On
January 28, 1874, for example, Williams saw Lawrence Barrett in
Hamlet. Williams' criticism of Barrett's performance not only assumes a single interpretation of the play, but also a single method
of making that interpretation.

> To-night's performance . . . was a good one. Full of
> excellent points and yet just as full of faults. Barrett's
> entrance was good--his manner evidently copied after
> Booth . . . . His opening speech, "A little more than
> kin, and less than kind," was also well done, but his
> "Seems, Madam" was a failure. A perfect piece of
> mouthing. Indeed he is too much given to this common
> failing among actors, and he will also rant. His first
> soliloquy was too much ranted, the following scene be-
> tween Horatio etc., describing the Ghost's appearance
> was good in all except the very last lines, 'Would the
> night were come etc.' These were said, first with too
> much levity and secondly with too great an effort. His
> first meeting with the Ghost was excellent;--he opened
> his address in a faint whisper--yet distinctly to be heard
> --(Barrett's whispers on the stage are always good.)--
> and then paused as if to recover from the shock before
> proceeding with 'Be thou a spirit of health etc.' [69]
>
> He was not so good in the following interview with the
> Ghost, and his acting, more than his reading, was full
> of effort. 'His rest--rest perturbed spirit' was well
> spoken, but the closing lines of this scene--"Oh, cursed
> spite etc" were a horrible rant.
>
> The second act was full of errors. The reading 'Words
> --words--words' was badly done,--and the last 'words'
> left off--a very great fault,--for this last word contains
> the very climax of the thought--also his 'Except my life
> --except my life--except my life!' was also said badly.
> The first 'Except my life' is a careless expression--the
> outburst of the moment and contains no reflection; the
> second, however, is more thoughtful--and a question,
> addressed to himself,--while the last--the answer to this
> question--is the depth of feeling, containing all of Ham-
> let's feeling. When the players come in, he does better
> --until he gets to the soliloquy which closes the act.

This, as all of Barrett's soliloquies are, was not well rendered. He talks too much to the audience.

In the Third Act, he was good throughout, with the exception of 'To be or not to be.' This was the worse read passage in the whole play and was absolutely horrid. He ought to have been hissed. In his interview with Ophelia, he was excellent, and it was full of little points which took. His manner of asking her where her father is, and the effect of her answer, together with his reply--or rather exclamation--was very good. The gem of this scene, however, was his last return, when he, cautiously, yet fervently, kisses her hand, while he looks so deeply into her eyes, as if seeking to give her to understand that what has just passed was all assumed behavior meant to deceive the King etc. His closet scene was, in the whole, the best of the play. It is hard to describe it; it was one of perfection from the first to the last, except, perhaps, the manner of his starting back on the ghost's entrance, which was somewhat unnatural, and not like any other actor I have before seen . . . . The remainder of the play is I think always a drag. The interest lags somewhat, and is no longer centered so deeply upon Hamlet . . . . and it is not until Hamlet appears in the graveyard that we feel again wrapt up in him. This scene, though fairly read, was not well acted . . . . His death was excellent. . . .

Williams' criticism throughout implies that there is a "right way" to perform each part of the play and that an actor may be tried at any point for a failure to conform to this "right way." Moreover, the "right way" rests, finally, not on psychological or aesthetic criticism, but on a traditional way of performing the part. The few instances in which [70] Williams gives a reason why Barrett's particular interpretation is bad is always backed by the argument, "not like any actor I have before seen" or "he did not do this the last time I saw him." Williams seems to assume that there is one practice which is acceptable for Shakespeare and everyone who knows Shakespeare knows the one practice. The criticism, in fact, has much of the fundamentalist's assumption of authority about it; and as a fundamentalist argues for his interpretation of holy writ by a claim to familiarity with the text, so does Williams imply the "rightness" of his dogmatism by constant reminders that he has read his Shakespeare well. On January 28, 1874, for example, Williams writes in his diary, "I had long before then been conver-

sant with the play [Hamlet], as I was a student of Shakespear
quite early in life and had by the time I was fifteen read him
through twice." At the same time, moreover, Williams does not
claim respect for his opinions in terms of a system of poetics in
an orthodox school. On January 5, 1874, for example, Williams
writes, 'Read another act in the Cenci, and read it carefully--as
I am studying the art of criticism--not after Horace--nor anyone
else, but after myself. "

Williams' criticism of Barrett's performance apparently is
not based on a notion of critical rules nor on an understanding of
any "natural laws" which Shakespeare followed, as Sheridan argues,
for example. Rather it is based on an almost-religious assumption. Shakespeare, in Williams' eyes, becomes an absolute, like
God, who has revealed Himself in one particular fashion; and all
true believers must follow the fashion.

Williams was, however, not a dogmatic man in other affairs.
When he wrote of other writers and of his own works, he was not
only modest, but he recognized the validity of a variety of opinions.
In spite of his statement that Barrett should have been hissed, for
example, Williams was a close friend and personal admirer of the
actor.[4] Only in the matter of Shakespeare does Williams show in-
tolerance, suggesting that his feeling for Shakespeare is better
labeled "worship" than respect. Worship calls for an order of
service, in this instance a prescribed method of performing a play;
and once that order has been established, the orthodox believer
judges all things by it, seldom reevaluating in large terms, as
Sheridan did the performance of Henry IV, to test the validity of the
relationship between the established order of worship and the nature
of the object being worshipped.

III

It is, moreover, seemingly in the nature of orthodox worship
to look to the "idol" for the primal goodly qualities, power and
awe. For [71] Boswell, Shakespeare is not a god, but a most human
artist, especially in his ability to create pity and move an audience
to tears. The "tender" emotions are, in fact, the ones that Boswell mentions in relation to Shakespeare in the Journal. On Janu-

ary 10, 1763, for example, Boswell attended the Drury Lane Theatre "and saw the Second Part of King Henry IV, where Mr. Garrick in the pathetic scene between the Old King and his son drew
tears from my eyes" (p. 134). On Thursday, May 12, 1763, he
again saw Garrick, this time in Lear. "I kept myself at a distance from all acquaintances," he wrote, " and got into a proper
frame. Mr. Garrick gave me the most perfect satisfaction. I
was fully moved, and I shed abundance of tears" (p. 257). It
should be noted, too, that Sheridan assumes that the aim in Henry
IV is to move the audience to sympathy for the dying king.

Williams, on the other hand, never associates pity with Shakespeare. For him, Shakespeare's greatness lies in his awesome
powers, his ability to provoke terror, his ability to stun an audience. On February 12, 1874, Williams and his father saw Tomasso
Salvini in the Italian actor's first performance of Othello in New Orleans.

> Went last night with Father to see Tomasso Salvini in
> Othello. Expected not to be pleased, as the perform-
> ance was to be in Italian, and could not understand it.
> Was however well read in the play & so could always
> tell what was being said tho' I did not see the points in
> the reading. Went to be, as I said, disappointed--and
> was so--most agreeably. I never enjoyed anything so
> much. Salvini is a great--a wonderfully great actor, of
> the Edwin Forrest school, but far more elegant and
> graceful in his bearing, with less rant and a voice at
> once the softest and most powerful I ever heard. His
> appearance and his acting in the first two Acts was but
> fair, indeed in some places only passable. His speech
> before the Senate was without proper dignity, and a
> great deal too much after the manner of the mere col-
> loquial. In the last three acts however he rose to a
> height, beyond my imagination. There were many points
> seen by those who understood the language which we fail-
> ed to appreciate. Points in acting however we could
> feel. His manner of throwing Iago down and then when
> about to tread upon him, evidently to kill him, shrinking
> back as if horrified at the thought of what he was about
> to do, and then raising himself with the air of an injur-
> ing yet injured man, was sublime.
>
> The whole of the last scene was great. His interview
> with Desdemona was agonizing, and the way he caught
> her by the neck & half dragged--half bore her into the
> bed-chamber, was terrible--it thrilled me to the soul &

I do believe had I [72] been near & free I would have forgot
myself & tried to rescue her. As it was I felt like
crying out to her to stab him in the back, as she could
have done with his dagger, accessible to her. When he
returned to the audience, his acting was awful. No
words can express it. Then his manner of throwing
himself on Desdemona and his heart's rending cry! His
stabbing of Iago, and lastly, the most terribly real thing
I ever witnessed on the stage,--his stabbing himself.
He thrusts the dagger downwards into his throat and
works it about. As he does so his whole frame--every
muscle--shakes and quivers, and then when he falls it
is with an effort of fleeting strength, and this is the
climax of natural acting, his limbs quiver and his leg
kicks. Nothing could be more harrowing and perfectly
terrible than this death scene. It only needed blood to
have been seen spurting from his throat to have caused
a general uproar in the audience,--who would then have
been positive that it was a real death they were witness-
ing.

Although Williams does assume "natural acting" as the standard for
his judgement, his notion of the "real" is obviously not the surface
realism of the world about him. Rather it is the "reality" of some
absolute, "the terribly real" as he calls it. Williams, in fact, dis-
approves of "natural acting" in the sense that a conversational tone
is judged to be "without proper dignity and a great deal too much
after the manner of the mere colloquial." It is the "perfectly terrible" which receives his final approval.

IV

These two concepts of Shakespeare, the eighteenth-century
English view of a superior human artist and the nineteenth-century
American view of a superhuman creator, obviously had their effects
upon the use made of Shakespeare's works. Boswell's casual and
fond acceptance of Shakespeare led him to expect a general casual
acquaintanceship with the main plays, and such works as Boswell's
life of Johnson contain allusions to these plays. Williams' attitude
of resentful awe, however, put the Louisiana playwright in a state
of rebellious subservience to Shakespeare throughout his career.

Williams' first commercial success as a playwright, Parrhasius, for example, was first written in imitation of Greek classical
drama. As soon as the play was successful, however, Williams
turned the single-act [73] classical version into two multi-act Shake-

spearian versions.[5] In the last years of his life, Williams delivered at least two addresses indicative of his attitude toward Shakespeare. The first, an address on the modern drama,[6] warned a-
gainst an imitation of Shakespeare by modern playwrights. The
second, "The Shakespear Myth," was a review of Wilbur Gleason
Zeigler's novel, It Was Marlowe, a romance, in Williams' words,
"woven around the theory that Christopher Marlowe was the real
author of the Shakespear plays." In this review, although Williams
admitted that "I cannot claim to be enough of a Shakespearian student or critic to go into the detailed analysis which perhaps is
needed to properly form a satisfactory judgement," he shows his
sympathies to any attack on the "Shakespeare idol" by concluding,
"It is nevertheless a fact, and one which I think more apparent today than ever,--that there is a mystery surrounding these monu-
ments of literature, known as the plays of William Shakespear. .
. ."[7]

   Williams' last play, Marlowe: The Buried Name, on which he
was still at work when he died,[8] is a dramatic defense of Zeigler's
"theory"; and, as might be expected, it is written in imitation of
"the plays of William Shakespear." To the end, the best that Williams was able to do was to try to change the name of the idol.
He could neither destroy it nor deny it. [74]

Notes

1. Williams' diary, which he kept from January, 1874, until March,
   1875, recently came into the possession of the University of Southwestern Louisiana library, Lafayette, La., through a gift of
   Mrs. Phillips Endecott Osgood, daughter of the playwright. In
   addition to the diary, Mrs. Osgood also turned over to the library copies (some of which are the original handwritten drafts)
   of over thirty plays, letters, poetry, and addresses. Williams'
   plays were produced in America and in England, and he was
   probably Louisiana's most successful playwright of the nineteenth
   century. All quotations from the diary are from the copy held
   in the library. Slight corrections in spellings have been
   made. [64]

2. Frederick A. Pottle, ed. (New York, 1950). All quotations
   from the Journal are from this edition. [65]

3. Eugene Aram, "A Play in Five Acts, Founded on Bulwer" (New
   Orleans, 1874), "Printed but not Published." [67]

4. Williams' only book of verse, The Dream of Art and Other
   Poems (New York, 1892), contains a poem dedicated to the actor "Lawrence Barrett." [71]

5. Parrhasius: Or, Thriftless Ambition was first published privately in New Orleans in 1879.   During the early 1890's Robert
   Mantell saw a copy of it and bought the stage rights from Williams.   The play was produced successfully in a number of A-
   merican cities, Philadelphia, Memphis, San Francisco, St. Louis,
   for examples, in its original single-act form; but with its success Williams made three-act and four-act versions and changed
   the single-incident plot into a double plot.

6. The Modern Drama: Its Literary and Moral Value, n.d.   A
   typed copy of the address is in the University of Southwestern
   Louisiana library.   Although not dated, the address was obviously written sometime after 1906.   Williams mentions "the
   late Henrik Ibsen," who died in 1906.

7. This manuscript is also in the University of Southwestern Louisiana library and is undated.   Zeigler's novel appeared in 1895.

8. The original handwritten copy of this play has been edited and
   was published by the University of Kentucky Press in its Modern Language microcard series, in 1961. [74]

A Final Note

Although from the examples given in this casebook, a student should be able to start with a notation in Dramatic Compositions and work his way through some final written demonstrations of his ability to do research, a guide, in brief form, might be useful. Obviously, the articles themselves are the best guides, and this list is merely meant to serve as a road map through and not a geography of the territory.

1. The starting place is Dramatic Compositions. Any play listed in this source was copyrighted. The Library of Congress still has some of the authors' manuscripts submitted for copyright protection, and, occasionally, if the student can locate any of the direct descendants of the playwright, he may find that the family has preserved old papers. The source lists the plays by alphabetical order, and thus it is necessary for the student to go through all of the entries for his particular interest--playwrights from the same area, plays on a particular subject, etc. Generally speaking, since this work has not been done, this original search through Dramatic Compositions is, in itself, the basis for a research report.

2. Even when copies of the "lost" plays are discovered, information concerning the playwright is necessary for editions, critical articles, and popular features. Many of these playwrights were at least locally known, and the various reference books for the separate areas are the most valuable secondary sources. Especially to be recommended are the various State Guide books, local histories, the telephone books, the newspapers. Sometimes, a letter to the last known address of the playwright will bring a response. Once, for example, I got a response from the playwright himself, then in his eightieth year.

3. Since the student is working, in the main, with materials

that have not been catalogued, it is sensible to publish as much as
one can as he goes along--letters to the editor, newspaper and regional magazine features, area journals.   The best single source
for markets is A. S. Burack's <u>Writers' Handbook</u> (Boston: Writer,
Inc.), which is brought up to date every other year.

4. All of the rules for any scholarship hold for these projects, but common sense should tell one that highly specialized ap-
proaches--imagistic studies, for example--to materials that are so
little known have little purpose.   The basic concern of this research
is to locate the plays, identify the playwrights, and demonstrate
how various plays and elements in the plays fit into--or fall into--
the general cultural history of the United States.   Engaging in con-
troversies about particular facts or opinions is not suggested.   It
is really not as important to answer a particular theory of a newspaper reviewer concerning a particular play as it is merely to record that opinion.   Of the more than fifty thousand plays written in
the United States during the years from 1870 to 1916, less than
five thousand have ever been edited or discussed.

Although this casebook has been designed largely for students
to use for suggestions with their research on the "lost" American
plays between 1870 and 1916, the same fundamental principles can
also be used for the unpublished plays in the United States for the
past fifty years.   It is, of course, necessary for the research
worker to obtain the permission of the copyright holder for those
manuscripts still covered by law; but this consent is not, normally,
difficult to obtain.   Obviously, living playwrights have more concern about their copyrighted materials than dead ones, and it is
not suggested that freshmen college students immediately write to
such men as Marc Connelly, Edward Albee, or Arthur Miller asking for permission to have microfilms made of their unpublished
copyrighted materials.   But all playwrights--even the major, successful ones--have dramatic compositions that have never been published, some that have never been produced; and when a scholar
demonstrates that he will treat such material with respect and for
some purpose, many playwrights are willing to give their permission.   One need merely read the "acknowledgments" in the various

biographies of playwrights in the Twayne <u>United States Authors</u> series for evidence of their willingness.